pulp EMPIRE

VOLUME FOUR

METAHUMAN PRESS

Cedar Rapids, IA

Published by
METAHUMAN PRESS
Cedar Rapids, IA 52403

 ISBN 978-1-4583-3654-5

Published simultaneously on the website *PulpEmpire.com*

CONTENTS

Introduction

By Nicholas Ahlhelm

By the time this anthology makes it to your shelf, it will already be well over a year since *Pulp Empire* first came to the internet and started its way to bookshelves.

As the proud papa of this project, it makes me smile every time I look at a copy of each of the first three volumes on the shelf. With stories that run the gamut of pulp storytelling, *Pulp Empire* has truly become something unique in the current pulp revival movement.

Within this book, you will find thirteen more stories of pulp action, mystery, and intrigue. The settings range from the Old West to the deepest corner of space, and pretty much everything in between.

This time around I am proud to say we have more returning authors than in any of our previous three collections. Four of our nine tales are from returning authors.

Not to discount our other nine tales by any stretch. Every

single one of the author's in this volume put their heart and soul in to the pages here. I think it's obvious as you read through our stories.

Pulp Empire may be a year old, but it's far from done. Already the next three collections in our ongoing series are in the works. At the same time, *Pulp Empire* will introduce its first themed anthology this year with stories of *Pirates and Swash-buckler*s.

Thanks for reading.

Doctor Shadows appeared last time in Pulp Empire volume two. He easily follows in the veins of the hero pulps of yesteryear, channeling the likes of Doc Savage and the Shadow. We open our newest volume as the good doctor returns to satisfy a...

Blood Debt

A Doctor Shadows Adventure

By Teel James Glenn

The world trembles on the brink:

The Empire of Japan was on the rise when it invaded and annexed Manchuria in 1932 in a thinly veiled conquest. They proclaimed it the independent nation of Manchoukuo that had conveniently 'asked' for help from the Children of Amaterasu-O-Mi-Mani the Sun Goddess, who felt divinely charged to rule the world. Every official of the new nation had a Japanese 'advisor.'

In the frozen north of the new 'country', near the Siberian border, the Russian founded city of Harbin is a hotbed of insurgent anti-Japanese activity. An impotent League of Nations does nothing but appoint committees, while across the sea. America does it's best to ignore the gathering storm clouds of war.........It is the fall of the year 1937…

A Sulsa warrior is loyal to his country and his fellow warriors. Fearless in battle, never takes a life unnecessarily, and always—acts for justice!!

Chapter I
An Obligation Assumed

Anton Chadeaux PhD., who the press had dubbed Dr. Shadows, drove his grey roadster at dangerous speeds on the icy evening streets of Harbin City. He did not have time for caution. The woman's voice on the phone had made that clear: "Come now to room twenty-one at the Hotel Moderne or I will be killed." She had said, and then the line went dead. Her English had been accented, possibly Japanese, and the fear in her voice was unmistakable.

Harbin City, built in the grand Russian style, was in fact often called the Moscow of the East, and so its broad avenues were bordered by sidewalks and squat stone buildings, but not well lit. The paved streets were slick with black ice, so it took all of Dr. Shadows' skill to maneuver the powerful roadster. He had been at a friend's home on Bolshoi Prospect in the nearby New Town, preparing for an evening out at the opera when the call reached him. That had been ten minutes ago.

Dr. Shadows pulled up to the elegant Hotel Moderne and leapt from the car almost before it rolled to the curb. He drew many curious stares as he strode across the lobby of the hotel toward the open cage elevator, but he was used to that. He stood six and a half feet tall and was handsome, with chiseled movie star features. This alone would have been enough to draw attention almost anywhere in the world, but it was his ashen grey skin and silver hair that drew most stares. They were a legacy of the herbal baths that had restored him to health after a terrible tragedy and combined to give him the aspect of having been carved from stone. That had given rise to his other nickname, The Granite Man.

The tall grey man knocked once on number twenty-one's door and was welcomed by a coarse male voice that said in Cantonese "Enter quietly, Ghost Healer, or the woman dies."

Inside the room, a burly Chinese sat in an overstuffed chair across the opulent sitting room of the suite. There was a beautiful middle-aged Japanese woman in full kimono with her arms bound behind her, seated on a footstool in front of him. The silvered steel of a knife blade was pressed against the pale flesh of her neck. Her skin was almost translucent, the 'alabaster' of the poets and the obscenely cold looking blade left a pink trail as the corpulent Chinese bandit dragged the tip across her throat.

Dr. Shadows found it hard to keep his eyes off the blade and attempted to concentrate on the face of the desperate man wielding it. It was a battle-hardened face, with sadness in the cunning eyes that seemed out of place. "You will hear my words, Ghost Healer," the man said with the Cantonese transliteration of Dr. Shadows' name. "Tonight the Kuomintang supported irregulars will board the train after it leaves the station. They will kill Baron Yashita and all those with him during the attack on the train."

The November sunset slanted through the ornate windows of the suite to outline the bandit and his prisoner in liquid gold. The woman's eyes pleaded with the Granite Man, who eased the door closed behind himself. "Threatening this woman will have no effect on that attack," the American said. "It can have no—"

"This is Madame Yashita, wife of the Baron," the Chinese said, "and she will die if I cannot end the life of that monster myself. Her blood is his blood and I will have the debt of blood paid in full." His voice was steady, with a calmness that was chilling; it was the voice of a man already resigned to death. "You will bring Yashita to me, to me alone to kill with my own hands by dawn or this woman dies."

"Yashita is a Japanese Secret Police official," Dr. Shadows said, "How am I to bring him to you or stop a train full of irregular fighters from killing him? I am one man."

"Ling Fu is a humble bandit," the knife wielder said tapping his own broad chest, "but even this one knows of the Grey American who has reason to hate the Japanese."

"Many people have reason to hate the Japanese." Dr. Shadows observed.

"But you are trained by the Sulsa monks of Korea," the bandit said, "and can do many things others cannot; or so the stories tell."

"You should not believe the stories you hear, Ling Fu," Dr. Shadows said, "I am just a man like you."

"Then as a man you will not want to see me kill this woman," Ling Fu said, "I will spill the blood of a Yashita by dawn—hers or his; it is your choice. If you cannot persuade him to come, she will die."

"Ghost Healer," the woman said, voice atremble yet with a firm resolve in her tone. "It is known you have no love for the Japanese people; I wish to incur no obligation from you; there is no shame in ignoring this bandit's request."

The Granite Man looked into the dark eyes of the woman and saw that she meant it, that there was a resignation in her to an inevitable death. It was that resignation more than anything said in the room that brought resolve in the American. "I have no problem with the people of Japan, Madame Yashita," Dr. Shadows said, "It is General Tojo and his military ilk that gets my attention. And yes, I know your husband has done more than his share to further the occupation of Manchuria—"

"It was Baron Yashita who ordered my village of Wo Fu to be destroyed," Ling Fu said, "and for that I will kill him myself."

"If you hate him so," Dr. Shadows said, "Why not let the irregulars kill him when they attack the train?"

"No I must see him die, I must hear his last breath. I knew I could not be sure of being first in the train. It is I who must collect this blood debt." The bandit's eyes glowed with the fire of an inner hate that his dead calm voice did not betray. "Yashita blood must wash my blade."

"Then I will do my best to bring the baron to this room by dawn," The Granite Man said. He looked like the statue of a war god come to life, his flinted eyes focused pinpoints of power. "But, Ling Fu, if you know anything about me you know that my promise is a thing of stone. You know what I can do; I promise you that if you hurt this woman, regardless of what happens, there is nowhere you can hide from me."

"This unworthy one would expect no less," the bandit smiled grimly, "but Ling Fu the bandit died when his family died in Wo Fu. Yashita will die either in the flesh or in his heart when this woman breathes her last breath."

Dr. Shadows looked into the eyes of the hostage and saw something there beyond resignation, but he could not say what it was.

The bandit took the knife from the bound woman's throat and waved it "When the sun rises there will be death in this room Ghost Healer, of this there is certainty."

"There is only one certainty in your life from this point on," Dr. Shadows said, "and that is me." To the woman he said, "Take heart, Madame Yashita, I will be back, no harm will come to you."

Once he was in the hall, the image of the woman's eyes hovered before him and quickened his steps; it would be a race to make the train.

Chapter II
Engine of Destruction

Dr. Shadows raced his roadster along Torgovaia Street toward the train station and considered the situation. He had contacts in the native Chinese city a few minutes' walk from New Town who could get messages to the irregulars that continually harassed the Japanese occupiers, but in no way exercised any control authority over them.

"And would they care about the life of one Japanese woman anyway?" he thought. "Perhaps not even if they had seen the fear in her eyes that I did."

The Granite Man pulled the car up to the stone edifice of the Harbin Railway Station which was the hub of the Manchurian, Chinese, Russian and Korean railway lines. He was conscious this time of the looks from the Japanese soldiers on guard outside the building. The dozen or so troops wore the uniform of the

Provisional Manchoukou Regime like all the Gendarmerie and city police who were also Sons of the Rising Sun. It was a masquerade for the rest of the world; the citizens of Harbin and the rest of Manchuria had spent five years crushed beneath the Nipponese boot.

A soldier stepped up to bar Dr. Shadows entrance with a gruff grunt and a gesture of his long rifle. The oriental came barely to the grey giant's chest, but his manner was as if he loomed over him. He obviously did not recognize the American adventurer and assumed he was one of the White Russian population that had settled the city originally. "No enter without a pass!" The Japanese said in Russian. He made a second menacing gesture with his long rifle to back the tall American up.

Dr. Shadows resisted the urge to just push the smaller man aside and instead answered in Japanese. "I have a pass signed by the military governor." He produced an excellent forgery made by his friend and associate Ki Nam Hoon that he carried whenever he went abroad in the city. It gave him free rein to conduct his private investigations.

The soldier saw his superior's signature and quickly stepped aside to let the tall occidental enter the station. If he was curious as to why a round-eye had a pass from a Japanese authority, he was well trained enough to not show it or dwell on it.

Once inside the European style railway station, the Granite Man made his way to the ticket window and purchased a coach class open car seat on the train. He raced to the steps of the coach barely in time, leaping up as the bellow of steam spewed from the great engine and the conductor yelled "All Aboard!" in several languages.

"Well," the tall American thought as the train picked up

speed moving out of the city, "I am seated on a train headed for an ambush purposed for a kidnapping with no plan; just the thing for a Saturday night in Harbin." He settled into a seat beside a White Russian officer who was reading the Rupor daily Russian paper. The headlines proclaimed how wonderful the Japanese government was, how the evil Jewish conspiracy was responsible for how terrible the train service had become over the last year.

The rest of the open seating railway car was full of a mixed group of mostly single men-few families risked train travel with the many irregular attacks. There were White and Red Russians studiously ignoring each other, going south for business, a few Chinese merchants who could still afford coach fare and two Koreans who had a thuggish appearance to them at the back of the car.

"Probably strong arm men for the Kempetitiai-the Japanese Secret Police." Dr. Shadows thought. He had a particular dislike for Koreans who collaborated with the Japanese, as many of his closest friends were Korean nationals who had been displaced or degraded by over the nearly thirty years of being forbidden to even speak their own language in their home country.

"The question is do they recognize me and if so, will they be a problem?" The Granite Man was an American citizen and so enjoyed the extraterritoriality of America's 'neutrality', but it was well known he agitated against the occupier whenever he could, raising money for the irregulars in the 'states and 'preaching' against the false state. He had also had direct confrontation with many agents of the Japanese. "My status will go directly to criminal after tonight," he thought.

He did his best to draw no attention to himself, keeping his fedora pulled down low and slumping in his chair like a weary traveler. He kept an eye on the Koreans and considered what he knew of the train from his brief chance to survey it as he ran onboard.

The night train was a short one with an engine and coal car followed by a flat bed car with a mounted gun and troop contingent. Two public cars in turn followed this, the first of which Dr. Shadows sat in. A first class/sleeping coach followed with a dining car, and then two cargo and passenger baggage carriages. The train finished with a troop car, the private coach of the Baron and a caboose with more troops.

"Not the best time to be working alone," he thought, wishing his associates in the Shadows Foundation for Justice were available, "but regardless, I have to move quickly."

The train was away from the lights of the city now and picking up speed. He knew it would continue along the Sungari River plain, gaining speed before it came to foothills and went up a grade that meant it had to slow. He had to make his move now, because that would be the most likely place for an irregular attack.

The Granite Man rose and made his way back through the carriage as casually as possible. When he exited the back door and moved across the gap into the second public car, he was conscious that the Koreans had risen to follow him.

He made his way through the second public car and they followed as well. "I don't have time for subtlety with my little ducklings," he thought, "so I'll do it the hard and fast way."

Dr. Shadows exited the public car and donned his leather gloves. He stepped to the side of the door and hung partially off the platform so he was not visible in the light from the open door. In a moment, the first of the Koreans stepped through the door and crossed to the next car. He was moving with some speed, obviously afraid to lose sight of his quarry. He was through the door to the sleeper before the second man was fully on the platform

As the second man, a gun in his hand, stepped to cross to the platform of the sleeper car and after the door had closed behind him, the Granite Man stepped from the shadows. The American grabbed the man by his coat and simply flung him off the moving train before he had any idea what was happening.

Then Dr. Shadows followed the first oriental into the corridor of the sleeping car. It was empty except for the Korean, who turned when the door opened and said.

"I don't know which compartment he went—" Then he saw the American and panicked. He attempted to draw a small automatic pistol, but Dr. Shadows pounced like a grey panther.

The Granite Man pinned the Korean's right hand as he went for his gun with his left. Then Dr. Shadows slammed his right fist into the slack jawed man's throat. The thug's eyes bulged as he gagged for air.

Then the American snapped his left elbow to the man's temple and the Korean dropped. Dr. Shadows caught him before he hit the floor and dragged him to the washroom at the end of the corridor where he bound the thug with the man's own belt. He gagged the man with his own necktie. Then Dr. Shadows tossed the automatic out the window and into the darkness of the Manchurian night. He preferred not to use guns if he could avoid it and a gunshot on the train at this point would definitely have it swarming with Japanese troops.

"I suppose I should feel some regret about the one on the platform," The Granite Man thought as he walked through the corridor of the sleeping coach. He remembered the Abbott's admonishment to "Take no life except to preserve life; your own or those you love." He remembered the pleading eyes of the captive woman even as her brave words 'released him' from obligation, and all guilt for the murderous Korean washed away from him.

Chapter III
Cargo of Death

Dr. Shadows went through the sleeper coach without drawing any undue attention or encountering any opposition. When he made his way into the dining car, several of the train crew took notice of him and began to talk amongst themselves.

One of the crew, a broad faced Chinese in a white serving jacket and an old style queue stepped up to him as he approached the rear door of the dining car. "Is there some trouble sir?" the waiter asked in Russian. "Can this humble one be of assistance to you in any way?" His manner was perfectly subservient, but the Granite Man had an inkling that there was something more behind the man's perfect polite manner.

Dr. Shadows answered in Cantonese, "There is no trouble, Honorable Sir, but I have need to have a 'discussion' with the most esteemed representative of the Japanese Emperor at the back of the train." He used as many code phrases for irregular activity as he dared and hoped the waiter was a patriot.

The smaller man regarded the grey giant from hooded eyes for a moment, and then smiled pleasantly. "Follow please, Dr. Shadows." He said in English. They made their way to the rear of the car through the kitchen, where the staff scrupulously found things to keep them busy and did not allow them to look up.

"I regret I do not have the key to the baggage car," the waiter said when he had opened the door to the connecting platforms.

"Your help is most appreciated," Dr. Shadows said, "I would suggest caution as the train hits the upgrade." The waiter smiled a more knowing smile this time.

"This one will be removing the train pin at the right moment," the waiter said, "the passengers in the train will be in no danger. Have a good 'talk' with the Baron."

The baggage car proved to be locked though it was a weak one, and the grey giant was able to pick it quickly. Inside the boxcar was pitch black. Dr. Shadows produced a chemically powered hand torch that cast a pale green light on the contents of the baggage car. It was a chaotic jumble of boxes and bags with no apparent organization. The Granite Man moved through it as quickly as he could and unlocked the door at the other end. Beyond was the boxcar that had been commandeered for military use.

The lock to the second boxcar proved as weak as the first and he was soon inside. This time the boxes were neatly stacked in shoulder high rows the length of the car. All the wooden crates were labeled as "Military Supplies for the Japanese Army." Dr. Shadows couldn't resist the chance to confirm the rumors that circulated in Harbin, so he paused despite the urgency of the mission and used a metal bar he located on the floor to pry open one of the crates.

"Even when you think Tojo's boys can't sink any lower," he thought as he looked at the packaged heroin and opium inside the crate. It had long been known that the Japanese forced many farmers to stop growing soybeans in favor of cultivating poppies. They also ran or franchised a number of opium dens with the Kokusai Union running the drugs throughout all of Manchoukou, but here was the proof that they also exported their filth. The crates were labeled to Kirin, Heliungkiang Mukden, Hankow, Tientsin and points beyond. All were addressed to the military commands in the various cities from where they would be distributed to all the franchised drug dens that the Japanese ran to finance their occupation of the country.

"Someday I'll put an end to this canker," he thought, "then I can—"

Suddenly some instinct warned the Granite Man and he twisted his body. He barely avoided a fatal wound as the edge of a ten-inch knife skated along his ribs.

Dr. Shadows shut off his light and jumped back as the body behind the knife slashed at him again. The American pulled off his topcoat and wrapped it around his left arm, just in time to deflect another hacking cut.

It was too dark in the boxcar to see the figure in front of him, but the Sulsa trained American had more than his eyes to rely on. He calmed his breathing and listened.

Beyond the sounds of the train clattering along and the sound of the wind whistling against the boxcar, the Granite Man could hear the ragged breathing of the attacker and the rustle of clothes as the man moved the blade back and forth. Then he heard a grunt and a guttural curse as the assailant knocked into a crate.

It was the Korean Dr. Shadows had left tied up in the lavatory.

"So much for my soft heart," the Granite Man allowed himself to muse, "Slugger always says I'm a sap for a sob story."

The man continued to swipe the blade back and forth, cursing Dr. Shadows' ancestry all the while.

The Granite Man realized he could not waste any more time in the boxcar and decided on a desperate gamble. He threw his coat high and hard against the side of the boxcar beyond where he guessed the knifeman was. When he heard the man react, the American sprang forward with a hard kick that connected to the man's hip. As the man stumbled backwards, Dr. Shadows continued his attack and slammed a back kick into the leading leg of the thrusting knifeman. The Korean went down and this time the American leapt in to finish the man. The two grappled in the dark with the Korean desperate to get his fingers around the Granite Man's throat. Dr. Shadows kept the superior position however, and with a powerful strike to the man's temple, ended the fight.

The American flicked his flashlight on again to confirm that it was the Korean and that he was dead. Then he found his coat and moved to the door of the boxcar. "I've lost enough time indulging myself," he thought. "The attack will be any time now and I have to get to Yashita first." The Granite Man had donned his leather 'battle tunic' before he exited his roadster and this allowed him to dispense with his topcoat. He peered out the end door of the storage car to be sure there were no guards on the platform of the troop car. Then he threw his topcoat into the black whistling night air. He had lost his fedora somewhere in the boxcar and had no time to search for it.

Off to the right the Sungari River shone in the dappled starlight as the train rumbled along. Ahead were the foothills. He knew that once it hit the upgrade for the hills, the danger of the attack would be greatest.

Dr. Shadows hopped up on the safety rail of the next car that held the guard contingent of Japanese troops. The only way to get beyond the troop car to the private car of Baron Yashita was to go over the roof. He pulled himself to the roof of the coach and lay flat along the edge.

The night wind slapped the Granite Man in the face like daggers of ice as the train rattled along. He had to keep his head turned and his eyes slitted to keep from being blinded. He could feel the vibrations of the train beneath him and he knew it was rumbling toward the ambush as unstoppably as a bullet from a gun.

The top of the train was windswept and soot covered, and had he not been wearing gloves, the cold rails that ran along its length would have frozen his hands in moments. He pulled himself along the rails with any effort to be quiet forgotten in the need to move swiftly. Fortunately, the racket of the train itself covered any noise he might have made.

It took him a full fifteen agonizing minutes to make the other end of the troop coach. When he did, he peered cautiously over the edge to observe the observation platform on the private coach.

The two Japanese soldiers standing guard on the platform outside of Baron Yashita's coach were more concerned with staying warm than protecting the man inside the car. They were huddled together, heads down and backs to the troop coach. It was a simple matter for the Granite Man to launch himself down on them and send them into oblivion with two deadly blows. This time he acted with no regrets; he never considered occupying soldiers to be innocents.

Dr. Shadows tossed the bodies off the train and grabbed the

handle on the private coach door. "Into the frying pan," he thought, then turned the handle and entered.

Chapter IV
An Urgent Appeal

Three of the four occupants of the private coach were sipping from warm saki cups when Dr. Shadows slipped quickly in and closed the door behind him. There were two uniformed officers, the Baron, and a bodyguard who stood beyond the other three.

Baron Yashita gave lie to the fact that stereotypes did not exist, for he was the perfect cartoon image of a yellow menace. Short, bow legged and with two front teeth that extended past his thick lips at twisted angles. He was dressed in formal pinstriped pants and shirtsleeves with a 'happy coat' short kimono over the top. His hair was thinning with tints of grey at the temples and was combed over in a pathetic attempt to disguise his onset of baldness.

The diminutive size of the Baron was made more apparent by the huge Japanese who stood beside him, massive arms crossed in a western style greatcoat that barely contained him. His hair was worn long in the *chonmage* style that made it was clear the giant was a *rikishi*, a professional sumo. It was an ancient wrestling form revered on the isle of Amaterasu-O-Mi-Kami, the Sun Goddess.

"Who are you?" the Baron asked in perfect un-accented English. "Not one of the ragged Russian irregulars, for certain; English or American perhaps?" His eyes were the break in the cartoon image, for they showed quick intelligence and a sharp mind inside the caricature.

"I am Anton Chadeaux, Baron Yashita-san," The Granite Man said. "And I must speak to you on a matter of great importance."

The little Asian stared at him for along moment, then smiled. "The one who spends so much time with the dog eater Koreans and the simple minded Chinese call 'The Ghost Healer?' How very quaint. I assume the guards are—"

Dr. Shadows made a dismissive gesture but kept his eyes locked with the Baron's. He was acutely aware of the two military officers standing there unsure what to do, their hands poised near their belt pistols.

The Baron stepped aside slightly so the large bodyguard had a clear field of play, but at the same time gave a hand gesture that that held the huge sumo at bay.

"You have been a thorn in the side of the Divine Empire of Japan for some time," the Baron said. "Up until now you have skirted direct confrontation or criminality though that is in the past. What important matter could an American interloper have to discuss with an official of the Emperor?"

"Your wife, Baron," Dr. Shadows said, "has been taken prisoner by a Chinese partisan who wants you in exchange for her." There was a moment of silence as the two officers, who did not speak English, looked to the Baron for explanation. He chose, for the moment, to ignore them.

"Mariko is a dutiful wife," the Baron said. "She will die for me without complaint. I have value to the Emperor. She is a mere woman." Then the nobleman explained the conversation to the two officers in rapid Japanese. The men were stunned for a moment then laughed.

“I was hoping you would give me reason to find redemptive qualities in the Sons of the Rising Sun,” Dr. Shadows said. “But your manner seems to have settled that.”

The Baron gestured and the sumo stepped forward.

“Taro here is a *yokozuna* of Sumo,” Yashita said gesturing to the man mountain behind him. “A champion. He will now educate you in this most ancient art and show you how a superior race disposes of mongrel annoyances.”

Dr. Shadows assessed his options as the massive wrestler shed his greatcoat for ease of movement. The man was only five foot ten, but easily three hundred and fifty pounds of compact muscle. He almost filled the space of the railway car. The Granite Man had no gun and he knew the two slim throwing knives, Ike and Mike, that he kept up his sleeve, would barely make it through the dense layers of flesh on the man.

If the fight lasted any time the whole mission would be compromised, or if they called for the troops he could not possibly hope to fight them. He could already feel the train losing speed as it began the upgrade into the foothills. The attack could not be far in the future.

The two officers also had guns—if they fired them, the odds of his bullet resistant tunic stopping the shells was not great, and the sound would bring the troops from the car ahead of them in a deadly swarm. "I really know how to get into trouble," the Grey Goliath thought. “I just have to figure how to get out of it and fast.”

The Granite Man was taller than his opponent with a longer arm reach but outweighed by a hundred pounds. If it came to grappling he knew he would be at a disadvantage, though not a crippling one. Dr. Shadows was the Sulsa Monastery’s champion at the ancient Korean art of Ssirum, that country's equivalent of Sumo. It was more ancient and simpler with the two players starting in kneeling position, using each other's sword belts for leverage, and then rising to a standing position before trying to toss the opponent out of the dirt ring. If any part of the body besides the soles of the feet touched the ground, that person was considered the loser. It was much like American 'collar and cuff' wrestling in that respect.

Sumo, on the other hand, had a complex series of rules and a heavy and formalized training regime that lasted years. The matches began with the two great bodies hurtling at each other in a concussive charge. Then they used a large number of slaps and body positions to win by tossing or forcing their opponent out of the ring. There were also many *kinjite* techniques—forbidden and illegal moves that echoed the battlefield origins of the sport and could be deadly.

"Okay, Big Boy," the Granite Man said in as insulting a gutter Japanese as he could manage, "let's play your patty cake games."

The impassive face of the Japanese giant registered the insult, but it seemed to only make him more determined to win. He began the ritual 'stomping' gestures that characterized the beginning of a Sumo match by going into a deep squat. In a moment he would begin his bullish charge.

This was the instant that Dr. Shadows had waited for and he sprang forward with Ike and Mike drawn. Before any in the train car could realize what he was doing, he launched both blades over the crouching head of the wrestler and into the throats of the two military officers, killing them.

The Sumo reacted with astounding speed, coming out of his

squat and charging at the Grey Goliath like a bulldozer. Dr. Shadows attempted to avoid the charge but the quicksilver wrestler, all the more amazing because of his bulk, was faster. The sumo collided chest to chest with the Granite Man and knocked him over.

The massive Japanese reached down to grab Dr. Shadows off the ground and literally tossed the American like a doll against the side of the car. Then he charged in again and repeated the ploy. He raised the American over his head and slammed Dr. Shadows into the opposite wall.

Dimly, the Granite Man could see Baron Yashita, torn between watching the spectacle of the fight and wanting to make it past the opponents to summon soldiers from the troop car. The American knew he had to stop that, but he also had to win the battle with the behemoth.

Dr. Shadows struggled to his feet, sure he had a couple of bruised ribs. The Sumo made a grunt of dissatisfaction that 'his toy' could even stand and charged in again. This time the Granite Man met the charge head on, smashing his shoulder into the meat of the broader man's chest. The two maneuvered with a rapid series of hand flails to get arms around the other (in lieu of seizing the ceremonial *mawashi* belt of the sport.)

In a flash, the Sumo had his arms around the Granite Man's middle and was squeezing him like a python. Dr. Shadows, his arms out flung above his head, grunted in agony as the wrestler compressed him in the massive arms.

"Crush him slowly, Taro," the Baron said with great delight, "Let him contemplate the futility of opposing the will of the Emperor before he dies."

*****

Chapter V
Hide and go Flee

Taro the sumo took great delight in tightening his grip slowly. He stared at the pale grey face of his victim with the narrow squinting eyes of a man who likes to hurt people. He increased the pressure with slow deliberate pressure waiting for the satisfying crack of the ribs he knew would come, the exhalation of life's breath and the death of his opponent. He had executed prisoners before that way for the Baron and it thrilled him like nothing other in life.

The Baron Yashita stood fascinated by the scenario before him, sipping from a saki cup in an apparently casual attitude. He made no move to summon help from the troop car or to examine or attend to the two fallen officers. Instead, he stood enjoying the sight of the American having the life gradually crushed out of him.

Dr. Shadows however, had let the massive wrestler gain the grip he had. The Granite Man knew that no single blow he could deliver would make it through the layers of muscle and fat on the sumo. There was no space to execute a Ssirum takedown or to do one of the spinning kicks that Sulsa Do had made him capable of, and so could not generate the power necessary to bring the behemoth down. The only alternative was to risk a close in strategy. So he appeared to play the monster's game, and despite the pain in his ribs, let the man grab him.

As soon as the sumo began to squeeze the Grey Goliath, Dr. Shadows focused his mind to a red-hot pinpoint. He utilized the intense concentration he had gained in his years of paralysis at the Sulsa Monastery. He raised his arms, and with an explosive exhalation of air, drove the points of his elbows down with sledgehammer force into the collarbones of the Japanese.

The giant's collarbones snapped with an audible crack. The wrestler let out a scream and fell back, away from the Granite Man. Dr. Shadows used the moment of release to leap into the air and execute a thrusting front kick to the man's head that snapped it back. The giant dropped to the floor, dead with a broken neck.

Baron Yashita actually dropped his saki cup in shock when the sumo fell to the ground. His mind had a hard time imagining that the giant could ever be overcome, especially by so unorthodox a means. Before he could react or cry out, the Granite Man sprinted across the room and knocked the official out with a simple old-fashioned right cross.

"Okay, Baron," Dr. Shadows said to the unconscious Japanese, "time to go save your 'dutiful wife'." He was suddenly conscious that the train was slowing down and the rocking motion had ceased. "They've uncoupled the aft section of the train," he thought. "The attack will happen any time."

He quickly shouldered the unconscious Baron Yashita and ran to the door of the car. He unlocked it and was out on the platform by the time the first gunshots from up front sounded. He jumped to the ground and raced off into the undergrowth with his burden across his shoulders like a sack of potatoes.

****

Once the Granite Man made it far enough into the underbrush to remain unseen from the rail line, he dropped the Baron behind some rocks and sat down with a groan. His sides were on fire from the fight and the exertion of the run. He was also bleeding from the slight cut from the Korean's knife attack.

The spot he had settled into was a little way up a slight incline and gave him a full view up the tracks for several miles. Less than half a mile up the line the train ground to a complete halt and the irregulars came swarming out of the darkness with guns blazing.

The Japanese soldiers had been alerted by the slowing of the train cars and had just enough warning to mount a defense. They fought well, contrary to many accounts of battles with the irregulars, repulsing the first attack with massed fire. It was a hopeless position, however, as the Russian and Chinese forces of the irregulars had good fire discipline and tactics. They held off after the first attack and began to work their way backward from the baggage cars.

Dr. Shadows tore strips from the kimono of the unconscious Baron to bind and gag the man. He then took off his tunic and improvised a binding for his own ribs. When he had re-donned his leather tunic, he set to deciding the next step. "I have to get this lump of nobility to the city now," he thought, "and while he's light, he isn't light enough to carry all the way."

Down below the irregulars had begun to work their way under the train car and began firing up through the floor of the carriage. The soldiers within fired back with little accuracy, wasting precious ammunition. The irregulars then began to pile wood that had been soaked in petrol under the cars. After they had drawn as much of the Japanese gunfire as they wanted, and once they were free from beneath the train, the irregulars lit the wood.

“War is never pretty,” the Granite Man thought, “least of all total war.” He made sure the Baron was solidly secured to a fallen tree and then moved down from the hillside toward the carnage. He moved through the light trees and brush that were scattered along the hillside using his skill at U Shin Bop, the Korean art of invisibility to remain unseen. It was a combination of stealth, psychology and camouflage that had given the practitioners of Sulsa Do a reputation akin to magicians.

This stealth allowed him to get within a few feet of a gathering of irregulars, former White Russian soldiers from their bearing, which were discussing the raid.

“They did not find him,” the tallest of the group said.

“He could not have known of the attack, Vladimir,” a second said. “Could he?”

“Sergi is right,” another said, “That scum Yashita must have been warned about the attack; how else do you explain he is not on the train?”

“I heard his guard was found dead.”

“Enough!” the first speaker said. “However he got out we must find him; killing a bunch of Japanese soldiers and burning some drugs is nothing if that architect of evil escapes! Have everyone search the area for him!”

The Granite Man backed away from the group. “Now they will be looking for us,” he thought. “I have to move Yashita now.” Then he noticed the group moved off to the side of the clearing they were standing in. They mounted horses there and spoke a few more words amongst themselves in preparation to riding off.

Dr. Shadows moved swiftly to one of the paths they had to ride past and scrambled up a tree. A few minutes later, as they rode out beneath him, he was relieved to see they were spaced. Some rode out in pairs, but most individually. The last rider was the tall one, Vladimir, and he was almost a full minute behind the rider ahead of him.

The Granite Man launched himself from the tree and pulled the rider from the horse and knocked him unconscious with a blow to the base of the skull.

"This is a lot easier than explaining, Vladimir," Dr. Shadows said to the unconscious man as he gently sent him down beneath a bush. "I'll donate a dozen horses to the cause when I can." He didn't bother to bind the man as he had every expectation to be long gone when he awakened. "If I'm lucky, he'll think he hit a low tree branch."

The Granite Man mounted the Russian's beautiful white stallion and rode back to Baron Yashita.

The kidnapped Japanese was awake and complaining when Dr. Shadows returned. The gag muffled his words, but it was pretty clear they were all obscene and pointed directly at the American and his ancestry.

"Nice to see you're all awake, Baron," Dr. Shadows said as he hefted the official and placed him face down across the withers of the horse. "I wouldn't want you to miss the ride back to the city to see your dutiful bride." With that the Granite man mounted and rode off toward Harbin, serenaded by the muffled curses of the Baron.

*****

Chapter VI
A Balanced Account

Meeting the dawn deadline would not have been a problem if Dr. Shadows could have ridden straight up Torgovaia Street to the Hotel Moderne, but he could not. Not with a kidnapped Japanese official on a stolen irregular horse and covered in blood. Instead, he had to leave the horse outside of town in a farmer's yard and carry the Japanese toward the suburbs.

All the way the enraged Baron continued to curse with an endurance of anger that truly amazed the American. "You might want to save your breath to try and talk Ling Fu out of killing you," Dr. Shadows said, "because nothing you have to say to me will change our destination." The Baron's answer was to stare daggers at his captor and begin cursing anew.

The Granite Man was able to steal a truck from another farmer (for which he left more than enough cash in the mail slot of the house) and hot-wire it. It was a battered old Model T that had been converted to farm use. He was able to drive to a block away from the hotel without being challenged.

"It is going to get a bit dicey from this point out," Dr. Shadows said to the Baron, "so I can't have you mouthing off so much." As if to prove the Granite Man's point, the Japanese began to mumble in protest again. Dr. Shadows wrapped his right arm around the man's neck and squeezed. The captive had barely a moment to register objection before the chokehold cut off the blood supply to his brain and he passed painlessly into a deep sleep.

The American set about to wrap the prisoner in some burlap he had taken from the back of the truck so that, at least a first inspection, it looked like he was merely carrying an ungainly package. He stepped back to survey his work. "Well," he said aloud, "anyone with half a brain will figure out what I'm carrying; fortunately most of the troops on the ground here don't even have that." He hoisted the unconscious Japanese on his shoulders again and tried to look nonchalant as he walked the rest of the distance to the hotel.

The streets were completely deserted at just two hours before dawn, but truly they were emptier than most night hours; kidnappings and robberies were still rife in Harbin. The Granite Man was not concerned with any casual encounter. His concern was that some of the city police might be abroad and demand a cut of whatever illicit activity he was engaged in.

He made it all the way to the rear door of the hotel before encountering a hotel guard.

"What have you got there?" the uniformed man asked. He was a Chinese, armed with a pistol that he brandished at Dr. Shadows as he walked down the street toward the loading dock of the hotel.

"I have a delivery for the party in room twenty-one." The Granite Man said in Cantonese. "Is there somewhere I can leave it or should I bring it up?" In the dark of the street the guard could not see Dr. Shadows' face and barely make out the shape he had over his shoulder. The question put him off his guard.

'Put it in the loading area," the guard said. He gestured with his pistol toward the back of the building. In the second the guard's eyes were off the Granite Man, he swung his right leg up in an axe kick striking the man a glancing blow on his head. The guard dropped unconscious.

Dr. Shadows rolled the guard into the shadows of the loading dock and then raced in the back door of the hotel. He went up the back stairs as fast as he could with his burden. He reached the floor of the hotel suite just as Baron Yashita came awake with a fresh string of curses.

"You can stop complaining in a minute, Baron," Dr. Shadows said, "We're almost at our destination." He moved down the empty hallway and stood in front of number twenty-one.

"This could be the biggest mistake of my life," he thought, "but like the Abbot said 'Doing evil is easy—you have to work at goodness'." He hefted the Baron to a more comfortable position. "This is sure defined as work."

He knocked on the door and waited.

"Enter, Ghost Healer," Ling Fu's voice called out with no sign of weariness, "We await you."

The Granite Man eased the door open but dropped the Japanese prisoner to his feet in the hall. The American held the squirming man at arms-length out in the hall while he slipped partway into the room. Inside he could see that the corpulent bandit was standing by a table of *zakuskist*, Russian hors d'oeuvres, picking at them with his knife. Madame Yashita was reclining, still bound, on the couch against the far wall.

"I have returned with the Baron Yashita," Dr. Shadows said, "Now you must release the woman." With the mention of her husband's name, the woman roused herself from a half doze and sat upright. Her face held an expression of hope.

"My husband has come to rescue me?" she asked in Japanese.

"Not exactly, Madame Yashita," the American said. "I had to appeal to his humanity." She looked at him oddly, then with a puzzled expression.

Ling Fu stepped up to the woman and cut her bonds, but

placed a hand on her kimono. "Show me this monster," he said, "then she may leave."

The Granite Man pulled the Japanese nobleman into the room and removed his hood and gag. He immediately began cursing vehemently.

When his wife saw that he was bound and had been brought by force, a light went out in her that had sparked with the American's arrival.

"You stupid woman," Yashita said. "How could you allow me to be put in this position; me, the representative of our most noble Emperor, treated like a common chattel for your sake? Why did you not take your own life for the glory of the Motherland? Stupid cow, you have jeopardized the conquest of this pitiful land with your incompetence? How will the Emperor ever re—"

With a strangled cry the woman pulled away from Ling Fu's grasp, yanking the dagger from his belt sheath at the same time. She whirled and with a fury that should have been beyond the capability of her tiny body, flung herself across the room and plunged the blade repeatedly into the chest of her startled husband. As she did, the kimono slipped off her shoulders and the account the Baron had written on her body over the years, was clearly visible in the uncountable scars that crisscrossed her alabaster flesh.

The bandit made a move to stop the woman, but Dr. Shadows was across the room and stayed his hand.

"No, Ling," he said, "It was your knife that has ended his life. Let that be enough; her blood debt was greater than yours and the account is paid in full."

Ron Draper joins Pulp Empire in this volume as he brings a quick and dirty little ditty that takes us straight back to the Old West.

Price of Survival

By Ron Draper

The desert rested uneasily under the glare of the sun—temporarily subdued by the heat. A rabbit peered out warily, blinked and returned to the safety of its burrow; a coyote, roused momentarily from its sleep, stretched lazily and turned its muzzle to the sky to sniff the torrid air; high overhead, an eagle, swept effortlessly along by the wind, turned its attention to the ground as the first pangs of hunger reminded it of the necessity to make a kill.

Below was the desert—silent, watchful, deadly, a savage environment where death patiently stalked the weak and unwary, the improvident and the foolish. In such a rigorous setting life was as fragile as glass, as easily snuffed out as the flickering flame of a candle. Only the strong and the vigilant survived. The bones of the victims can be found in the parched sand, bleached white by the relentless rays of the sun.

Matt's lean, muscular body swayed rhythmically as he guided the buckboard through the jagged piles of lava rock, which loomed like tall, silent sentries against the blue of the sky. The heat was oppressive, heat-sapping.

Nancy sat beside him. The thin layer of dust that covered her face like a powdery mask did not conceal her dark young beauty. Nor did it hide the fear in her eyes.

"How much longer?" she asked.

"A few more hours."

"Will we get there before dark?"

"God willing. We started early enough."

She shivered. "Good. I would hate to spend the night out here. I want to sleep in my own bed tonight."

He was glad they only went to the settlement a couple of times a year. It was not an easy trip. The journey across the desert was arduous in itself, without taking into account the ever-present dangers that stalked them.

But it was a necessity. The buckboard was piled high with provisions they had bought to see them through the winter—beans, flour, coffee, a pair of new, store-bought clothes for each of them to replace the ones worn out during the previous year. They didn't need a lot. Their garden provided them with vegetables and there were always deer to shoot for meat. They were lucky to have a cow to provide milk and cheese.

The cattle they raised were a cash crop. A few were sold to provide money for their needs but most were kept to increase the herd. He visualized the day when cattle would graze the lush grass that grew on the foothills of the section of land deeded to him by the government. With a bit of luck he could become a man of means.

It was a dream he and Nancy shared, which was why they had settled on a homestead in this remote area, thirty miles from the nearest settlement, an hour's ride to the nearest neighbor. They wanted a place to call home, a place where they could raise a family.

Others would follow. He was convinced of it. It was only a matter of time before newcomers showed up to help tame the rough country. One day there would be neighbors and schools and churches.

If only he had a son to leave it to.

He patted the worn black bible that rested on the seat beside him and turned his gaze to the heavens. It would happen. Someday there would be friends who lived nearby and a son to replace the one they had lost.

God was good. In the meantime, he had his faith to sustain him.

For now it was enough.

*****

The Indians appeared without warning. Nancy saw them first. Matt heard her sharp intake of breath and then followed her gaze. There were three of them, nearly hidden in the shade of a gnarled juniper tree, legs loosely gripping the withers of the wiry Indian ponies they straddled.

Matt touched the stock of the Winchester repeater tucked under the seat.

"Easy, Nancy," he said.

The Indians sat motionless as statues. They were naked from the waist up, long black hair adorned with a single eagle feather. They were young, early twenties or late teens, Matt judged. Each of them cradled an ancient muzzleloader, relics from the War Between the States. The weapons were old and tarnished but none-the-less lethal.

Folks at the settlement had warned that a few Indians had wandered off the isolated reservations they had been forced onto after the last skirmish with the army. The Indian wars were long past but a small number of malcontents still roamed the frontier, begging for food and stirring up trouble. Who could blame them? They had lost everything dear to them as the flood of white settlers continued to drive them from their lands. Was it any wonder they struck back when they had the opportunity?

The largest of the trio edged his pony near the buckboard and gestured that he wanted food.

Matt hesitated. Was it wise to encourage them? He had heard sad tales about people who gave food to Indians. Besides, there was plenty of game in the mountains. All they had to do was hunt for it.

He turned to his wife. "What do you think?"

"Give it to them. Maybe they will go away." Her face was chalky white, her lips two thin lines. He could see she was near hysteria. Her nerves had been bad ever since she lost the baby.

"All right," he said.

He kept his fingers on the rifle as she poured a sparse amount of beans and flour into two empty sacks. Then she added several chunks of jerky. The Indians watched greedily. When she finished it was a pathetically small amount of food.

"Sugar? Tobacco?" the Indian queried.

Matt shook his head. "We're short ourselves."

The Indian grunted and stared hard at Matt. His eyes shifted to the Winchester rifle cradled across Matt's knees and after a moment's hesitation he reached out a hand to grasp the food. He gestured to his companions and they swiftly disappeared into the desert.

"They're gone," Matt said needlessly.

"For now."

"They won't be back. No reason to."

He had never been more wrong.

*****

Matt awoke with the sun the following morning, as was his custom. He stoked the coals in the pot-bellied stove and put coffee on to heat while he started the chores. There was no need to milk, as Old Bessie, their milk cow, was dry. She would calve soon and if it was a heifer they would have two cows to milk in a couple of years.

He would let Nancy sleep a little longer. After the strain and turmoil of the days before, she deserved it.

They had arrived at their cabin just before dusk the night before. After toting their provisions into the house they had fixed a bite to eat and then spent an hour discussing their hopes and fears. They had such high hopes of building a ranch and raising a family. Nancy was distrustful of the Indians they had seen. He did his best to quiet her fears.

As was their habit they read a chapter from the bible and then knelt together to say their prayers.

When they crawled into bed Nancy initiated the lovemaking.

She was frantic to get pregnant again and insisted they have intimate relations nearly every night. Matt did nothing to discourage it. She was an exciting woman and he enjoyed making love to her. There was nothing wrong with a man enjoying sex with his wife.

They both had slept well afterwards.

He got his mare out of the barn and saddled her, planning to do a hurried check on their herd before waking Nancy.

The sun was just coming over the horizon when he saw the Indians. They were on the ridge, overlooking the cabin, making no effort at concealment.

Why were they still here, he wondered?

They rode the skyline with savage grace, their bronze bodies catching the light of the morning sun. They seemed to be headed toward the cabin. He wondered why. Did they intend to beg for food again or were their intentions more sinister?

He realized how vulnerable they were. It would be a simple matter for them to lie in wait and ambush him while he was tending the stock. Their old muzzleloaders were not as deadly as his Winchester but they would do the job. And with him dead, Nancy would be at their mercy. He knew what Indians did to white women.

Abruptly he came to a decision. There were times when quick, brutal action was required for survival. In this savage land it was kill or be killed, eat or be eaten. Only the strong survived

It was better to be safe than sorry.

As the Indians crossed a clearing less than fifty feet ahead of him, he raised his rifle and took careful aim. His first bullet hit the lead Indian in the chest and knocked him off his horse. Before the others had time to recover, he shot the second one. The last

Indian gazed about desperately, trying to locate the source of his danger before deciding to make a run for it. His momentary delay gave Matt time to pump another cartridge into his rifle. Before the Indian's horse had taken a dozen leaps, Matt hurried off a shot. The Indian winced but kept going.

Matt slammed another round into the chamber. Taking careful aim at the fleeing Indian's back, he said a silent prayer and squeezed the trigger. The Indian was only yards from safety when Matt's bullet caught up with him. He jerked convulsively and then slumped down on the horse's neck. As the horse sidestepped, the Indian slid weakly off his back.

Matt realized his hands were trembling.

The horses scattered but he was not alarmed. Horses could tell no tales, even if there was someone to listen.

He led his horse to the bodies. In death they seemed younger and less frightening.

He knew where there was a small cave nearby which would provide concealment for the bodies. One by one he loaded the Indians on his horse and took them there. After deposited their bodies inside he covered the entrance with rocks to keep coyotes from eating their flesh.

When he was finished he rubbed his hands together, feeling a twinge of guilt but also mindful that he had done exactly what needed to be done.

He bowed his head and said a silent prayer for his victims.

It seemed like the Christian thing to do.

We go from the Old West straight out in to space. New Pulp Empire contributor Scott Taylor still gives us a bit of that frontier feeling as Magnus Rucker and Delroy McIntosh make…

Planetfall

By Scott Taylor

The big twin Rotex engines screamed in protest, the airframe of the Dauntless creaked and popped, and the pilot gripped the yoke so tightly his knuckles ached. Still, there was nothing that was going to change the fact that Captain Magnus Rucker was about to auger in.

"Strap in, Tosh," Rucker yelled into the com, "This doesn't look good."

The digits on the range to surface meter plummeted, the rate of descent was slowing, but not fast enough.

An alarm sounded just seconds before the tiny craft shuddered and lurched sideways. "Flame out on Wilma! Tosh, see if you can—"

"I an' I is on it, Cap." Delroy McIntosh said in his thick

Jamaican accent. He was up and out of his harness, being buffeted against the bulkhead he clung to for support. Keeping one hand clasped on the overhead supports, he crossed the cargo bay to the starboard engine control panel. Starboard was Wilma, port was Roxanne. Wilma was the temperamental type.

Tosh grabbed the big yellow lever marked PRIME, cocked it, then punched the glowing green button labeled START. A screech like metal fingernails scraping a chalkboard made Tosh wince and curse under his breath. "Don't plan on Wilma makin' it in time for the party, Cap."

"Damn." Rucker punched the roof of the cockpit. "Well Tosh, it's been nice knowin' ya"

"Likewise."

The Dauntless broke through the cloud cover, and the flat, red sand surface rose up to meet them. Rucker pulled back a bit on the throttle for Roxanne, tapped the fore thrusters to keep the Dauntless out of a spin.

There was no doubt they were going down, but Rucker would try to make it survivable. If possible.

His seat was jumping around under him, the yoke continued fighting his efforts, and his helmet kept slamming against the cockpit canopy. A gigantic sand dune came rushing toward him, impossibly fast. Red sand filled his field of vision. Then blackness.

*****

"Kiss me neck back, what the 'ell are we supposed to do now, mon?" Tosh kicked at the sand. The sandy surface had absorbed the worst of the impact, but the Dauntless had plowed in deep.

"Why didn' you jus' follow the bleedin' nav beacons?"

"I did, Tosh. Right down to the meter. We were in the navigable zone." Rucker stood on the rim of the crater they had just created.

"Don't seem all that navigable for me," Tosh mumbled.

"Well, there's oxygen. Temperature is within habitable limits."

"Yeah, jus' crucial. At least I can be able for breathe while I are starvin'. You see anythin' from up there?"

Rucker scanned the horizon with the nocks, switched to infrared, then back to visible. "I don't know…looks like something at seventy-nine degrees…and something else out farther at one twenty-five. Yeah, something big out toward the horizon at one twenty-seven." He pushed the nocks to max magnification, the view flickered, then stabilized into a grainy image of twisted metal. "Let's pack up what we can haul, and head out to one twenty-seven, relative Dauntless. That thing is definitely man made."

"Alree," Tosh said, grabbing a Mag rifle from the weapons rack. "But if it gets dark out, and some big bad ugly comes up and wants to yam on you, I'm goin' let it get a bite out your ass, at least."

Out on the trackless waste, an enormous cratered moon hung in the blue daylight haze above their heads. Rucker and Tosh plodded across the dunes of sliding sand. The wind rippled Rucker's shirt and tugged at Tosh's dreds.

Within two hundred meters of their crater, they stumbled across a half buried oxygen cylinder, then what looked like a length of hydraulic hose. Next Tosh found a large chunk of titanium sheeting, crumpled and scorched. A piece of shattered cockpit canopy here, a Pendragon outdrive revolution shaft there.

"Mon, this whole damn place be littered with broke parts for ships."

At the crest of the next dune, Rucker raised the nocks again, and got a better look at the shape on the horizon. It looked like one of the big Pre-Consortium freighters, the kind they called Dreadnaughts. Easily a kilometer long, this one's back was broken, and it laid half buried in the sand.

They passed by several chunks of what was once a luxury passenger liner and the burned out hulk of a revenue patrol cruiser. Finally, as the light of day began to fade, they arrived at the long shadow cast by the crippled dreadnaught.

Both stood in awe of the enormous mountain of metal laid out before them. They had seen these giants in flight, in their natural element. Even so, this massive train of crumpled metal laid out before them seemed to be impossibly immense.

Finding a way in was not a problem, a thousand splits in the skin of the craft made entry easy enough. Rucker slapped at the light bar on his flight vest, the amber glow created a small pool of light in the cavernous hold.

"Cha," Tosh said. "This mother be huge, yeah?"

"First things first, Tosh. Food, shelter."

"Alree, mon," Tosh said, shining his own rifle mounted light on a bank of storage bins. "Hey, Cap. Look 'pon this." He pointed at the latches of the bins, which all appeared to have been cut open. "Looks good for been a plasma torch used."

"Chances are that didn't happen pre-crash." Rucker scanned the floor, strewn with detritus and red sand blown in from outside. "Look over here, Tosh. Empty ration cans, remains of a fire. Blankets."

"Well, for someone set up house, must be some grub somewhere…"

The Dreadnaught, being the size of a small city, would take weeks to search thoroughly, and the two men were bone weary. So after a search of the immediate area, they made do with a meal of Foodbrick from their own rations, and Rucker sat up for the first watch while Tosh wrapped himself in one of the grey blankets and shut his eyes.

Rucker sat in a shaft of light from the enormous moon, rifle across his lap, his back against a sandblasted girder. He listened to the sound of the wind, moaning through the rents in the hull, and wondered about the fate of the dreadnaught's crew.

Probably most had died at their duty stations. Perhaps that was best. Maybe he and Tosh were the unlucky ones, stranded on this shithole, to await a slow wasting death.

An occasional gust of wind blew a handful of sand against the hull, where it made a noise like static on a radio. Tosh snored lightly. And then there was a new sound.

A low rumble, with an accompanying high pitched squeaking noise; the unmistakable sound of a tracked vehicle. "Tosh," Rucker reached out and shook his friend's shoulder. "Tosh, get up. Something's moving out there."

Tosh sat up, rubbing the sleep from his eyes. "Sounds big."

"Lights out, Tosh. Let's get a look at them before they get a look at us."

"No argument."

Out into the moonlit night, skittering across the still warm sands, Rucker and Tosh kept low, following the racket toward the mechanical beast.

Rucker had seen something like it before, it was a mobile

drilling rig, its large square platform a few hundred meters across, with a central tower of girders that rose to scrape at the night sky. It had a pair of gigantic tracks on it that chewed at the sand and propelled it along at little more than walking speed.

Originally intended to drill this dry landscape for water, or some other precious liquid, from the looks of it, it had been retasked decades ago. Layers of makeshift structure had been tacked on haphazardly, bits of flotsam and jetsam welded or riveted onto the framework to create crude shelters. Cables ran everywhere in a discordant tangle providing power or communications where it was convenient.

Silhouetted in the lights dangling from the metal framework, hundreds, maybe even a thousand people swarmed. Rucker watched them through the nocks, talking, moving about like tiny insects, bartering with one another. Living their lives in this strange mobile city.

"I don't like the looks…where you think they goin'?" Tosh asked, keeping his voice low although there was no chance of being overheard. Not from this distance. Not with the racket that thing was making.

"Yeah…straight for the Dauntless." Rucker lowered his nocks. "Wreckers. Picking over the bones of whatever falls out of the sky."

"I think it best we tell 'em the crew ain't done with the old girl yet." Tosh picked up the Mag rifle, checked the charge.

"C'mon, shouldn't be hard to catch up with that thing." Rucker took off at a trot across the dunes, Tosh slung the rifle across his back and followed close behind. They approached the hulking monstrosity from the shadow of one of the giant treads as it ground through the sand, leaving a deep furrow in its wake.

The clamor of the machinery was deafening, so Rucker directed Tosh with hand signals.

Follow me. Keep out of sight.

Rucker waited for the tread to pass, then cut around behind it and grabbed one of the slowly rising steel plates at the rear. The first ten meters were the toughest, Rucker and Tosh hanging on, legs dangling while the tread lifted them off the ground. After that point, the tread went around a cog, and the angle changed, making it possible to lean against it as they rode up, and finally, they were able to stand on the plate as it traveled the top of the track.

From here it was just a matter of hopping off the steel plate and onto the first convenient spot. Except that there weren't any. They rode along on the clattering beltway, examining the cowling that covered the top of the track, and no access presented itself to the upper side.

Rucker looked to Tosh, and the look on his first mate's face made Rucker grateful for the clamor that kept communication to hand signals. Rucker shrugged, and then Tosh shot him a hand signal.

They started walking backward, jumping the gaps between the plates, buying time while looking for a way off. A couple of access panels faced the tread, but they had no handles or latches on them. An electrical cable hung down from the cowling, tantalizingly close, but to reach it would take a leap of faith, then a hand over hand crawl above the gnashing and grinding drive gears.

Rucker was studying the cable, calculating his chances, when he took a bad step and wedged the heel of his boot into the gap between plates. He tugged at it, tried to work it back and forth, but only succeeded in twisting his ankle. He was being drawn inexorably forward, toward the point that the tread took its downward trip.

"Tosh!" he yelled. But Tosh was busy looking for an escape, and couldn't hear Rucker over the racket of the machinery.

The boot was integrated into his flight suit, so slipping it off wasn't an option. Rucker reached into the cargo pocket on his thigh, and grabbed his small laser cutter. It would make short work of the thick flight suit, with the downside of taking Rucker's foot off as well. He decided on a better use for the thing. He threw it at Tosh.

It hit the big Jamaican squarely between the shoulder blades, and got his attention. Tosh jogged the few steps back to where Rucker struggled, and clasped both hands around the ankle of his boot. He pulled, hard. The veins on his temples stood out and beads of perspiration formed on his brow. But he couldn't break the grip of the treads. Thirty meters from the edge and moving slowly, Tosh unslung the Mag rifle and grabbed a red plastic magazine marked THERMAL from his bandolier.

He slotted the magazine into the rifle, then drew back the bolt to chamber a round. Twenty meters from the edge now, Tosh took aim over the side, down into the drive gears and squeezed the trigger. A flat *whump* and the rifle bucked, launching its projectile. A spark of light so bright that it was blue at the edges burned at the point of impact.

Ten meters from the edge. Tosh worked the bolt again, ejecting the plastic casing and chambering another thermal round. *Whump.* Another bright arc of thermal energy lit the inside of the gear housing, sparks of white hot metal began popping from the still churning gears.

Two meters from the edge. Then, a terrible rending crash, like scrap metal in a blender, and the tread ground to a halt. The platform slewed to one side as the remaining track continued to drive forward. Rucker looked over the edge, now barely a meter away, and whistled.

"Well, so much for stealth," he said.

*****

Mordecai Stubb had a pretty good thing going here, and he wasn't about to let these two clowns mess it up for him. Leader of the wreckers, lord mayor of Crawlertown, he was a bandy little troll of a man who got what he wanted through intimidation and coercion.

But now these two, the cowboy who liked the sound of his own voice and the big black guy with the dreadlocks and the attitude, had to go and survive the crash of their ship. Mordecai didn't like survivors. They complicated things, and Mordecai liked things simple.

He sat in a high backed chair that had once been the pilot's seat of a Talon fighter, his boots kicked up on the grey steel desk in front of him. He took a long drag from a little black cigarillo, then exhaled blue smoke in Rucker's direction. "So, let me get this straight, Ruger—"

"Rucker. Captain Magnus Rucker."

"Captain?" Mordecai made a face like he was sucking on a lemon. "Military's been disbanded for awhile now."

"Nevertheless."

"Alright, *Captain*. You make some kind of piloting error that causes you to plow in on our humble little world, here, then…"

“There was no error, the nav beacon—”

“*Then*,” Mordecai slipped his feet from the desktop and sat upright. “Then, in order to elicit the aid of the local people, you decide to sabotage their very means of their existence, thereby endearing yourselves. Is that about right?”

“Well, when you put it like that…” Rucker looked up over Mordecai’s shoulder, as if the wall behind his head had just become very interesting. “…it just sounds so…”

“Imbecilic? Irresponsible?”

“I was going to go with flashy. Listen, Tosh here is a mechanical genius. He can fix practically anything. Should be no problem getting your little…community…back as good as new. Better even. Right, Tosh?”

“Ya, mon. I can have the old girl runnin right as rain in no time. All I gonna need is some—”

Mordecai slammed a meaty hand flat down on his desktop. His beady eyes bore into Rucker. “What *I* am going to need, is payment, you moron. We live hand to mouth out here, shifting through the sand to live on what falls out of the sky. If I have to spend time, resources, and manpower fixing your screwup—”

“Oh, is that it?” Rucker smiled his best Trust Me smile. “Don’t worry about that one bit, Morty. I’m sure that what I’ve got in the cargo hold of the Dauntless will be *very* interesting to you.”

“Magnus—” Tosh said, and glared at the Captain.

“Now, Tosh, we’re going to have to work with our new friends here.”

Mordecai sized the two up for a moment, then turned to one of the greasy brutes standing by the door. “Josu, fuel up a couple of scramblers, get two teams ready. You are going to take the

Captain out to his ship, and get an inventory of the cargo. Meanwhile, Mr. McIntosh, here, is going to get started on the repairs to our fair city."

*****

Rucker shielded his eyes from the intense light of the blazing sunrise as he watched the six-wheeled scramblers being lowered to the desert floor. Josu supervised the operation, directing the group of seven other men as they cranked the clattering winches by hand, and the vehicles slowly descended on cables from the underbelly of the platform.

"Look like you been give a nice group of playmates, Cap," Tosh said, nodding toward the cluster, all of whom had the build of a gorilla. "You should see the lot they give me to help fix the tread. Real bunch o' winners, for sure."

"Have you looked at the damage yet? What's the preliminary?"

"Not too bad. Look like the splines be sheared off for the main driveshaft, and the mesh gears be all fused, but them could build up an interstellar cruiser with the spares they got."

"I don't think parts are the problem, its know-how. Mordecai doesn't strike me as the type that surrounds himself with the best and the brightest." Rucker kept his voice low and his tone conversational. "Listen, Tosh, that joker is bad business. I can feel it. You and me, we're nothing but an inconvenience to him, standing between him and the salvage of the Dauntless."

"Ya mon, I caught the vibe." Tosh reached to touch the sling of his mag rifle, then remembered that it had been 'stowed' for him. He felt naked without it.

“Well, take your time on the repairs to this rig, I’ve got a feeling that our value will be greatly diminished once this monstrosity is mobile again.”

“Alree. What you gonna do about the cargo?”

Rucker kicked at a pebble. “Hell, Tosh, as long as I can keep them from finding what’s hidden in the front landing gear bay, I don’t care if they take it all.”

“Hey, flyboy!” Josu clapped his hand on Rucker’s shoulder, startling him. “Time to mount up.”

The scrambler lived up to its name. Built for speeding across the dunes, its low profile and wide stance kept it stable while its knobby tires slung rooster tails of sand into the dry air. Josu sat in the driver’s seat, applying throttle with a lever in his right hand, steering with a pair of foot brakes. The rest of the passengers rode like the cargo, clutching on to the chassis wherever was convenient. They charged up the face of the dunes; felt a momentary weightlessness as they crested the rise, then held on for a skidding plunge down the next face.

Josu, who was obviously experienced at desert recon, had no trouble locating the spot where the Dauntless had gone down. Arriving on the rim of the planet’s newest crater, Rucker jumped off the scrambler as it slid to a stop. Looking down over the rim, at his beloved craft in the bottom of the bowl, Rucker’s pulse quickened. The wind was already blowing drifts of sand against Roxanne’s engine cowling, the nose was even further buried than before. The desert was slowly claiming the old bomber.

The men from Crawlertown busied themselves unloading their gear, sand blowers, automoles, and plasma cutters. “Whoa, there guys,” Rucker said. “What are the cutters for? We’re just here to get a look at the cargo.”

“No tellin’ what we’ll run up against. Cutters are just part of the standard loadout,” Josu said between grunts as he lugged a mechmule off the scrambler’s deck rack.

“Just remember, salvage rights extend to the cargo only. First person that cuts on my ship is going to find out what happens when I get cranky.”

“We’ll do our best to see that it doesn’t come to that.” Josu chuckled and slapped Rucker on the back, a bit harder than was friendly.

Rucker stretched his mouth into a tight grimace, the nails of his clenched fist bit into his palm. ”I appreciate it, buddy.”

*****

Tosh had difficulty telling where the machinist left off and the machine began. Metal pistons, a greasy drive chain and a bundle of electrical wires stuck out from the left sleeve of the grungy coveralls. A human arm extended from the right, but its skin and bone had been augmented by metal banding and plastic tubing.

“Hey mon, you Hogarth?” Tosh had to speak loudly to be heard over the whine of a grinder.

“Who’s askin?” The machinist looked up from his work. His face had burn scars covering half of it, and a camera lens protruded from his left eye socket. The focus ring of the lens clicked and then spun a quarter turn. “Hey, you’re the one who fubared the drive gears on the number two track, aren’t ya?” His voice sounded like it was coming out of a cheap loudspeaker.

“An accident…me mate was stuck…”

“Haw! Good one. An accidental discharge of two thermal

rounds—right into the old gearbox. Whoops!" When Hogarth laughed, Tosh had the sensation of biting on tinfoil.

"Regardless, you the machinist, yeah?"

"Well, what's it look like to you?" Hogarth held up the mechanical appendage. The grinding wheel at the end of it retracted, and a three pronged claw blossomed, then clicked shut with a snap. "Made it myself. As a matter of fact, I guess you could say I've made most of myself." More tinfoil laughs.

Now that the man had turned from his workbench, Tosh could see that aside from his human head and right arm, a good part of the man was indeed manufactured from scrap. "Nice work," he said.

"Well, I work in what I'm given." Hogarth's arm ratcheted as he retracted it. "So what brings you into the belly of the beast, here? Surely you've got enough spare parts and grunt labor to rebuild an outdrive without my help."

"Always best I get to know the local craftsmen, when I got a job need doin'." Tosh picked up a tiny cylindrical object and squinted carefully at it. "This here be a Sponstill reticular rod?"

The focus ring of the camera lens whirred. "Yes. Yes it is. That is a good eye you've got there my friend."

"This be some very fine work. You make this?"

"Yeah, although I'll never get a call to use it. There isn't a Sponstill subreactor within four thousand klicks of here, I'm sure."

"So, why make it for?"

"Dunno, to keep in practice maybe? These Crawlertown goons don't have much need for a machinist. These are mostly find-and-replace type of guys. Don't have the imagination to realize the value of a fabricator."

"I hear that," Tosh said. "So, how do you fit in? How do a flash gent such as yourself wind up in the belly of this beast?"

"Crashed. Long time ago," Hogarth's cheap speaker voice crackled. "I was a machinist's mate on a long range recon cruiser, the kind they used to send scouting for pirates in the shipping lanes. Anyway, we got caught in this weird gravity well here, and down she went. Nasty crash. I was lucky to survive at all."

"Tell I bout it brother. We been caught in that same freaky grav. Like nothin' I ever seen."

"It's the moon. That huge mother stays in an almost geosynchronous orbit. Plays all hell with the gravity fields."

"Don' help that the nav beacons be mislaid. We followed em right on in here."

Hogarth's human eye avoided contact with Tosh. "Yeah, the nav beacons..."

Tosh snorted. "Tell you what, mon. I and the Cap get off this here rock, first thing I'm doin' is blow all hell out of some bleedin' beacons."

A tiny pincer deployed from Hogarth's arm, extended on a delicate silver shaft, and plucked the reticular rod from Tosh's fingers. "Listen, you're an alright guy, so I'm gonna shoot straight with you. You ain't getting off this planet. If you're lucky, and do as Mordecai tells you, he may let you live past your usefulness, but I wouldn't count on it."

"So that the way it be?"

"That little toad calls the shots round here." An acetylene flame burst from a brass nozzle on Hogarth's arm, and the pincers maneuvered the rod into the blue arc, cutting it in half.

*****

The little toad stood on the bridge of the crawler, pudgy hands clasped behind his back, and looked out across the windblown expanse. Rucker sat in a metal chair, feet splayed out in front of him. Josu stod silent in the doorway, hairy arms folded across his chest.

Mordecai spoke first. “So, Captain Rucker, I hope you had a good time on your field trip with Josu.”

“Yeah, it was wonderful. Charming little planet you’ve got here, really.”

“It’s not much…but its mine.” He turned to face Rucker. “Josu tells me that your cargo is intact and has been inventoried. Your shipping manifests all check out and match the load that you’re carrying. Everything looks on the up and up.”

“Oh, yeah. Up and up.”

“And that, Captain Rucker, is why I don’t trust you. Your paperwork is too correct. As if you didn’t want to be questioned at any Consortium checkstations.”

“Hey, now, where’s the trust? Coming from you, that really hurts. I mean it-“

“Shut up, Rucker. I’m not playing games.” Mordecai’s dark eyes were like little pebbles; his tongue darted out to wet his thin lips. “I have yet to meet the Captain of a ship carrying cargo of any kind that doesn’t have a hoard of contraband stashed away somewhere aboard his vessel.”

Rucker put on a hurt face. “Wait a minute; you think that I’m some kind of smuggler?”

“I think that you’re human. You’re a man trying to make a few extra credits on the side. I just want to make it perfectly plain to you that I know. I know there is something more valuable than

Foodbrick and Gojuice on your little ship, and I'll find it if I have to rip out every rivet."

"You can't do that! Salvage rights extend to cargo only. My ship is—"

"Your ship is on my planet, Captain Rucker, stuck, just like you are. We are a long, long way from any Consortium Enforcers, so I guess that salvage rights are what I say they are."

Rucker's hand went to his hip, where his plaspistol should be holstered. He touched empty leather. "You're holding the cards, Mordecai, but I'll tell you this—there is nothing on that ship that's worth your life."

Rucker stood, scraping the chair legs across the floor for good measure, and made sure he jostled against Josu as he walked out the door.

"He's lying to you," Josu said after Rucker was gone.

"Don't you think I know that?" Mordecai kicked the empty chair, toppling it over. "I'll find what he's hiding if I have to look in every last crevice—"

"No need for that." Josu was smiling broadly. "I overheard him this morning, talking to that dark skinned fella. He's got something hidden in the front landing gear bay that he doesn't want us to find."

Mordecai grinned like a greedy child. "Excellent work, Josu. I mean truly outstanding. But…didn't you say the ship was nose in? Buried pretty deep?"

"Yeah, It's gonna take some manpower to get it cleared. But manpower is something we've got."

"You've got that right, Josu. Get a team out there tomorrow morning, I want that ship uncovered by the time this platform is mobile again."

*****

Work progressed on the ruptured track, Tosh supervising a team of grunt labor as they tore down the damaged assembly. As Hogarth predicted, most of the pieces that would be needed for the repair could be found in the stockpiles on board the crawler.

Tosh had found the storage decks littered with looted items gathered from the debris field of the desert. Not just gears and hydraulic pistons, but plasma injected chill units, complete tachyon waste incinerators, blue wavelength radiation deflectors, and gaseous singularity containers, virtually anything that looked halfway useful was thrown on the pile. Sorting through the mess was the most arduous part of the job.

Tosh followed a trail of hydraulic oil, left by a faulty piston in Hogarth's left leg. It made the machinist much easier to find among the flotsam of the cavernous storage bay. Hunched over a pile of junk, Hogarth tugged on a heavy pulse generation tube with his mechanical arm. The entire pile of debris moved with each heave.

"Hey Garth! How you doin' mon? Does I good to see you gettin' some exercise."

Hogarth looked up from his work. "Gonna have to increase tension on my drive chain," He said, clutching at his mechanical arm with his human one.

"Well, you know how much I need the help of them skilled…hands."

"Hands my butt, it's this thing you need." Hogarth hoisted the mechanical arm and shot a jet of white hot flame from the welding tip.

Tosh kicked at a shock light lens. “Sure be a good deal o’ junk here. You got a pretty good idea what’s what down here?”

Tinfoil laughter erupted. “More than half of me came from down here.”

“Alree, that’s cool, mon.” Tosh fished a flask out of his cargo pocket. “Want a nip? Some Cack I picked up back on the mining station at Cerberus.”

Hogarth’s voicebox squelched feedback. “I haven’t had Cack since…well it’s been awhile.” He took a pull from the flask then winced as he swallowed. “*That* is a truly horrible batch,” he gasped, then took another swig before handing the flask back to Tosh.

Tosh tipped the flask, wheezed. “S’pose a guy was lookin’ round down here for some means of propulsion. Something has enough lift for gettin’ an interplanetary bomber out of this suck ass grav well.”

“You’re still on about that, huh?”

“You know, ‘don’t give up the fight’, and all that.”

“I told ya, Mordecai won’t allow it—”

“Him aye the captain’s problem. I’m the nuts and bolts. Thrust to weight ratio, what you got?”

“Well, for pure power, there’s the Throm-Sturgeon twenty-one.” Hogarth gestured broadly toward a hunk of machinery on the left. “It’s a heavy lifter for sure, but…”

“But I’d need a reactor the size of a starcruiser just to power it up. What else you got?”

“These little Pitts antigrav units would work if you arrayed them around the ship,” Hogarth said, plucking a small purple orb from a heap of junk. “But they’re all missing their networking chips. Besides you’d need a whole crapload of ‘em.”

Hogarth stumbled around the various piles of hardware, tottering on his mechanical legs. "Probably your best bet is a Burtson Liquid Plasma booster. It's a one-time use deal. Strap it on for takeoff and then jettison the damn thing."

"That's the ticket. And you got one of those rude boys stacked up in here somewhere?"

"Yeah, but it won't do you no good. I told you, Mordecai's not lettin' you go anywhere."

"And I told you, let the Cap worry for that sawed off runt. What's it gonna take for me to get the booster?"

Hogarth scratched the back of his neck. "Two things. First, I'll take that flask of Cack off your hands."

"Done." Tosh tossed the chrome flask, the mechanical arm whipped up and an electromagnet grabbed the flask out of the air.

"You say two things, what else you need?"

"Take me with you."

*****

Rucker stood on the upper deck of the platform, leaned back against the sandblasted metal railing looking at the moon looming low overhead, the reflected illumination making the night a bright one.

"Here's what I still don't understand, Tosh…"

Tosh waited, but Rucker seemed to have lost the thought. "Yeah? What's that Cap?" he asked at length.

"Well, the gravity of this planet, judging by its density and diameter, should be roughly equal to three point six E's. That moon up there, probably one point nine, maybe two. Even combined, that's less than six E's…"

"Yeah, that's big pull, mon." Tosh looked up at the moon. The central drilling tower stood silhouetted in the huge blue disk, stretching to a dizzying height. It looked to Tosh as if he climbed the tower to the very top, and stretched out his hand, he could just reach the surface of that moon.

Rucker was still talking, "…it's about appropriate approach angles for the pull encountered, sure. That's what the nav beacons are for. But here's the thing, came in flying *between* this planet and that moon. The gravitational forces wouldn't have combined. If anything, they would be somewhat offset by one another."

Tosh was still staring up, but now his attention was focused on the tower. He wondered why the people on the crawler left it there, it had to be hell in a windstorm. Maybe they used it as a lookout tower.

"Don't you think that's strange, Tosh?"

"Hmm?" Tosh realized his thoughts had been drifting, he had barely been listening to the Captain. "Here's what I think be strange, Magnus. I been spent most of my life in a flight suit, crew for one kind of tub or another, and I never met a pilot with the natural talent as yourself. So, if you tell me that you don't understand why a grav field is actin' the way it does, *that* is strange to me."

"Say, what are you boys doin' out here?" Josu emerged from the shadows in the stairway, his mouth was smiling, but his eyes didn't.

"Just takin' in the night air, Chief," Rucker said.

"Hate to hose down your little party here, but the upper deck's off limits to you two."

"What gives? Morti think we're gonna sprout wings and take

off from up here?"

"Let's don't forget that you are uninvited guests in our humble home." Josu cracked his knuckles. "If I have to toss you down these stairs I will."

Rucker stood up straight, brushed at an imaginary speck on his shirt. "C'mon Tosh, I can tell when we're not wanted."

*****

The next dawn Rucker watched Josu lead two teams of men in scramblers out into the desert, travelling in the direction of the Dauntless. They didn't return until almost dark, sweat stained and filthy. The next day the same two teams of men left just after sunrise, and returned right before dark.

Meanwhile, work progressed on the tread, despite Tosh's Herculean efforts of procrastination.

The third morning the two scramblers left out and disappeared over the dunes as before, but this time they returned to the crawler after just three hours. Rucker watched from the entry port as Josu leaped off the still moving vehicle and mounted the gangplank. Josu shot Rucker a very nasty look as he passed.

Josu strode through the cramped passageways in the interior of the crawler. The look on his face cleared the way for him, men flattening themselves against the bulkheads as he passed. He went directly to Mordecai's private quarters, and threw the door open without knocking.

Mordecai sat at his breakfast, fork full of scrambled Chembryos poised halfway to his mouth. His eyes were still bleary with sleep and whisps of his hair stuck out like a rooster's comb. He put down his fork slowly. “What the hell, Josu. Are you mental?”

“It’s empty! Three day’s digging, and the damn thing’s empty!”

“You’re talking about Rucker’s ship? You’ve got it uncovered?” Mordecai stood and gathered his tatty terrycloth robe over his round belly.

“Yeah, we got the damn thing dug out, I popped the landing gear hatch up front, and guess what? Landing gear!” Josu slammed his fist down on the table, the fork jumped off the plate and clattered onto the floor.

“Take it easy, you meathead. He’s probably got the goods hidden behind some kind of false panel.” Mordecai smoothed his hair. “You’re lucky he didn’t have the thing booby trapped. I’ve seen that happen before, and it ain’t pretty.”

“Let me have five minutes with that cocky bastard. I’ll let the boys take a tooth for every day they spent digging. He’ll talk.”

“But will we understand what the hell he’s sayin if he ain’t got no teeth?” Mordecai shook his head and chuckled. “Cool down, Josu. He’s got you riled. That Jamaican has been given enough time with the tread, get his ass up to my office. Once we’re mobile again, you can do what you want with Rucker.”

*****

No one offered Tosh a chair in Mordecai’s office. Instead he stood in front of the gray steel desk and waited while Mordecai pretended to be engrossed in the paperwork spread out before him.

“Ahem,” Tosh cleared his throat.

Mordecai didn't look up, just held out an index finger and grunted. More time passed in which Tosh considered the consequences of snapping Mordecai's index finger off and shoving it in various orifices. Finally, Mordecai put down his pen and looked up at Tosh.

"Well, you've been given three days and plenty of labor. What's the status of my tread?"

"Me best guess is we have her up and runnin' in four more day."

"How about by nightfall?"

"Tonight?" Tosh's eyebrow arched.

"Yes tonight. You've got until nightfall tonight to get that tread operational."

"Can't be done. I still got to rewind the main drive motor, set up the power inverters and don' even get I started on the state of—"

"Listen to me, you puke." Flecks of spittle flew from between Mordecai's gritted teeth. "I don't need a complete overhaul, just get this pile of junk mobile, and make it happen by sundown."

Tosh scowled. "Alree, alree…I think something can be done. But I gonna need you to cut off the reactor for about fifteen minute."

"Oh, *that* is not going to happen. No way."

"But, if I throw power to the motor directly, there be a good chance she gonna kick back a spike that could—"

"You're the mechanical genius, figure something else out. That reactor stays lit, no matter what."

Tosh threw up his arms and stomped out of the office. His ranting could be heard echoing all the way down the corridor until the bang of a slamming door cut it off abruptly.

The rest of the day Tosh worked at a feverish pace, pushing his team of brutes hard. They made astounding progress, and as the shadows grew long the tread was reassembled. Tosh stood atop the housing for the big motor's power input, directing a sweaty group of men shouldering lengths of thick cable.

"No, no…look, the blue go to red, and the red go to blue. I told you we got to set it up in a parallel—What the bleeding hell are you doing with that Deiner resistor, Lumpy?"

A dull looking man with a unibrow and a sagging lower lip blinked and dropped the cylinder he had been holding. "Uh, I dunno."

"Well, get that out of here and grab a *reverse* Deiner, or you gonna blow us all for hell." Tosh jumped down from his perch, turned to his friend Rucker. "This lot is thick, mon," he said, gesturing over his shoulder with his thumb.

"Speaking of thick…" Rucker said, nodding his head toward Mordecai and Josu, who had ascended the stairway and were approaching.

"Just look what can be done when you've got a little motivation," Mordecai said to Josu. "Here I was under the impression that it might take four days to get this far, but damn if it ain't done in one." He looked out over the railing where the last of the sun was just winking below the horizon. "And right at sundown, just like I asked. It really makes me happy when I get what I want."

"Well, it ain't done right," Tosh said. "Are you gonna take the reactor offline?"

Mordecai sneered. "I told you, not gonna happen."

Tosh gave Rucker a baleful look and shrugged. "Alree, then. There nothin else but for to throw the switch." Tosh stepped to the side and bowed slightly. "Would you like to do the honors?" he said to Mordecai.

"And get my ass fried? You'd like that, wouldn't you? No, that's fine, I'd just as well see you do it."

"I'd rather not."

"It's not a request. Do it," Josu said, leveling a plaspistol.

Tosh sighed, then stepped up to the big lever and gripped the handle. He winced and turned his head away, then began to pull down. "Here go," he said, then grunted and pulled the lever down hard.

The cables snaked out across the decking jumped, and the deck of the crawler lurched forward slightly. The group on the deck held their arms spread to steady themselves.

It began to grow brighter, then brighter still. The lamp hung directly overhead buzzed and glowed with an insane intensity until it burst in a shower of sparks. Next, the lights further away exploded, and then the lights next down the line.

A crackling hum tore the air and cables writhed and sparked on the deck. Tosh yelled "I told you so!" over a whining noise that rapidly increased in pitch and volume. The smell of ozone hung heavy and the pops and flashes of shorting equipment lent a strobe effect to the scrambling of terrified men running for shelter.

Bolts of electrical fire arced; showers of sparks followed one after the other cascading across the deck. Soon a blue ball of light blossomed at the base of the tower throwing the scene into sharp black and white relief. The wiring leading up the tower itself broke free and began whipping about, sparks flying wherever they struck, like the stinging tentacles of some horrific beast.

The whine escalated until it became deafening. Mordecai

jammed the palms of his hands against his ears, as if trying to keep his head from exploding. Josu gaped and pointed at the top of the tower, his mouth was moving but his shouts were drowned.

For a moment it seemed as if a new sun had been born meters above the deck. The top of the tower blossomed in an intense disc of pure brilliance that spread the width of the entire platform, then winked out, leaving everyone on deck blinded in the sudden dark, their ears ringing in the sudden silence.

Luckily for both Rucker and Tosh, neither was still on the deck. Moments after the first light blew, Tosh kicked a reel of cable over the side of the crawler. The end had been made fast to the railing, and as pandemonium broke out, the captain and the Jamaican went over the side, slithering hand over hand down the cable to the desert floor.

Sprinting through the sand to the area shadowed by the massive tread, they shielded their eyes when the intense flash lit the desert floor. Rounding the corner, Rucker skidded to a halt, confronted by the hulking shadow of an enormous man.

"C'mon, the scrambler's over here," Hogarth's loudspeaker voice crackled.

Rucker tried to get a good look at the shape in the shadows in front of him. Certainly a big man, unnaturally big, and somehow odd shaped. "This your friend, Tosh?"

"Ya mon, this' Hogarth. Let's do the intros later."

There was no debate about who would drive, Rucker vaulted into the driver's chair and quickly familiarized himself with the controls while Tosh and Hogarth clambered onto the deck. Tosh checked the straps that held the big Burton booster lashed to the rear of the scrambler. "Garth, you alree for an agent of Babylon."

"I'll take your word for that," Hogarth said.

"Hold on to something," Rucker yelled from up front. The knobby tires ground into the sand and the scrambler surged ahead. Rucker threw it into a skid to the left, then satisfied that he had his bearing, he jammed the accelerator fully forward.

Wind rushing past their ears and sand pelting their face, they sped through the night, their path illuminated by the blue glow of the enormous moon. Rucker used the wreck of the freighter that he and Tosh had sheltered in as a waypoint, his navigator's instinct led him directly to the crater that held the Dauntless.

Sliding to a stop on the crater's rim, Rucker shut down the scrambler and leapt onto the top of one of the knobby tires, to get a look over the edge of the rim. "Ah, there she is, Tosh! Isn't she beautiful in the moonlight?"

Tosh busied himself around the back of the scrambler, helping Hogarth unbuckle the booster. "You disabled the other scramblers?" he asked the machinist.

"Yeah, I got to them, but there's still the Manta."

"Nothin' we can do about that, except for hurry ourselves up."

But hurry was no help. Before the last strap was unbuckled, a yellow glow at the crest of a nearby dune and a whine like a vacuum announced the arrival of the Manta. Hovering about twenty meters over the sandy ground, the flying wing crested the dune, and the twin searchlights trained their intense beams on the scrambler.

Rucker, Tosh and Hogarth stepped out and stood abreast, squinting into the bright light, hair blown back by the high speed fans providing lift to the Manta. Rucker caught his first good look at Hogarth, then elbowed Tosh. "You didn't tell me this guy was half Swiss army knife," he mumbled.

“I’ve got extremely sensitive microphones built into my ears, Captain,” the loudspeaker voice said.

“You got a can opener in that thing?” Rucker asked.

The Manta leveled, then descended and settled onto a pair of landing skids that deployed from the underside. The canopy opened and two figures, one stubby and wide, the other built like a gorilla stepped out of the cockpit and into the glare of the lights.

“Where do you think you’re goin’, Rucker?” Mordecai shouted over the whine of the Manta’s fans.

“Just out for a drive.”

“Time for jokin’ is over.” Rucker heard the distinctive clack of a mag rifle chambering a round. “Josu, go take a look at what’s on the scrambler.”

Josu took a step forward, but was checked when Hogarth stepped into his path. The mechanical arm whirred and swung around, a plaspistol barrel protruded from the end pointed directly at Josu’s chest.

“So, you’ve chosen sides, huh?” Josu spat on the ground. “Shoulda’ let you stay in that burned out hulk we found your sorry ass in.”

Josu held his mag rifle out in his right hand, letting it dangle by the strap. “Alright then, have it your way,” he said before dropping the gun into the sand.

Josu’s left hand concealed a small laser cutter, and while Hogarth’s attention was drawn by the falling rifle, Josu swung the cutter in a sweeping arc and jumped to the inside of the plaspistol barrel. The cutter sliced neatly through the main, auxiliary and backup power lines protruding from Hogarth’s chest.

The heavy mechanical chassis sagged and then collapsed, a

fizzling sound and a trickle of blue liquid leaked from the severed lines.

"Woohoo! Take *that* you clockwork freak!" Josu kicked sand onto the immobile pile of scrap, then retrieved his rifle. He strode the last couple of meters to the scrambler, and knocked the side of the booster with his rifle butt.

"Now how do you suppose this thing got here?" Josu raised the mag rifle high over his head and brought the butt down hard on the booster's glass plasma containment chamber. It cracked, but did not break, so he struck it again, then a third time with growing ferocity until the plasma oozed out, dripping thickly into the sand.

Satisfied that the booster was ruined, he turned the rifle on Rucker.

Mordecai spoke up. "My friend Josu is plenty mad, Captain. Seems he spent a lot of time lookin' for somethin' on your little ship, and he didn't find it."

Rucker squinted into the lights and fan blown dust, trying to get a good look at Mordecai. "I'm afraid I don't know what you're talking about," he shouted into the wind.

"Drop the act, you stupid stick jockey." Josu jabbed the rifle barrel at Rucker's ribcage. "I heard you talking to your buddy, I heard about what's hidden in the front landing gear bay."

"If you know so much, why didn't you find anything?"

Josu reversed the rifle and slammed the butt into Rucker's stomach, doubling him over.

"Josu!" Mordecai called. "You won't get anywhere buttin' heads with him. Put a round in the Jamaican, then he'll talk."

"Right," Josu said, and whipped the rifle up to bear on Tosh's chest. "Nothin' personal," he said.

"WAIT!" Rucker shouted.

Josu sighed and lowered the rifle. "Feel like talkin' now, huh?"

"Yeah...yeah...just take it easy. There is something. Up in the front landing gear bay."

Josu raised the rifle again. "I've searched it, there ain't nothin' there."

"No...it's there. It's behind a secret panel. You've just got to open it up."

Josu looked back at Mordecai and ginned, then to Rucker. "So, how do you open it?"

"Well, that's the thing. You need a fifteen newton-meter Torquesman tool to get it open, and I don't carry one on the ship for just such an occasion as this." Rucker sounded almost apologetic.

"So you've got it locked down and don't carry a key?"

"Seemed like a solid plan at the time."

"Son of a..." Josu kicked at the sand.

"Josu, you moron," Mordecai called. "You've got a freakin' tool box right there!" He pointed at the fallen Hogarth. "Just grab what you need off that lame bastard's arm."

Josu's face lit up. "Ha! Great idea." He walked over to Hogarth and crouched down next to the big mechanical arm, then began tugging at the tool selection apparatus. "Here it is. Fifteen newton-meter, you sai—"

Josu never finished the question. He had forgotten that Hogarth still possessed a human arm, and that human arm required no power. In fact, that human arm was quite powerful on its own, as Josu found out when it clouted him on the side of his head.

Josu reeled, and the club-like arm struck again, then Hogarth gripped the barrel of the mag rifle and wrenched it from Josu's dazed grip. Hogarth flung the weapon toward Tosh, who was already in motion. A bolt of energy from Mordecai's weapon struck the scrambler in the spot where Tosh had been standing moments before.

Tosh caught the rifle, dove and rolled in the sand, coming to a halt with a bead on Mordecai. Tosh didn't hesitate a moment, the trigger was pulled as soon as the shot was lined up, and Mordecai went down with an antipersonnel slug in his chest. Dead center mass.

Josu staggered to his feet, wiping the blood from his busted lip with the back of his hand. Rucker went toe to toe with him, taking a vicious uppercut from the thug for his trouble. Rucker countered with a jab to the nose, followed by a haymaker that landed against Josu's temple, sending him reeling.

Josu took two unsteady steps to the left, then stumbled directly into the port side fan of the idling Manta. Flesh and bone were no match for the tritanium blades, and the last of Josu was a clattering noise followed by a lumpy soup blown out through the exhaust port.

"Ee-yew! Him done for sure." Tosh said.

Rucker stood wiping flecks of spray from his pant legs. "I think he ruined these pants, though."

"That ain't all he ruined…" Hogarth's unamplified voice was a husky croak, barely audible. He strained his neck to raise his head, looking at the booster with his human eye. "The booster's busted but good." A luminous white fluid oozed down the housing of the booster and pooled in the sand.

"Yeah, that thing is toast," Rucker said, still trying to get the

Josu off his boots. "Lucky for us we don't need it."

Rucker looked up to see both Hogarth and Tosh staring at him as if he had lost his mind. "What?" Rucker said. "Don't tell me you haven't figured it out yet. The freaky gravity? The nav beacons? Tosh took care of all that for us when he backfed the reactor power through the main grid on that piece of crap crawler. Brilliant plan by the way, Tosh."

"Natch," Tosh said. "A nice diversion, that. But how do it help us gettin' off this rock?"

"Think about it Tosh. That damn tower, the one on the crawler. Why leave it standing?"

"Yeah, it did cross my mind..."

"Mordecai had himself a nav beacon, lord knows how he got it, but he got it, and he installed it up on the tower of that rolling scrapheap of his. Then, once he led a ship astray of the lanes, he'd hit it with an impulse grav generator, pulling it right on out of the sky like it was stuck in some find of heavy gravity well. I'm thinking it was the grav generator that made that huge flash when its core collapsed."

As understanding came to Tosh, a mask of rage descended on his features. "They be a clottin' bunch of coolie. How many they bring down and kill? How many? And all for greed." Tosh looked at Hogarth, his body broken, skin burnt by the crash that marooned him on this planet. A crash that was orchestrated by Mordecai and his cohorts. "A bullet were too good for his stumpy carcass."

"Probably so, Tosh." Rucker strode to the rim of the crater, looked down on his beloved Dauntless sitting in the moonlight. "I'm gonna go start preflight. You think you can plug the tin man back in?"

"Ya mon, everything be cook and curry in no time."

"Good, 'cause I'm gonna need the both of you to go over Wilma with a fine tooth comb before we take off. I want to make sure we dust our heels of this place but good."

Kenneth W. Harmon debuts with one of the grittiest stories Pulp Empire has ever published.

Sex Sales

By Kenneth W. Harmon

"Now there's something I could hang my hat on," Tagert said motioning with his chin toward the blonde dancer twirling around a pole in front of a half dozen howling men.

Kushing, the heavy-set bouncer turned his wide face to the stage. A smile flashed over the ends of his full mouth. "Two hats actually. Names Candy."

Tagert pulled a flask from inside his coat and took a slug of whisky. "New girl?"

"Like a virgin."

Tagert snorted as he returned the flask. "That ain't no virgin."

Prince's "Little Red Corvette" blared inside the Kit-Kat Club at ear bleeding volume. Tagert drummed his fingers across the railing. On the secondary stage, tucked in the shadows, Lulu staggered around the platform like a drunk. Black mascara streaked the length of her cheeks. She'd been crying again.

Tagert glanced back at Kushing who eyed a small group of frat boys sitting at a table. They had ordered a pitcher of beer after first arriving. That had been over an hour ago. Kushing looked at his wristwatch. Kushing once worked as a professional wrestler. He nearly killed a drunk who dared pulled a blade. Beat him into a pile of hamburger. Tagert shook his head. Someone needed to tell those college boys to get busy drinking.

Prince faded away and Candy teased the crowd with a final shake of her double D's. Dollar bills fanned around her garter. She strutted to the curtain, paused in the opening, and blew a kiss toward some poor fool who tumbled over backward in his chair. Kushing straightened. Under the flash of strobe lights, he looked more bear than human. "Gotta go talk to those boys."

"Try not to break any bones," Tagert called.

Kushing laughed.

Tagert pushed off the railing. He made his way past the tables, to the DJ stand. Rowdy Rick Harris, the club spin master, saw him and stabbed his right pointer finger into the air, as if John Travolta prancing on the dance floor in his perfect white suite. "Tagert my man, how they hanging?"

He'd known Rick for ten years. A college dropout who had a genus IQ and the work ethic of a sloth, Rick remained stuck in the 70's. He drove a *Smoky and the Bandit* Trans Am and listened to the Doobie Brothers on eight tracks. Rick swished harder than a horse's tail swatting flies. It nearly got him killed when he asked the wrong customer for a blow job. "What's happening with Lulu, Hawk at her again?"

Lulu's boyfriend was a former football player Hawk Wilson. He lasted two weeks in an NFL camp before blowing out his knee. Now the only hits he made were to Lulu's face.

"Yeah, she ought to find herself another pony to ride." Rick leaned over the counter to snort a line. Give me a second, got to start some music."

KC & the Sunshine Band's "Get Down Tonight" soon blasted out of the speakers. Rick grabbed his microphone and kissed it like Mick Jaggar. "Now on the main stage, direct from Los Angeles, city of the bad angels, I give you Vanessa. And on stage two, that Russian nuclear hottie, Anastasia."

Tagert's crotch started to tingle as he watched Vanessa work the pole. She'd performed a similar trick on his pole a few nights back and he was up for more. Anastasia glared at him from stage two. She remained pissed that he'd dumped her after only one date, but to his mind, she was all bite and no swallow. Rick pointed toward a fresh line of coke. "Go ahead, I got more."

Tagert waved him off. "I'm here on business."

"Ah," Rick said. "There's still a lot of cop in you."

Tagert laughed under his breath. It had been nearly ten years since the city fired him for beating a handcuffed suspect.

"A couple of your vice buddies came around earlier. Ross and Paget."

"Yeah, their all right."

Rick shrugged. "As long as you keep plying them with free booze." He snorted the coke and sighed. "You here to see Big Mike?"

"That's the plan. He available?"

"Before eleven on a night Betty's working, are you kidding me?"

Betty was the only black girl working at the club. She had one of those perfect bubble butts that some men loved to rub against. Big Mike was one of those men.

"Damn," Tagert said reaching for his flask again. "Big Mike knows I got a lot on my plate. Why'd he call me up here if wasn't going to see me?"

A loud crash thundered over the music. One of the college boys lay crumpled on the floor like a piece of paper. Kushing snatched another boy by the crotch and lifted him over his head. He growled and slammed him onto a table, which shattered with a crack, beer flying. The boy moaned louder than a carnival girl entertaining a donkey. Kushing grabbed them both by their collars and dragged them toward the front door. Shaky Jake, one of the club regulars, held open the door. Kushing heaved what was left of the frat boys out into the rain. "Don't come back you son of a bitches or I'll make you bleed."

Kushing tugged his jacket into place. His gaze came to Tagert, and he offered a mock salute. On stage 2, Anastasia finished her routine with a prolonged grind. As she strutted off stage, she raised her right hand to offer Tagert a different kind of salute.

"Damn, you really pissed that girl off," Rick said as he changed records.

"I'm lucky to have survived."

Rick laughed. "Hey, there goes Betty."

Tagert watched Betty slither onto the main stage like the serpent in Eden. "Big Mike should be in a good mood," he said pressing past Rick on his way to the hallway that led to the club offices and dressing rooms. Yellow light beamed down from a single bulb hanging on a wire. The narrow passage smelled of booze and cheap perfume. Big Mike's office was at the end of the hall. Tagert stopped outside the door and listened. Satisfied that Big Mike was alone, he knocked and waited for the familiar,

"Get your ass in here." How Big Mike could identify him from the sound of his knock remained a mystery.

The door opened with a squeal of hinges. Big Mike sat with his feet crossed on the top of his wide oak desk. A fat cigar dangled from one side of his mouth sending up a thread of gray smoke. When he looked at Big Mike, Tagert saw Jabba the Hutt. All that was missing was Princess Leia in chains. Tagert had known Big Mike from his days on the vice squad. They had a special arrangement. Tagert wouldn't hassle Big Mike for code violations, and in return, Tagert had his choice of Big Mike's girls for thirty minutes every Friday night.

When Tagert lost his job, Big Mike brought him in on his blackmail schemes. Nobody was safe. Professional athletes, movie stars, and politicians all fell victim. The scam was simple. Big Mike made connections with hotel workers, maids, bellhops, and concierges, anyone with room access willing to risk their job for a thousand bucks. Whenever a celebrity visited the club, Big Mike arranged a private lap dance. If the girl worked her charm, she'd soon be invited to the celeb's hotel. Tagert then drove the girl to the hotel and waited until the hotel worker came along to unlock the door. Video camera in hand, he slipped inside the room to capture enough action for a steamy internet clip. Kushing always went along to keep the peace in case the victim spotted Tagert. It happened only once, with a soccer player from the Brazilian national team. He kicked like a mule and Kushing had to break both his legs. The scam worked because Big Mike never got greedy. He asked for fifty thousand dollars in return for the tape, no more, no less, knowing the celebs could afford the price. They paid without protest rather than explain themselves to wives or girlfriends.

Tagert dropped onto a chair in front of the desk. Big Mike's cigar failed to mask the tang of semen. "Betty's looking good tonight."

Big Mike leaned forward to tap ash into a coffee cup. "I hadn't noticed."

"That new girl looks interesting."

Big Mike sank back in the chair. He puffed on the cigar and blew a smoke ring toward Tagert. "Just can't keep it in your pants can you?"

Tagert couldn't help but smile. "So, I take it you have a job for me. Who's the unlucky bastard?"

"Businessman from upstate."

"Businessman. You sure he'll pay?"

"Oh yeah, he'll pay."

Tagert coughed as the smoke cloud enveloped his head. "Who's going with me, Angel again?" Angel Rodriguez, a street-wise Puerto Rican, worked most of the blackmails. She had the face of a saint and a body that would bring Satan to his knees.

The end of the cigar glowed red as Big Mike inhaled. He blew another ring. "The new girl Candy."

Tagert felt his eyebrows gather. "How old is she?"

"Why?"

"I don't know she just doesn't look that old to me. In fact, I think I saw her face on a milk carton last week."

"Probably did. Don't start having a conscious. You're not a cop anymore."

Tagert pushed out of the chair. "Which hotel?"

"The Westmoore."

He started to open the door.

"Tagert."

"Yeah," he said over his shoulder.

"Don't take Kushing on this one."

Tagert felt suddenly vulnerable as if charging into a gunfight without wearing a bulletproof vest. "Why the hell not?"

"I wanna kept this one private."

"I don't like going without Kushing."

"You can have the fifty grand."

Tagert's jaw dropped. "Don't screw with me."

Big Mike rocked forward to crush his cigar in the coffee cup. "Money's tight for you. Take the offer and be grateful."

Tagert pictured his shithole apartment and wreck of a car. Yeah, money was tight, and he'd gladly sell his soul to be out of debt, but something about this deal smelled like a fart in a crowded elevator. Why couldn't Kushing go with him, and why was Big Mike using the new girl Candy? Big Mike never used a dancer for his scheme until they'd worked at the club at least six months. "All right, I'll take the job."

"Of course you'll take it," Big Mike said pouring Wild Turkey into the same coffee cup that he used to put out the cigar. "Sex sells, my friend, that's why we're all fat and happy."

Tagert left by the backdoor. He entered the dark alley running behind the club. The stench of rotting food hung in the air. A rat darted out from behind a trashcan. Behind him, the Doobie Brothers *China Grove* echoed through the walls. He turned up the collar on his coat and walked to his rusting sedan, a former police cruiser that he'd purchased at auction. A cold October rain seeped from a moonless sky. Tagert climbed into his car. He tossed a box of half-eaten pizza into the backseat and waited.

An hour passed before Candy stepped out of the club wearing a trench coat that fell just past her knees. She clutched the coat against her throat while looking up and down the alley. "Here we go," Tagert said and flashed the car headlights to let her know he was there.

Candy ducked into the rain and ran to the car. Tagert opened the passenger door. She slid onto the seat with a big smile. "Hi, I'm Candy."

He studied her face. The full mouth painted a garish red, delicate nose, high cheekbones, and ocean blue eyes. Too young, he thought, much too young. She was a China doll waiting to shatter. She lifted her long blonde hair from inside the coat and let it fan behind her. "Name's Tagert." He turned the key and the cruiser growled to life. "So you and Big Mike go back awhile?"

She continued to smile as if to patronize him. "I think you know that answer."

He shifted the car into drive and turned on the windshield wipers. From the corner of his eye, he caught her watching him. "I hope you don't mind my asking, but how old are you?"

"Old enough to know better."

"But young enough to do it anyway."

"The cop in you is talking," she said crossing her legs.

His eyes traveled the path that led from her slender ankles to mid thigh where the coat bulged to reveal skin. Tagert tried to gulp down his desire. "Big Mike's been telling you stories."

"No, I heard it from the other girls."

He turned onto Huntington Street. There wasn't a lot of traffic in this part of town at night and he quickly brought the car to speed. "That so, what do they have to say about me?"

"They like you, especially Anastasia."

He stifled a laugh. "I thought she hated my guts."

"Well," she said folding her arms across her chest, "she's not happy that you won't see her anymore."

"I have my reasons."

She smiled again. "I won't ask."

He accelerated onto the interstate. Tires hummed over the asphalt painted in white streaks by overhead lights. "The Westmoore's uptown. High class all the way. I'll need to see Tommy, he's a concierge, he'll give me the room key."

"You won't need Tommy."

Tagert watched as she dug inside a pocket on her coat. "I will unless you're doing this in the backseat."

She shot him a glance through narrowed eyes. "On top of the pizza box?"

A tinge of embarrassment raced along his spine.

Candy produced a shiny gold plastic card. "I have the room key."

"You got that from the mark?"

"There a problem?"

His knuckles whitened across the steering wheel. "I've been doing this awhile and never heard of a mark leaving the girl his room key. He seems kind of reckless."

"He knows me," she whispered in a flat, detached voice.

If he'd been driving on any road other than the freeway, Tagert would have pulled over. "What do you mean he knows you?"

"I've said too much." She turned to stare out the window.

The vein that snaked along his right temple started to throb as blood pounded inside his brain. Everything about this scam felt wrong. His instincts said to turn around, but he had fifty thousand reasons to ignore his instincts.

They passed the remaining drive in silence, which amplified

the splatter of rain on the windshield, and the squeaking of the wipers. He parked on the street a block south of the hotel. Candy stepped onto the sidewalk and drew her coat snug. Tagert collected the camera case from the trunk and joined her. "Come on," he said, "let's get this over with."

Bright light flooded the lobby of the hotel, which stood empty except for a couple of lesbians who cuddled in a dark corner, and the night manager Derek, who acknowledged Tagert's presence with a sly grin. Candy walked with purpose to the elevators. It was obvious she knew where to go, so he followed without a word. Mirrors lined the walls of the elevator and from every angle Candy looked beautiful. Tagert clenched his teeth as the elevator climbed. It's just a damn job, he told himself, but had a hard time believing it. The elevator stopped on the eighth floor and the doors peeled back with a metallic chime. She stepped into the corridor and held up the door key.

"Room 802. Give me ten minutes." She handed him the card.

Tagert stared at the card and then up at her. A smile trembled over her lips. She started to turn away and he caught her by the arm. "I'm not trying to pry, but I've got to know the score here. I've done this a hundred times, but never like this. Big Mike doesn't want Kushing along. He offers me all the money if I'll do it. The mark knows you, and gives you his room key. I've got to know what I'm walking into."

"Why, why do you have to know?"

"Hey, my ass is on the line here, either you tell me or I walk, fifty thousand or no fifty thousand."

"You're not a priest."

"Hell no."

"But you want my confession."

“I want the damn truth.”

Her chin sank toward her chest. “I’m seventeen.”

Tagert swore under his breath. “All right, anything else I need to know?”

“I ran away from home. Big Mike took me in and gave me a job. My father tracked me to the city.”

“He wants to take you back home.”

Her tear-filled eyes rose to look him in the face. “Not exactly.”

A stabbing pain jolted his skull. He tried to massage it away, but the pain intensified. “If your father knows where you’re at why doesn’t he want to—” A thought hit him and bile rushed into his throat. Tagert turned from her to collect himself. “The man in room 802,” he said over his shoulder, “is your—”

“Father,” she said. “When Big Mike found out why I ran away, he said he’d help me.”

Tagert faced her. “Your father leaves you alone or Big Mike sends the tape to your mother.”

Candy brushed her tears onto the back of her hand. “That’s the plan.”

“So there’s no money involved.”

“Big Mike will pay you.”

Tagert walked to the window at the end of the hall. He pressed against the cold glass and stared out at the black buildings. What am I doing? He thought. Big Mike expects me to walk into that room and film Candy screwing her… His right curled into a fist.

“Tagert,” she called behind him in a soft voice.

He took a deep breath and turned. “Make it fast, I don’t have all night.”

From gritty crime, we move in to gritty fantasy. Craig Comer brings us a tale with all the traits of great sword and sorcery.

The Augurwraith

by Craig Comer

Saja gagged as the tanner's breath washed over her in warm huffs that reeked of fish and ale. The man leaned forward from his perch upon the stoop of the guildhall, and pulled her close, his hands fumbling along her waist and rump.

She considered for a moment to let him have his way. Her father had left her with few choices, and almost all ended with her lying upon her back. She cursed her father for the thousandth time that day, wishing him dead, and at the same time wondering if he still lived. She hadn't seen him for three days, since the Feast of Raast, where the denizens of Kuthahaar had celebrated those of the Sultan's royal blood, the Kitame, the Children of Light.

The tanner forced his mouth to her neck, and its warmth broke her from her stupor. She shoved at the man's chest. He raised a hand to strike her, and she quickly lowered her head, staring at his sandaled feet in meek submission.

"Please," she said. "My father's always been loyal to the guild. It is said you protect your own."

The tanner smirked, revealing rotted teeth that pointed like daggers. "But your father's not in the guild, no more than the boys who collect dung for the vats."

"He sells you oak bark and lye, gathered from across the Seas of Abthinar. You need him!"

"Phaw, forget that doddering fool. There are a dozen others who would give us as fair a price for their bark and lye, and they wouldn't squander it all in cups at the taverns." The tanner rose. His eyes roamed her body. "Come inside, and we'll find work for you."

He grabbed her arm, and she slapped it away. Staring up at his leering face, she knew whatever work the tanner would offer, it was his bed he wanted her in. She took a step back, and his smile dropped.

Jerking forward, he snatched her close again. His fingers dug into her shoulders; his chin crushed down on the top of her head. She shrieked and tried to bat him away. He growled and threw her to the ground.

"Leave, then!" he barked.

Saja glanced about, but though the street was busy, no one stared at her. No one cared. The Immortal City of Kuthahaar was never kind to those without wealth or power, and less so to those without family or guild to protect them. Despair bubbled in her gut again, but she pushed it down. Her father had always taught her that panic during a negotiation produced only two effects: a spoiled stomach and an empty purse.

She settled her shoulders and drew her face blank. "I will find him," she said, though the words brought little comfort.

As she spoke, two other men emerged from the guildhall. They wore the simple vests of craftsmen, and the mark of the Tanner's Guild emblazoned their arms in red ink—a scraping blade resting upon a stretched rawhide. The first tanner mumbled some rude comment, and the others laughed.

Saja seethed. She silently cursed her father again, and the Tanner's Guild, and the Sultan, who allowed lechers to prey upon the desperate. She felt a chunk of sandstone under her palm and grasped it, eyeing the three men. She pictured the tanner clutching his nose and howling in pain, but then thought better of hurling the stone. She could perhaps outrun two, but three certainly pressed her luck. Besides, she still held a small hope the guild would take her in. Maybe if she came again later and spoke with someone else.

The tanner saw the stone as she dropped it, and his eyes went cold. Saja did her best to ignore him. Rising, she scraped off the silt and muck that clung to her dress. In the Tanner's District, buckets were kept to collect the leavings from animal and man alike, for use in the tanning process, but the slop of refuse still soiled the ground. And in the air, baking under the noonday sun, the stench of the vats hung thick.

As Saja strode away from the guildhall, she passed a few peddlers hawking pottery and craftsmen's tools from the backs of their carts, while wagons of fresh skins and rawhides trundled along. She dodged one of the wagons and almost collided with a beggar who shuffled by with his arms tucked into his robes, mumbling to himself. She heard giggling from a shadowed corner between two squat buildings, and spied a pair of harlots watching her. They wore sheer linen dresses, with paint caked upon their eyes and cheeks. They know, Saja thought with a shiver. They can see I will soon be one of them. The notion plunged her heart into her gut, and her eyes welled.

A year ago, she'd been in love with Tarim, her father's apprentice. A year ago, she thought she'd never dream of another man. Her entire life lay before her, scripted like the sweet tales from a mummer's stage. But then the winds had changed, and her father stole her future.

One of the harlots stepped forward, but the other caught her arm and flicked her gaze at something behind Saja. The first altered her step into a graceful pivot, so that her back faced the street. Saja frowned. She peered over her shoulder and gasped. The tanner and craftsmen followed her, trailing only a few dozen paces away.

For a moment, she only stared. An icy hand of fear gripped her spine and wouldn't let go. Then, with a gasp, her knees buckled and she lurched forward. Weaving through the street, she quickened her pace, her mind racing with what the men would do to her if they reached her. When she glanced backward again, the tanner gave her a mocking grin.

She stumbled in a wagon rut and heard the two craftsmen laugh. She was only sport to them, she told herself, something to pass the afternoon. Soon they would tire of their chase. She just needed to keep moving.

But she felt them edging closer. The hot sun melded with the imagined heat of their breath upon her neck. The gentle breeze was their fingers reaching out to clutch her dress.

The street forked, and Saja darted down an alley pressed between a salting house and a dyer's shack. The footsteps slapping the dirt behind her echoed louder, coming closer until they seemed like they were her own.

As she broke into a run, a shadow flittered across the corner of her vision. Only it was higher than it should've been, as if a giant hawk had suddenly swooped down beside her. A loud grunt sounded, followed by a thud.

Saja heard the tanner curse, then the shriek of another man. She stopped and spun around, shocked at what she found. A lithe man in a shirt of green silk had his back toward her, blocking the alley. He balanced on his toes like a dancer, with a dagger held in one hand. Even Saja could tell the man was dangerous.

One of the craftsmen clutched at his arm, blood weeping through his fingers. The other was crumpled upon the ground, moaning softly.

The tanner sneered and brought his hands up in fists. "This is unwise, thief," he said. "We are guildsmen. We are protected. The Horned Man will hear of this and string you from your toes!"

The silk-shirted man shifted his dagger so it pointed toward the ground but remained silent. The tanner lunged at him. To Saja, the punch was as quick as an asp's strike, but the thief danced to one side and brought the butt of his dagger into the man's temple. The tanner grunted and was struck again. This time he fell to his knees.

Saja winced, but instead of a death blow, the thief stepped back and allowed the other guildsmen to regain their companion. They did so with wary eyes that never left their assailant, gathering the tanner between them, and backing away.

Once they had fled the alley, the thief turned to Saja. "Run!" a voice shouted within her, but her feet remained still. His face was fair, except for a scar that ran along his nose like a dividing line between his cheeks. Dark locks fell almost to his shoulders, and the black trousers he wore were for a much larger man.

He smiled at her. "I suppose asking for a kiss as reward would defeat the whole noble gesture," he said. "But perhaps you would give me your name? Such a detail will make for a better tale, when I tell my friends of your rescue."

Saja started. The anger she'd felt earlier welled up again. "Rescue? After what you've done, no guildsman will show me kindness! No proper work! No food!" She knew she sounded ridiculous and ungrateful, but she was tired of men pretending to be her savior only to leave her desperate and alone.

"They wouldn't have helped you before. Their kind is… let's say, less than honorable." The thief glanced at his bloodied dagger. He quickly wiped it clean and tucked it into his boot.

"I am called Lucendes," he said. At Saja's reaction, he added, "I am from the southern march of Maeldon, though I've lived in the Immortal City for many years."

"My father trades with the Maeldonese. He says they are desert rats of impure blood, who scurry about hoping for the Sultan's favor."

"Then I can see he knows them well," said Lucendes, widening his grin. Saja huffed and turned to leave, but Lucendes fell in beside her. "A moment, Saja," he said, placing a hand upon her arm. "I did not just chance upon you. I have come to add my blade and wits to your formidable quest."

Blinking, Saja stammered, "You know my name?"

"You wish to save your father, but the Tanner's Guild won't help you. So you are caught in the winds, without friend or family."

"You knew? But then why did you ask?"

Lucendes shrugged sheepishly. "I may have overhead some

of your argument with the guildsmen. Your voice held such misery, I could not rip my ears away. It is a fault of mine, this burden of altruism."

"I didn't see you," said Saja. She frowned, trying to recollect the thief's face from earlier, then shook her head. It didn't matter. "But you are mistaken. I have no quest, only a need for food and work." She swiped his hand from her arm and added, "Honest work."

This time it was Lucendes who frowned, if only for a fleeting moment. She had caught him off-guard. Good, she thought.

"But what of your father?" he asked. "Wouldn't his freedom answer all of your problems?"

Saja shook her head. "He's a drunk, and he owes money to many people. He could be a captive of the Sect of Raast or the Horned Man, or perhaps dead."

"To have such debts, he must've been a mighty man once. And maybe not so long ago? Tell me of him, and I will find you a warm meal."

"Why?" Saja asked.

"Perhaps I like to help people. Perhaps your father owes me money, too." Lucendes' knowing grin returned. "Perhaps I desire you. Does it really matter why?"

Saja stared at the thief. Of course it mattered. But she couldn't ignore her stomach for another passing of the sun, and the thought of food for so simple a price was too tempting. She didn't care if it meant soiling her father's name further. He'd vanished only a few days ago, but he'd disappeared long before.

With a curt nod, she spun and marched away. Lucendes followed, guiding her with occasional grunts as they left the Tanner's District and entered the Cupper's Warren. There, the ringing of hammers filled the alleys and the smoke of stoking fires billowed in the streets, increasing the afternoon heat.

Saja spoke of her father, of his trading caravans, and of the life that had been hers. She told him of the raiders who'd burned an entire shipment of oak bark and slain the dozen guards who accompanied it. How the loss had crushed her father and forced him into debt, and how losing a few contracts through ill luck had caused that debt to swell.

And last, she told him of Tarim. "Those my father owed forced him to sell his apprentice to the Kitame, in order to recover their losses," she said, straining to keep her voice as flat as possible. "My father sold Tarim like he would any of the goods from his caravans."

"He became an augurwraith, a bodyguard for one of the royal blood," said Lucendes. "Such horrors the privileged deliver upon the poor. It is a blessing the Sultan outlaws the practice except to a certain few."

Nodding, Saja dropped her gaze. "They came for him one day. We knew it meant his death, and still he went willingly, to become a creature of the spirit world, bound to one of the Kitame." She blinked back the tears welling at her eyes. "One day he was as a son to my father; the next he was gone."

Lucendes studied her. "You cared strongly for this Tarim," he mused. Pursing his lips, his eyes flickered to the sky. Then he grinned and turned to Saja. "After you have eaten, we shall go to see a friend of mine. He may be able to help us."

Saja started to protest, but Lucendes cut in. "Did you know it was possible to speak with an augurwraith? Even one not bound to you?"

Saja's heart thumped. Speak with Tarim again? What would

she say? What would he? The bustling of the city around her faded, and she allowed herself to be led away as if lost in a dream.

"That is," Lucendes continued, "if you have the right kind of friends."

*****

Her belly full, Saja followed as Lucendes approached the hovel of his friends. It was perched between a slaughtering pen and a grain house, with a flat roof that buckled in its center. The thief halted at the slatted wood door, but instead of knocking, he slipped his dagger through the crack formed at its frame. The door creaked as he pushed it taut against its latch, scraping his blade up and down, searching for the release.

Saja gawked at the blatant thievery. She scanned the near empty street, wondering if anyone watched, when the latch suddenly clicked free, and the door swung open.

A man with shoulders as wide as a bull's stood within. "You!" he cursed at Lucendes. He wore no shirt under his vest, and Saja could see his muscles flare.

"Me," said Lucendes, ducking low and throwing his shoulder into the man's gut. Both stumbled backward, spilling into a room filled with the scent of burning incense. Heavy tapestries hung on the walls, blocking the outside light, and a heap of overlapping rugs covered the earthen floor.

Another man, small and plump, sat at a table in the far corner. His robe was finely cut, something Saja's father would've worn. He bolted to his feet, sucking in a tight breath and eyeing the open door, the only exit Saja could see.

The larger brute swiped at Lucendes' head, but the thief ducked under the blow. He caught the underside of the brute's arm and used it as leverage, slamming his knee into the man's side.

The brute grunted. He clutched his ribs and bent over. But instead of attacking, Lucendes leapt out of the man's reach.

"You think I'd not remember that ruse, Raj?" he asked. Raj glowered, standing upright. The pair circled, Raj in a crouch with his hands raised before him, Lucendes springing lightly upon his toes.

With a deft flick of his wrist, Lucendes sent his dagger sailing at the other man's head. He rushed after it, chasing the toss that flew wide and clattered against one of the tapestries.

Raj didn't flinch as the blade spun past. Instead, he stepped forward into Lucendes' path. The thief tried to swerve, but his foot caught in one of the thick rugs. He stumbled, and Raj's arms seemed to swallow him in a crushing embrace.

"I remember, too," the brute said.

Lucendes squirmed, trying to loosen the larger man's grip. His face turned red from the strain. He kicked his legs out and battered his head against Raj's chest, but neither was effective.

Saja realized her knuckles had grown white from clutching her dress. She released her grip and glanced down the street again. She could run. What were the promises of a thief, anyway? These obviously weren't his friends. But he'd fed her, as he said he would, and rescued her from the tanners. Thoughts of the roasted pigeon and beets caused her stomach to gurgle in contentment.

And the chance to speak with Tarim again. Even to discover the fate of her father. The boon was worth a small amount of hope.

She stepped inside. Movement to her left caught her attention. The robed man edged toward her, hugging the wall. His gaze swung from the grappled pair to Saja. She swallowed, unsure what to do.

"Get the door," Lucendes gasped, as if reading her mind.

Right, she nodded. She spun out of the entrance and grabbed the door. But as she tried to swing it closed, the robed man darted forward and caught its edge.

"Child, I would advise you to move," he said. His voice held a note of panic in it, despite the stern warning.

Saja pulled back, and the light from outside flooded the man's face. He squinted and tried to step through, but as he did Saja slammed the door shut again, causing the man to yelp in surprise. She lowered her shoulder and pressed, to keep him pinned, then rolled her back flat and slid her rump to the floor, wedging them in place.

The wood pinched against her skin as the man tried to shove her out of the way, but his arm was trapped at his side, and he didn't have enough strength or leverage. Saja gritted her teeth. Determination welled within, fueled by hope.

In the center of the room, Lucendes threw himself from side to side, forcing Raj to stagger. Like a ship lurching across rough seas, the pair threatened to tip. Lucendes brought both his knees up, and the sudden weight caused Raj to lose his balance. His arms slackened, and Lucendes slipped to the ground.

The thief tumbled away and came to his feet. He knocked into the table, spilling some of the scented oils that burned within clay pots. Snatching one of the chairs, he hurled it.

Raj batted the chair aside as he stalked forward. Lucendes

waited until the last moment, then tossed one of the pots. The burning oil splattered across Raj's bare chest, and he howled in pain.

Grabbing another chair, Lucendes smashed it into the larger man. He swung again, breaking the chair across Raj's temple. The brute blinked, wavering, then slumped to the ground. Lucendes looked up at Saja and grinned.

"Hurry," she barked at him. Her back felt like it was on fire, from the strain of keeping the door forced shut. He strode over and grasped the plump man, pulling him into the room as Saja shifted out of the way.

"I have need of your services, Khouri," said Lucendes.

The plump man blustered. "The last time I helped you, I had to flee the city. And you never paid!" He shook his head. "I will do nothing for you."

Lucendes righted one of the overturned chairs and sat the plump man down. Then he held up a finger and moved to where Raj lay sprawled across the floor. Yanking the man's belt purse free, he shook it, the coins within clinking together. "Here," he said, tossing the bag to Khouri. "My debt is settled."

"I should've guessed you'd seek me out again," said Khouri.

The thief shrugged. "You're an augur. You should've seen me coming."

"An augur, Lucendes, not a Seer. My visions are not that precise. Though in truth, I've had dark dreams of late. It seems they foretold a visit from the Blessed One's best assassin."

Lucendes' eyes flickered to Saja. Her own widened in shock. "An assassin of the Blessed One?" she whispered. The hope she'd felt earlier evaporated. The prophet kept an iron thumb on perhaps half the thieves in Kuthahaar. His attention was one to avoid, not covet.

"Did he not tell you?" asked Khouri, with a chuckle.

"It changes nothing," Lucendes snapped. "We've come for you to divine the location of her father."

The augur's gaze became intent upon the thief, and his laughter increased. "Why bother? You know it already. I can see it on your face!"

Saja started. She swung her gaze between the two men, taking a step toward the door. "Was it a lie?" She shuddered. "You promised. You fooled me into believing."

Lucendes shook his head. "I kept things from you, but the words I spoke of the other matter were the truth. You will see your father's apprentice again. Khouri holds the power to summon an augurwraith."

Khouri jerked. "You told her of this? It is knowledge punishable by death."

"I know where your father is kept," Lucendes continued, ignoring the augur. "If he still lives, I will free him from his captors."

Saja took a breath to quell her panic. The thief—no assassin—was trying to negotiate with her, she realized. "Why would the Blessed One want to help my father?" she asked. "Why would you want to help me speak with Tarim?"

"Ah, now it makes sense," said Khouri, rubbing at his jaw. "I can see a vision without need of my scrying bowl. The Blessed One moves against the Horned Man, to take control of protection for the Tanner's Guild. It is well known to certain ears." He turned to Saja. "Your father will be found with one or the other."

"He is with the minions of the Horned Man," said Lucendes. "For the debts he owes them, they will make him suffer the wrath of their god."

Anger flared within Saja, washing away her fear. Her father had brought her trouble. Again. She stared at Lucendes, seeing a coiled snake. He'd rescued her from the tanners because he needed her. He'd wanted to use her all along, just as they had.

"You would allow me to see Tarim," she said, "but only if you can also use him as a weapon in your fight. That is why you concern yourself with the supposed rescue of my father."

"He needs you," Khouri agreed. "An augurwraith is a terrible creature—a warrior of the shadows forged from the same mystical powers that birth clairvoyance and precognition, but blended with the strongest of death magic. It is not surprising the Kitame use them as personal bodyguards. Not quite human anymore, they are not quite dead.

"An augur's wraith, yes, an omen of death. Trying to summon one not bound to you is beyond dangerous. It is something only a master augur would dare attempt. You might as well challenge the will of the Sultan!"

"Strong emotions can sway them to their old life," said Lucendes. "It has been done before." Khouri sighed and nodded, conceding the point, though he continued to mutter under his breath.

"And if I refuse?" asked Saja.

Lucendes turned to her, an almost apologetic look upon his face. "Then you will not see your father, nor your Tarim, again."

Damn them all, thought Saja. Her hands knotted into fists at her waist. Spite boiled within her, and she wished for nothing more than to storm away from Lucendes and deny him his nefarious designs. But where would she storm to? The question had plagued her for days, yet she had no better answer for it.

She couldn't meet the assassin's eyes, so stared for a time at the intricate rugs splayed across the floor. Her mind raced, searching for better options but finding none. Finally, she nodded.

"I suppose I will not be able to refuse, either?" asked Khouri.

Lucendes picked up his dagger. "No," he said, without bothering to veil the threat.

*****

Despite the sun's absence, the day's heat continued to infest the city as if some great hearthstone burned unseen. Saja and Lucendes strode through the alleys of the Tanner's District, guided by the light of the moon. The streets still held a host of denizens, but the peddlers had gone home and the craft shops had closed. The only hint of commerce remaining came from the jovial chatter spilling from the district's alehouses, and on occasion, from the moans of pleasure emanating from the shadows.

It'd taken Khouri the afternoon to prepare the summoning totem—a lock of Saja's hair tied around a garnet-encrusted glass medallion, steeped in an unction of oils—and Lucendes had used the time to set his plan in motion. He'd returned to the augur's house wearing a loose robe of green over his shirt and trousers. It hid the half-dozen daggers he now carried. To Saja, he'd given a small knife, and its weight at her hip felt strange, like an unwanted reminder of the bond between them.

As they crossed a star-shaped plaza at the convergence of several streets, three men in similar green robes joined them. Saja regarded the men, then peered into the shadows. "Only three?"

she asked.

"Our strike needs to be fast," said Lucendes. "Too much commotion and the Seers will send the city guard. They watch the city from above, like falcons circling, but with Magi enhanced eyes. It is how the Sultan keeps his peace." He pulled his lips tight, not quite the grin he wore earlier in the day. "But don't worry, we have all the strength we need." Saja thought of the totem he'd tucked beneath his shirt, and nodded.

The assassins marched on in silence, each knowing what was expected of them. Saja's heart battered her ribs so hard, she thought they'd shatter. For her sake, she hoped these other men were as good as Lucendes. She concentrated on taking deep breaths, trying to keep her mind from the bloodletting to come.

Thankfully, she didn't have to wait long. Two of the assassins peeled off from the group as soon they turned down a narrow street lined with sandstone buildings. They quickly disappeared into the darkness, and when Saja stared after them, Lucendes slapped her rump.

She spun on him, raising a hand to strike him back. But he caught her wrist and wrapped his other arm around her shoulder. Laughing loudly, he leaned into her as if they were an amorous couple returning from an evening out. The remaining assassin dropped back, giving them space.

Saja fumed but went along with the ruse. Lucendes led them down the street in a slow procession, chortling and babbling nonsense. He tapped at Saja's shoulder as they went, and at first she thought he was trying to get her attention. But then she realized: he's counting!

They approached a storehouse flanked by a pair of taller buildings. In its center, a pair of double doors stood open, but guarded by a half-dozen men.

Lucendes stopped tapping.

"The lookouts are dead," he said. "Now it is our turn." He strode toward the guards, leaving Saja behind. The other assassin joined him, pulling two long knives from his robe. The men at the door started and fell into a line behind a brawny thug. Some of those in back glanced warily up and down the street, but the leader glared at Lucendes.

"The Blessed One sends his greetings," said the assassin.

The thug spat. He raised a hand, as if to make a threatening gesture. Instead, he gurgled and dropped to his knees, a dagger sprouting from his throat.

Lucendes and his companion rushed forward, blades flashing silver in the night. The minions of the Horned Man recovered from their shock and met the assassins with cudgels and staves.

Wood cracked against stone and metal whooshed through the air. Two of the guards fell before Lucendes as he spun and stuck with his dancer's grace. He was not a snake, Saja thought, watching him, he was some sly cat of the desert.

He flung a dagger at another of the guards, catching the man in the thigh, then turned toward Saja. "Come!" he barked.

Saja clamped her teeth together, to keep her gut from spewing out, and hurried forward. By the time she'd reached him, he'd swung shut one of the doors and was pushing hard against the other. His companion battled against the remaining guards, slashing and hacking like a madman, forcing them into the street.

"Get inside," said Lucendes. Saja ducked into a massive foyer lit by a pair of braziers. Footsteps clapped across the tile floor from the far side, where a score of the Horned Man's thugs raced toward them.

Lucendes slammed the door shut behind Saja. She opened her mouth to scream, but it'd long since gone dry. "Lucendes," was all she was able to gasp.

The assassin appeared at her side. He held the crossbar meant to wedge the doors in place, but instead, he heaved the beam at the newcomers. It clattered along the floor at their feet, causing them to slow and jump out of the way.

Lucendes reached into his shirt and plucked out the totem, handing it to her. As Saja felt the cool glass, a shiver went up her arms. The last time she'd seen Tarim, he'd run a hand through her hair as they strolled through the potters bazaar. Would he remember?

"Do it now!" Lucendes said. "As Khouri instructed!"

Saja glanced up. The thugs were almost on top of them. Raising the totem, she hurled it at their feet. She found her voice and shouted, "Tarim, son of Yusri!" The totem shattered, and a flash of white light seared Saja's eyes, blinding her.

She stumbled backward into the doors. Dark shadows grew solid as her vision returned. All but one.

"Tarim," she whispered. He was clothed in the fine vest and shirt of one of the Kitame's guard, with a silk sash of blue wrapped around his waist. Hanging from a belt was a curved sword.

He wasn't the boy from Saja's dreams. That Tarim was more solid, somehow more real. The Tarim before her was blurred, as if the details of his face—the glint of his eyes and ridge of his cheeks—weren't fully formed. Or perhaps they were just hidden from this world.

The augurwraith studied the foyer, taking in the minions of the Horned Man, who'd stopped in horror of their new adversary.

It shifted its gaze to Lucendes, and finally, to Saja. Joy swelled in her chest, then dwindled to nothingness.

No recognition showed in its features.

The creature drew its giant blade and snarled. One of the thugs dropped his stave and ran. The augurwraith turned and sprang forward, cleaving a path through the other men. Where its sword met flesh, great rents blossomed. Its movement was a drifting mist, its already blurred features seeming to dissolve and reform with each step.

A man with a short sword hacked at the creature's back, but the steel slid through the augurwraith like a stick through a spider web, pulling tendrils of mist in its wake. The creature slashed low, and the man clutched at sundered legs as he fell.

The remaining minions bolted for the far reaches of the room, where a pair of doors and a corridor led off to other parts of the storehouse. The augurwraith pursued them, its whirling blade a dark streak of shadow.

Saja trembled, not quite comprehending what she saw. Tarim. And the creature. Existing together, yet not the same. They couldn't be. She took in the butchery, and something steeled within her gut. No, she thought. This couldn't be how she remembered him. With a determined step, she strode forward.

Across the foyer, the augurwraith disappeared into the corridor. Saja quickened her stride. She'd reached halfway to the edge of the room, when Lucendes grabbed her shoulders.

"Let it be," he said. Saja tried to shrug him off, but his grip tightened.

"I have to see him," she said, "the real Tarim. My Tarim." She squirmed in his embrace, straining against his wiry arms. Her hand found the knife at her belt, and she drove its butt into his gut.

He shuffled back, releasing her, and they glared at one another. Lucendes' face was a tense mask, his skin pulled tight around his eyes and lips. Saja knew if he lunged with his dagger, she would die.

But the assassin relaxed and shook his head. "It is foolish to hope such things," was all he said.

Saja ran. Bodies lined the corridor, leaving a trail easy to follow. She rounded a corner and hurried down a flight of stairs, as a scream echoed from below. Her feet hit dirt, and she leapt toward an open door just as a stout man with graying locks burst through from the other side.

Saja grunted as they collided, and the wind was knocked from her lungs. She was thrown back and landed hard on her rump. The man cursed, staring down at where her knife stuck from his chest. His knees buckled, and he dropped.

Saja blinked, but she had no time to dwell upon what she'd done. Scrambling to her feet, she padded around the man and peered through the door. The augurwraith stood within, stalking a man who already clutched at a flayed hand. Several tables lay overturned and broken, and in the far corner, a trapdoor rested open against the wall.

But it was the form huddled against the near wall that halted Saja's breath. Her father lay with nothing but a soiled cloth wrapped about his waist. Purple welts covered his body, and caked blood matted in his hair.

She rushed to his side, and the movement brought the creature spinning toward her, sword raised high.

"No!" she roared. "You are Tarim, son of Yusri, not this creature!" Fury burned within her chest. At her father and the guild. At Lucendes and the thieves of Kuthahaar. And at Tarim. The apprentice had wounded her deepest of all. She'd thought to tell him of how much she loved him, but now as she stood before him, she felt only the anger of betrayal.

"You could've run," she said. Tears streamed down her cheeks, and her body shivered. "We could've hid from my father and found a life together. But you abandoned me and ripped that life away."

The augurwraith's face remained hard, but it lowered its blade. "You are wrong, Saja, daughter of Sukahn," it said.

A voice gasped in wonder. "Tarim, I dared not truly believe." Saja's father gawked at his former apprentice, then racking sobs overtook him. "What have I done?" he cried.

"You did what you thought best," said Tarim. He turned his gaze to Saja. "As did I, no matter how much it hurt you." He paused, and the silence seemed to suck the air from the room. "What is done, is done. You must find a way without me."

"Is that all?" she asked, though she knew Tarim's words for truth. He'd tried to save her and her father the best way he could, the only way left to an apprentice bound to a penniless drunkard of a master.

The apprentice shimmered as if its shadowy form was suddenly taken by a gust of wind. "Do not seek me again. It only brings me pain." Tarim's face grew sorrowful, then began to fade.

As the augurwraith dissipated, Saja felt a void open within her. A great hunk of her old life ripped away, and with it went the false hope she'd tucked deep in her heart, one she'd never admitted existed, even to herself. The hope Tarim would return to her. In that void, Saja realized she would need to forge resolve and strength. He'd given his life for her future, and she meant not to squander that gift. She'd rescued her father once but would need to do so again. She loved him still and would not abandon him the way he'd abandoned her.

Across the room, the remaining minion of the Horned Man stared at Saja in bewilderment, clutching his bloodied hand. "Run, fool! To the Under!" barked Lucendes. The man jumped at the assassin's command and scampered to the trapdoor, disappearing down a hole in the floor.

"Saja," said her father, shoulders jerking as he continued to sob. "I ruined us. Who will trade with me now?"

"Don't worry, papa," she replied. She helped him to his feet, then grinned at Lucendes. "I am your new apprentice, and I believe the Tanner's Guild will soon be sending you more work than you can handle. And at a very favorable price."

The assassin laughed. "Perhaps," he said. "The Blessed One does take care of his own."

David Perlmutter returns for his third consecutive volume as he continues to push the boundaries of great pulp. This time he brings us perhaps his strangest story yet.

Jody Ryder and the Martian Marxian Invasion

By David Perlmutter

It was a blustery, cold fall day at the Hudson High Bowl in the city of Hugopolis in the year 2350. Despite, or perhaps because of, the drop in temperature, the action was white hot. Hudson was locked in tight combat with its great rival Clinton High, but now, at the last minute, needed only one more touchdown to achieve victory. There was only one way for this to occur, but fortunately she had already proved herself worthy of the glory that would soon be hers. The canine population encased within the dome, part of the remnants of "civilization" that had managed to endure following the extinction of the human race more than two centuries before, was collectively on the edge of its seats.

"She" was Jody Ryder, the star athlete of all of Hudson High's sports teams. Her tenacity and mighty powers of endurance, in addition to her astonishing speed and strength, made her one of the most formidable power sources, in sports or any other endeavor, in this or any century. The Clinton defense well knew this, for she had torn holes through them all day to a record five touchdowns. The sixth was soon to come.

After the snap, the quarterback slipped the ball to Jody, and she, with her blue eyes gleaming beneath her white helmet, sped off in her dark maroon jersey, white padded pants and white cleated shoes before anyone could catch her. Some burly members of the Clinton defense began to pursue her, but those who were able to keep up with her were soon dispatched by an astonishingly mighty right arm. At length, she arrived at the goalposts untouched and spiked the ball so hard that it was not recovered from the turf until several weeks later. (They lost more footballs that way!) As the gun went off ending the game, Jody doffed her helmet, and with a smile that displayed happiness, passion, power and arrogance in one gulp, displayed the top part of her orange-and-white pelt and looked for all the world to be a perfect goddess, despite the streaks of grease beneath her eyes and the quite obvious gaps in her teeth, victims of many prior contests, sporting and otherwise.

Jody stood in the embrace of the crowd, the hero of the game as always, before retiring as always to the dressing room. There, in the brief private moments before her colleagues arrived, she removed her jersey and pads and opened her chest, revealing a complex grid of technological and mechanical bric-a-brac.

Hitting herself with a fist to relieve what she euphemistically called "heartburn" within her "rib cage", she then shut her chest tightly. A press of a couple of buttons on the wired control box on her wrist and her appearance abruptly shifted to her favorite civilian gear: a white tank top and grey shorts. Then, placing her athletic bag on her shoulder, she ran out of the stadium before anybody could catch or find her.

For Jody Ryder, despite her athletic glory, had another job conducted secretly that meant even more to her. She was a superpowered robot hero, and her duty was to fight crime and evil no matter what the cost to her or anyone else. And being alone and isolated far more than she would have liked was part of that cost.

*****

Jody Ryder, also known by her code name, "Folklore 3", was the third attempt by the United States' Services of Intelligence to combat the forces of evil within and outside of planet Earth, of which there were plenty. The two previous efforts, it should be said, were both unqualified failures. Stagger Lee, or "Folklore 1", was a model designed as a typical ray-gun toting enforcer, but his positronic brain was damaged during the manufacturing process, and instead he became a villain of monumental proportions who constantly beleaguered his creators. At the other extreme was Shine, or "Folklore 2", who also suffered from a malfunction in his positronic makeup: he was physically powerful but was too cowardly to emerge from the lab, barricading himself behind a wall rather than performing his appointed tasks. Feeling that it had been a mistake to construct the robots using male DNA as a source, the higher-ups ordered that female genes be substituted. The third time, so to speak, was the charm.

Constructed from unbreakable Terullian steel, the strongest in the galaxy, Jody Ryder was molded into the shape of a "typical" canine teenage girl. This appearance, chosen by lot, was determined to be the most inoffensive of the ones suggested; who, after all, would suspect an innocent teenager of being a superpowered robot? And this time, the positronic brain machine actually worked! Jody Ryder was therefore, a superpowered robot with the appearance of a teenage girl, and she carried herself in public so well that few citizens suspected her of being anything else in her civilian guise. Aside from her athletic prowess, there seemed to be little on the surface that distinguished her from her peers. But when crime or other nefarious activity presented itself within her vicinity, she underwent a miraculous transformation. With a push of the buttons on her wrist transformer, she became a mighty hero clad in a red one-piece bodysuit with "J.R." prominently stitched in white on the front (a tribute by the technical staff to an equally mighty canine heroine of a previous era, who dressed similarly.). It was then that she was able to display to her opponents—and the world—the full range of her mighty robot powers. Among these were the strength and speed of an entire army of soldiers, as we have already seen, as well as heat-seeking lazers within her eyes that could melt any metal at first touch, experimental guns and swords concealed strategically within her brawny forearms, and the ability to blow herself up like a bomb and take all her opponents out if such circumstances were required. Fortunately, Jody had not yet had to use this last function—and a good thing, too, for it would have meant *her* end as well as that of her enemies. All in all, she was a formidable and powerful opponent when at full power, as her ever-growing list of foes was swiftly coming to realize.

Despite, or more likely, because of, her great power, American intelligence was determined that she act for them and not against them. For this reason, the top brass had insisted not only on making her female but also on making her teenage in mind and spirit, and specifically of the kind that was modest, thoughtful, intelligent and, above all, respectful of her elders in her words and intentions. While they certainly did not wish to have complete control over every aspect of her life, hence their allowing her to pursue "normal" teenage activities at Hudson High, they still insisted on monitoring her to prevent her from rebelling against the prescribed role and plans they had in mind for her. For this reason, she was to be powered not by batteries, as was the case with most robots, but with a specialized power source of alternating current electricity wired into her wrist communicator that recharged her dwindling strength and abilities every twelve hours. It was the duty of a special attaché monitor assigned to her not only to ensure that she was re-powered at that time but also that she was docked power for any overt displays of rebellion, temper or insolence towards the established line of behavior. This is where Sam, captain of the Hudson High cheerleading squad and Jody's only real friend in the world, came into the picture.

*****

Samuel J. Poodle, more familiarly known by the diminutive form of his first name, was as outgoing and popular as his friend and charge Jody was shy and retiring. Early on in life, ensnared by the love that dared not speak its name, he had embraced all the passion and theatricality in life that such social stereotyping threw in his way. Not that it spared him that byproduct of being a unique individual: bullying by those who considered him too much of a "threat" or a "freak". That was, in fact, how he and Jody first became acquainted, when she heroically inserted herself between Sam and the local bullying cartel and took a hail of punches meant for him. She then proceeded to expose said bullies to a furious barrage from her well-lubricated metal paws, earning her both the friendship of Sam and his eternal loyalty, though this, as she would later discover, came at a price.

Sam's ebullience and very evident *joie de vivre* made him an exuberant contrast to Jody, who more often than not kept her inner self in check in public. They were very much the odd couple, but had a strong affection for each other than endured in spite of, and because of, the frequent harassment on campus of both of them for their "different" status. No matter what was said about one, it was said, the other was sure to come to their friend's defense.

Jody's masters at American Intelligence were impressed with Sam as well, enough so that they agreed to give him the position of being her monitor. This, of course, put strains on their relationship that only they knew about, since the public revelation of their intelligence activities was out. While Sam was made to understand point-by-point the duties of his role as monitor, and that he should not hesitate to punish his friend should she transgress her boundaries, he was torn. He admired Jody, loved her even, and were she not made of metal he easily would have given up his latent tendencies to be with her; she felt similarly towards him, but was limited in her own way as to how she could show it. So he tended to bend the rules sometimes regarding her conduct. Well, a lot of the time. Well, most of the time. He and Jody agreed that the rule system was kind of old fashioned, and they subverted it whenever it needed subversion, which was fairly often; the rules were, in fact, somewhat out of date. About the only time he took power away from her was when she made him mad, but that was rare; *he* made *her* mad more often, in which cases he had to duck and cover to hide from her wrath.

They were an unlikely but strongly united pair, and seemed destined to remain that way. At least, that was how it seemed until this day—that of the first Martian Marxian invasion.

*****

Sam had a homing pigeon-like ability to track Jody, not only due to his close proximity to her but by the beeper-cum-stun gun he used to both keep track of and punish her when it was necessary. So when she didn't put in an appearance after the game, he knew exactly where to find her. Still clad in his maroon-and-white cheerleading jersey and the maroon skirt he favored over the traditional male cheerleading pants, as well as holding his coconut-sized maroon pom-poms in his white-furred armpits, he passed up his chance to "score" with Jody's football colleagues *yet again* to play nursemaid to her surprisingly vulnerable ego.

Incredibly, the most powerful robot dog on Earth was still psychologically a teenager and she needed, as many teenagers do, to have her ego constantly massaged in spite of the great level of success she had achieved and likely would continue to achieve in the future. This frustrated Sam to no end; he would eventually outgrow the tempests of adolescence, but Jody would not. Until she ceased operation permanently, he had been told, Jody would be his responsibility. Not only would he have to accompany her on her missions, but he would have to constantly be "there" for her when she needed emotional support. And this part of the job was what really stuck in Good Neighbor Sam's craw, although he had until now been too much of a gentleman to let Jody know his true feelings.

Nevertheless, being "there" was getting to be a full-time occupation for Sam, and he was starting to tire of it. Not that he didn't like having a piece of the superhero action; that he liked. He was just tired of being her handmaiden in the off-hours. Metaphorically, he had pulled too many thorns out of her paw to expect nothing in return. And that was all he seemed to be getting from her. She could ramble on for hours about her insecurities and fears, and dutifully he offered solutions and answers. But the next time, she was still complaining. Wasn't the advice he gave her good enough? Or was she just going to be a whiny, clinging crybaby for the rest of her warranty?

When he caught up with her, sitting and sobbing beside her favorite oak tree in Riverside Park, he was determined to let her know the facts. But it wouldn't be easy on either of them.

"You wanna talk, J.?" he said as he sat down beside her.

"What is there to talk about that *you* don't already know about?" she answered, wiping away the artificial tears that had streamed out of her artificial tear ducts.

"But you won the game." Sam replied, stating the obvious.

"*This* time, Sam. *This* time." Jody repeated, pessimistically. "I was just lucky that Clinton wasn't on the ball tonight. But how'll I make out against Kelvin? Or Silver Heights?"

"*You* need to have more confidence in yourself, Miss Ryder. You're on the fast track to being a great athlete, if you don't let your female problems get in the way."

"Says the guy wearing a *skirt*."

"I told you, it's more COMFORTABLE for me!"

This led to one of the robot girl's few displays of her outward emotions, as she unleashed a sonic boom of a belly laugh that threatened to rupture the hearing of all within earshot of it.

"Oh, Sam!" Jody said when her fit of humor had ended. "You always know what to say to loosen me up."

If it had ended there, the previous anecdote would not have seemed out of place in the typical teenage photoplays so common during this period. But Jody had one particular weakness that was very much an Achilles heel: once she got started with something, she did not know when to quit. Had she not been a superpowered robot, this attitude might have caused trouble for her, and, worse, might have given her questionable social status. Especially concerning what actions she was now about to perform.

With a gleam in her mechanical eyes, Jody stared longingly at her male companion, and, with her superstrength at full power, slammed him against the tree behind them. Sam whimpered fearfully. Any other boy, if in this position, and especially with a girl as beautiful and powerful as Jody was, would have jumped at the chance, but Sam Poodle was *not* any other boy. He knew what he wanted and what he liked, and this was not it!

Desperately, he tried to resist her actions, but his strength was no match for hers, especially when she was physically and/or sexually aroused, as was the case now. But Sam knew he could still best her if he pulled rank, and he decided to do just that.

“Stand down, Folklore 3!” he snapped firmly. “This isn’t part of your programming!”

But she didn’t snap to attention or anything like that. If anything, she seemed even more turned on.

“Come on, Sam!” she said in a trilling, almost desperate whine. “I wanna mess around a bit! And you know you’re the only guy I can do it with!”

That was it, as far as he was concerned. He reached into the pocket of his skirt and pulled out his controller, turning the “punishment” knob over to the highest level: “super naughty”.

“I hate having to do this to you, Jody…” he said “…but you asked for it. And I mean, you *really* ASKED FOR IT!”

He pushed the button, and the device did its work. Abruptly, Jody Ryder was bombarded with the electricity that fueled her super muscles. Only this time, it was being used to restrain rather than empower her. As she uttered a bloodcurdling scream, her superpowers were robbed from her and she sank to the ground, helpless. She landed just as Sam wanted her to, on her knees looking up at him. Temporarily disabled, Jody watched as Sam walked up to her and slapped her face so hard that she yelled and cried again.

“Oh, shut up, you little BABY!” Sam spat out, bitterly. “I’m through being your nursemaid!” He reformatted the dial so that Jody’s power was restored to her, though she still felt the mental and physical pain he had inflicted upon her. Very deeply, in fact.

“What the hell was THAT?” she bellowed at him. “You can’t just drop me down whenever you wanna play Marquis De Sade and give me a beatdown! There’s procedures and stuff that they…”

“…told me about when I agreed to be your monitor!” Sam

finished her sentence. “Yeah, I know that, girlfriend! But all the times we bent the rules together—and ALONE, in your case—could get me disbarred and you turned into scrap iron! Is that what you want?”

“No.” Jody said, defensively. “But I also don’t want my friend to become my ENEMY just ‘cause he can break me with a push of a button!”

“Is it my fault that I want to keep my job?” San snapped, crossing his forepaws over his sweater and walking away with his back turned to her. “Not that you would know ANYTHING about that!”

“What the hell have YOU got to be so smug about?” answered the robot, grabbing his arm and spinning him around. “You have no idea what kind of pressure I’m under, okay? NO IDEA! I’m lettering in every sport at Hudson, and they practically expect me to carry all of ‘em on my shoulders ‘cause the guys aren’t men enough to stand up and be heroes! I have a full course load of work to do, and the teachers treat me like CRAP just ‘cause they assume I’m a dumb athlete, so I have to constantly prove to them I’m not! And let’s not forget the fact that I have to run around in my red undies every time some stupid bunch of aliens or some evil genius who’s trying to get revenge because he got denied tenure starts causing trouble, and I have to punch and kick and shoot blasters out of my eyes and generally make myself look like a pompous windbag ASS that none of the boys want to date! That’s a full working day, Sam, AND DON’T YOU FORGET…”

She would have thundered out the final word of that sentence, but Sam, pushed to the edge, had firmly placed his paws over the vocal chords and mouth of his charge, preventing her from uttering anything further.

"You listen carefully, spark-plug-for-brains!" he fumed, in an aggressive whisper. "Your life is a goddamn BED OF ROSES compared to mine! Have you got any idea about what I go through? The stares? The insinuations? The JOKES? You should, 'cause most of the time when they happen, YOU'RE THERE! Bad enough I get laughed at and mocked for being a fruit, but it gets magnified double, triple even, just because I have to be your handmaiden, your boss, your psychiatrist, and every other damn thing you need from me! Jody, I have no problem being your friend and your monitor and all that, but you gotta stop relying on me for EVERY DECISION! Seriously, girl, you gotta give me some space! I can be a friend, for sure, but you have to get your thing together! Have confidence in your brain power like you do your muscle power! Trust yourself, like you do me! BE A REAL GIRL, for once in your life!"

Releasing his grip on her throat, Sam allowed Jody to get her breath back and then gave her his strongest "you're my best friend in the whole world" hug. She responded in kind.

"You're right, Sam." Jody said softly. "About everything. I was out of line. But I'm just so LONELY! You're all I have, friend wise, and I figured, if I was going to do that with anybody…"

"You know I don't swing that way, J.R." Sam said, stroking the fur on her artificial pelt. "And you also know that I can only take so much. Or, at least, you do now. If it's any help, I can help you out with the kids in school; I know most of 'em good anyhow, and it wouldn't take you long to make cute with some of them. But you gotta start behaving yourself and stop taking me granted, with everything! Understand?"

“Okay, Sam.” Jody replied. “You sound like you know best about this.”

“I do.” he said. “You just need to listen to me.”

*****

The reverie between Sam and Jody was, however, destined not to last. For, at that moment, Jody began ringing like a telephone, with appropriate shaking and sound effects. This meant only one thing: headquarters was calling, likely with a new assignment for them. Jody and Sam both groaned. Why now? This was the *last* thing they needed!

In any event, Sam lightly pressed Jody’s belly button, and a small television screen emerged from her stomach, the principal means by which communications occurred between her and headquarters. Immediately, on the small computer monitor-sized color TV screen, the image of H.W., the director of American Intelligence, and thus Jody and Sam’s immediate superior, made its appearance.

H.W. received immediate respect from his charges, not simply the respect due a person of his superior age but because of his experience and appearance. Thin-eared, large-eyed, bespectacled and clad in his favorite blue suit, not to mention his black fur rapidly turning gray, H.W. looked for all the world like one of those Milquetoast middle-management types, but he was much more than that. After a distinguished career as a teenaged star soldier, he made millions drilling for oil and mining oort on Uranus and Neptune. But that wasn’t enough, at least not for him. He was from a patrician family that insisted upon giving back to the universe that gave so much to them, and that meant public service, preferably politics. He was fortunate enough to be friendly with the current President, and was therefore trusted with the task of running the American Intelligence network, but it was a slippery slope. Elections were coming up, and if the new President felt he wasn't doing the job well enough, he'd be fired for sure. And if H.W. got fired, then all of the projects he had nurtured at American Intelligence would be cut or scaled back, which meant that Sam would be out of work and Jody would be permanently decommissioned. It wasn't anything personal, they were told, it was just the way things worked in their business. Even though none of them particularly liked it. So they were all determined to do their best job at all times, though this was not necessarily what would keep them working.

In any event, the robot girl and her companion snapped to it when their boss appeared to them within the limited confines of Jody's console screen.

"Evenin', Jody…Sam." H.W. said, in his distinctive Northeast-by-way-of-Texas accent. "Hope I'm not interruptin' anything."

"Funny you should say that!" Sam remarked, hoping to report on Jody's recent "malfunction". But Jody gave him a look that clearly said DON'T YOU DARE, and he trailed off. For he, of all dogs, was most familiar with what she was capable of doing to an enemy, and it was certainly *not* something he wanted done to him.

"You're not, H.W." Jody said. "You know I think anything you have to say is important!"

"I know that, too, darlin'," answered H.W. "but let's not let my wife find out I think that way!"

The robot and the bureaucrat laughed like they were old

friends, which, for all intents and purposes, they were. Sam folded his paws and glowered out of view and of earshot. It was partially because H.W. was so friendly with Jody that he was willing to allow her to bend the rules to achieve her goals, the very rules Sam was supposed to be enforcing on her. Of course, he couldn't complain about this, not having the protection accorded by a high rank, but he resented their closeness. Especially when Jody kept rubbing his nose in the fact that she was on good terms with the boss when Sam brought up procedural issues. Jody might have been his friend, but theoretically she was also supposed to be his employee. Instead, he was being treated as an appendage, almost an accessory. And he did not like that.

"Can we get *on* with it, *please*?" Sam snapped at Jody and H.W., not only to break up their mutual admiration society but to get Jody to re-recognize his authority over her. Jody turned around and shot daggers at him with her eyes. It was as if she, and not he, was in charge, and she preferred this situation as much as he did not.

"Can you stop acting like a *snot* for one minute, SAMUEL?" she snapped. "H.W. is as much my friend as you are. Why can't I have a friendly conversation with him?"

"You can." he answered. "but not THAT friendly! Jody, he's your boss! So am I, for that matter! And you never treat me with the respect you're supposed to give me!"

"'SUPPOSED' to give you?" answered the robot, angered. "You're lucky I don't cream you RIGHT NOW! 'Supposed' to give you respect! Right!" Those last words were said under her breath, but Sam could still hear them. So *this* is what she thought of him on the job, huh? Well, he'd fix *her* soon enough!

"You were saying, H.W.?" Jody said as she returned her attention to her "real" boss.

"Right," said H.W. "'Fraid I haven't got much time, so I'll come right out and say it." As always, he shot his paws out in front of him at the end of each sentence to emphasize the point. "I'm not gonna lie to you—it's bad."

"How bad?" Sam asked.

"We're dealing with *War of the Worlds* REVISITED!" said H.W., with surprising calmness.

The planet Mars, due to its isolation from the rest of the solar system on a social basis, had been unaffected when the planet Earth had imploded nuclear gas that destroyed the human race and elevated the canine race to its place. It had also refused to allow the new canine race to explore and colonize within its lands, or to interbreed with its citizens to create new hybrid races, as the other races of the galaxy had graciously done. As a consequence, relations between Mars and Earth, never very cordial to begin with, had declined to the point where war was not just possible, but a constant and visible threat. Even with the formidable negotiation skills of H.W. and his associates, the Martians refused to bend. It became increasingly more difficult after the Martians involuntarily chose to do away with democratic government in favor of a Marxist experiment that Earth did not approve of. As a result, Mars had begun a constant series of attacks on Earth, and this was another one of those occasions. Hopefully, Jody would be able to repel this attack, just as she had on the previous half dozen occasions. Or, at least, that was what H.W. was implying.

"I thought Ogg learned his lesson last time," said Jody, referring to the self-appointed Supreme Commander of the

Martian Armed Forces and her constant nemesis. "They didn't know what hit them when I was through—or at least that's what I thought."

"I thought so, too," said Sam, "but we forgot about…"

Jody glared at him again, and again Sam was forced to clam up.

"I know what you mean." said H.W. "But you know those Martians!"

"And they've just gotten meaner since Ogg set up that whole Marxist government thing," agreed Jody. "That makes it even more of an imperative that I beat them back."

"Hey!" interjected Sam. "There are two of…"

Again came the glare and the slump back into silence.

"I don't mind that he wants to impose that totalitarian lifestyle on his people, within reason, of course," Jody continued. "But I'll be damned if he tries to bring it down on us, too. I mean, who wants to walk around in green polyester and chanting praises to a semi-human being all day, anyway? Yecch!"

"So I take it you're going to take the job again?" said H.W.

"Damn right I am!" Jody said with her typical arrogant determination. "And this time, he *really* won't know what hit him!"

"All right, then!" said H.W. "Just let me know when you've done it, and I'll check it under 'done'!" His image disappeared from the screen, which retracted back into Jody's body.

Sam raised his lips in imminent objection mode. Was it not *his* job to accepts assignments from H.W.? And wasn't *she* supposed to nod and say "Yes, sir" like a normal intelligence agent? Friendship was friendship, but business was also business. And Jody did not seem to know the difference. But once again

Jody suppressed his tirade with one of her own.

"SHUT UP, Sam!" she snapped. "I haven't got time for you to run your mouth off again today- ONCE was enough! The Martians are probably mobilizing AS WE SPEAK, and you want to waste time complaining about *me*? Just go home and change and I'll pick you up in twenty minutes."

"Change?" Sam uttered with wounded pride. "What for?"

"Because I will *not* perform superheroic activities with a boy who thinks a SKIRT is the height of fashion!" Jody snapped again. "Come on! Move!" For the time being, Sam was compelled to act as was requested of him. But inside, he seethed.

"This is the last straw!" he said to himself. "She's pushed me too far this time. Let's see how strong she feels when her power runs out and her monitor isn't there to save her!"

*****

Unbeknownst to either Jody or Sam, their seemingly private spatting had been observed, by no less an intimidating figure than Jody's sworn enemy. Even now, along with his already formulated plan to invade Earth, he was scheming to rid himself of his nemesis and her boy-toy for good. After charting out plans for an invasion of Earth that he felt was destined not to fail, General Malachi Ogg, the Supreme Commander of the Martian Armed Forces, had sequestered himself in his planet-viewing parlor for several days straight to keep an eye on Jody Ryder, his robotic foe from Earth, who had thus far thwarted all his chances for invading Earth with her pluck, grit and superpowers. The reason, he explained to his aides, was so he could pick the moment when she was the weakest or most stressed to invade. If she was in no condition or had no desire to fight, she would easily surrender to them, and the Earth would be THEIRS! (Cue evil laughter.)

It was not for nothing that General Ogg was the Supreme Commander, after all. Through his guidance and his frequent, overtly repressive discipline, the Martian Army was now the most feared fighting force in the galaxy despite the fact that, physically, the Martian race most closely resembled a troupe of green-skinned circus midgets. But with disparity in size comes recompense in other areas of physical and mental growth, and those favored Ogg and his contemporaries. Their intelligence especially was superior to that of other galactic life forms, with the result that they were second to none when it came to military strategy and its applications. But "none" still existed in the form of Earth. While Mars had succeeded in establishing colonies and trading posts all across the Milky Way, and Ogg was constantly praised (by force of his own hand, mostly) at home for his work, it was not enough for him. Earth stood in his way—laughing, mocking, cajoling him. Earth and its population of resourceful, intelligent canines was what stood between the Martians and an expanded, galaxy-wide influence, and Ogg hated them for that. Especially Jody Ryder and her constant meddling. He would have given anything to have them—and especially her—toiling in the Martian copper mines under the sting of his own personal lash. Having seen the dispute between Jody and Sam occur with his own eyes, on his planet's far advanced telecommunications system, Ogg knew he had his foes at a disadvantage. Physically and emotionally, she was pushed to the limit, and she'd quite clearly crack under the strain of defending Earth yet again. He rushed out of the viewing room and was immediately surrounded by his identical, fawning aides.

"It's time." he said with determination. "Make sure the men are ready to go."

The aides erupted in a chorus of "Yes, sir"'s as they rushed off to implement his orders. The general was left alone with his thoughts, and they were very evil ones, too.

"By tomorrow night…" he said determinedly to himself "…Earth will be MINE! And the head of that busybody robot Jody Ryder will be here on my desk—as my own personal ASHTRAY!" (Cue evil laugh again.)

*****

While this display of villainous vitriol was going on, Jody Ryder, having converted to superheroic mode, was now standing in front of Sam's house, impatiently waiting for her partner-in-justice to emerge from his abode in an ensemble that pleased her.

"Hurry up!" she shouted, as she tapped her foot furiously on the ground. "I'm digging my own grave here!"

"All right!" said Sam, with an equal amount of testiness. "I'm coming!"

Sam emerged shortly thereafter. His sweater was the same as before, but wisely, for his sake, he had removed his skirt in favor of a pair of green corduroy pants. Jody, seeing him re-outfitted, was considerably more pleased with his appearance.

"There, now!" she said "Doesn't it feel better to be dressed in *normal* clothes, for once?"

"*You're* one to talk about dressing normal, champ!" Sam retorted sarcastically. After all, most non-superhero types didn't wear red bodysuits with their initials stenciled on them, even in this more advanced time. And especially not after Labor Day.

"Ha, ha!" returned Jody, catching his sarcasm and returning with her own. "Just hold my paw, shut up, and leave the comedy to me!"

"Just like I leave *everything else* to you, huh?" Sam thought. Fortunately, he did not say this, or his life might have ended then and there. Instead, he did what he was told, and Jody took off with all the rocket power available in her chassis.

Sam was only able to keep his promise of being silent for a minute before Jody shifted into second gear and began moving faster. At this point, his falsetto shriek began blending seamlessly with the hum of Jody's internal engine. She still heard him, however.

"Stop being such a BABY!" Jody snapped. "You're just lucky that I don't take it all the way."

"*You're* just lucky I haven't thrown up yet!" Sam replied.

With Jody firing on all cylinders, it wasn't long before the pair had reached the outskirts of Earth's atmosphere and had exited it altogether. Sure enough, they encountered the first initial strike force of Martian troops, who fired on them. Jody fired back, with the blasters in her eyes as well as the gun in her right paw; her left held Sam and kept him from dropping, though he remained completely petrified.

A couple of minutes later, the fleet was entirely destroyed, and Jody and Sam were on their way to the heart of Mars itself.

*****

Sitting comfortably at the intersection of the Gogol, Pushkin and Nabokov rivers, Muscovy, the capital city of Mars, displayed all the affluence and wealth one would expect from the seat of an interplanetary Marxist empire. Like Hugopolis, its Terran counterpart, it was the place where everyone in the planet eventually came to stay, at least for a little while, if they wished to truly "make it" in this thriving society. Ever since General Ogg and his militant cohorts had seized power in a bloodless coup twenty years earlier, everything had been restructured and reconditioned to build Mars into a glorious empire. As already noted, there was a string of Martian outposts all over the galaxy, competing for space and financial resources with that of Earth. The Marxist empire was notorious for muscling its way into territory held by others, especially Earth's. And since Mars was now the only truly alien race left in the universe, no way was Earth going to allow "foreigners" to take over territories that "rightfully" beyond to them. Hence, the advent of American Intelligence efforts to counter this Martian expansion, especially in the person of Jody Ryder.

Said person, accompanied by her frightened associate, now began their descent into the Muscovy area, in the face of one of the dust storms that were so common on the Red Planet. Jody cut her rocket boosters down with the pressing of a few strategic buttons on her chest, and they landed, slowly and smoothly, within the City Square. Or at least Jody did, on her feet; Sam was dropped unceremoniously, face first, on the ground.

Sam, with his mouth full of gravel, uttered something unintelligible and unprintable to Jody, but she had no time for any more talk from him. Especially when General Ogg and his minions, with all the force that could be exhibited in such small frames, were hastily approaching them. Jody quickly tucked Sam under her arm like the footballs at home and placed him gently on a marble bench in the north corner of the square.

"Now, you stay here and let the grown-ups talk!" she said, and walked off. Sam said nothing, but he didn't need to. He knew his revenge would come, soon enough.

Jody's timing, as always, was immaculate. She assumed her favored stance just as Ogg and his associates, apparently not knowing of her presence, entered the center of the square, and suddenly found themselves face to face with Jody, paws on hips, bigger than all three of them put together.

Ogg wasn't afraid, however. He'd dealt with her before, and he'd deal with her the same way. He signaled this mentally to his colleagues, who got the message right away.

"So, Folklore 3," he said with typical combative arrogance. "Earth sent you back again, huh? What makes you think I have any intention of invading your pathetic planet?"

"Don't lie to me, Ogg!" Jody retorted, not moving a muscle or even arching her eyebrows. "I just chopped down your latest invasion force on my way in here! Did you *really* think that those paper planes could seriously conquer Earth, let alone get past *me*?"

"You can raise hell all you want, Ryder," answered Ogg, "but Mars have its way! And not even *you* can stop us!" (Cue evil laugh once again.)

"Ah, g'wan!" said the robot, dismissively with a mocking tone. "You can't fool me with that act! Earth has more people than Mars—plus better morals! They won't let you conquer them even if you do succeed in landing an invasion force—and judging by what happened just recently, I seriously doubt that!"

"You are severely trying my patience with that patented Terran arrogance of yours, Ryder!" the Martian commander replied. “You of all beings should know what happens to those who cause me displeasure…”

Jody put her left paw up in typical crossing guard fashion.

“Spare me the lecture, Ogg!” she said. “I’ve heard you say that speech so many times that I know it by heart. ‘I will have you bowing at my feet kissing my toes, no matter how badly it hurts your back. You will be enslaved cleaning my stables and killing the lions and hydras of the Martian wilderness’. Puh-lease! What *you* need to do is concentrate more on what’s going on here on Mars and let we Earth people live our lives in peace! What’s the matter? Not enough going on in town on Saturday night to keep you satisfied? Obviously not, if you keep trying to conquer Earth as much as you do. But you gotta quit it, Ogg! Just *give it up*! You and I, we’ve been through this routine too many times already, and, speaking for me, I’m SICK of it! This whole “invade the Earth” routine sucks loads, and it doesn’t solve ANYTHING! And I’m putting a stop to it NOW, whether you like it or not!”

The ray-gun from her right arm exposed itself to back up her claims. Her internal mechanism loaded it up to fire at the Martians as she continued to speak.

“And don’t think I’m kidding,” she snapped with finality. “Because I’m not!”

But then it happened. The very forces that powered Jody Ryder now conspired to betray her. Abruptly, her ray-gun reassembled back into her right arm, and she uttered a piercing scream as her superpowers, taking the form of a blinding beam of light, exited her body. She fell to her knees, powerless.

Ogg smiled at this moment, as did Sam, farther away in the shadows. They had both long hoped that this moment would occur, but for different reasons. And it seemed now both of them had what they wanted.

"What happened?" the stunned robot uttered softly to herself. She had never lost power during a mission before, having always been careful to time her work with Sam to avoid such eventualities. But now, she realized what was going on and uttered the appropriate response for the occasion, a profane expletive that was heard all across Mars and even forced some Earth mothers to cover their childrens' ears.

Ogg, seizing the opportunity of seeing his mighty enemy brought down to *his* size, rushed towards her. Grabbing her bodysuit, he balled his left hand into in a fist and held her above him with all his Martian strength in his right.

"How does it feel to be on *my* side of the ledger, Ryder?" he sneered with contempt. "Things worked out just the way I wanted it, for once."

"You *planned* this?" Jody snarled.

"Of course I planned it, you stupid Earth girl!" Ogg answered back. "You know as well as I know that I know DARN WELL how you Earth robots operate! And I especially know how *you* work, my dear! So, naturally, I thought to myself, the fabulous Ms. Ryder can't possibly act at full power *all* the time—she has to be powered up sometime! So I figured that I should just hit you when you weren't ready for it!"

"But how could you possibly know all about my energy cycles?" said Jody.

"That's what SPIES are for, honey!" Ogg said, arrogantly spitting Martian saliva in her face, where the acid within began wearing away her pelt and metal exoskeleton. "You'll find that, if you examined your planet more closely, there's quite a few of us

Martians in your government and civil service—just look for the little ones! Back in the 1950s, the human beings caught on pretty quick to our little plan of infiltration. They called our men COMMUNISTS, and drove most of them to their DEATHS! But that won't happen this time, because you DOGS are too stupid to tell the difference between people of their own race and those NOT OF THIS EARTH! (Once again, cue evil laugh.)

Jody was enraged and wriggled in his grasp impotently with what little strength she had left as he spoke those words.

"You FIEND!" she screamed. "I'll…"

"*You* won't be doing anything, Ryder!" Ogg answered with cruelty in his voice. "I'll see to that!"

And so, General Ogg began in a long-desired dream—beating up his nemesis Jody Ryder in combat. Ordinarily, her speed and strength, coupled with the fact that she was virtually indestructible and invulnerable at full power, would have been enough to discourage him. That, and the fact that she was, after all, a girl. But those barriers were gone now, and he now felt free to treat her as he pleased. And he wanted payback for all the damage she had caused to his home, his reputation, his plans for a new and better Marxian Mars. Beating her up would not resolve all of the hatred he felt for her, but it would have to do for now.

And so, he proceeded with his "smack down". A rapid fire series of punches, coupled with the occasional kick, promptly found their place within the damaged face of Jody Ryder. Ignoring said person's constant cries of "Ow!" and "Quit it!", he slowly but deliberately smashed her big black nose, ripped off large chunks of her synthetic pelt to reveal the robot beneath, tied her artificial ears together, and stuck his bulbous thumbs into the circuitry of her mechanical eyes, temporarily but effectively blinding her. Finally, before she could even attempt anything in the way of feeble retaliation, he leaned back and delivered a roundhouse knockout punch that left the robot champion of Earth sprawled and dazed on the ground, too weak to mount a challenge.

She had been knocked to the very corner in which Sam was now standing, with confident smugness, above her. Slowly getting to her feet, she told him what was up.

"Ogg tricked me into coming here when my powers expired so he could beat me up!" she told him. "You gotta recharge me so I can fight back!"

Sam thought for a moment about this desperate request. Then he said, slowly but effectively:

"No!"

"WHAT???" Jody was breathing fire. Sam had never said "no" to her before. Why now, when she needed his help the most? He let her know *that* right away!

"Consider this punishment for disobeying your monitor!"

"You're going to pull rank *NOW*? Why, you arrogant little JERK! I'll…"

"What can you possibly do to me without your powers?" Sam taunted impudently. "Even *I* could beat you up *now*, and you know what a BABY I am!"

Before Jody could respond, she was pulled to her knees by Ogg's aides, who gagged her mouth and tied her once-powerful arms together. Pointing with their guns, they ordered her out of the courtyard, following her out. The General himself approached Sam, who pouted a final stare at Jody as she was led off.

"Inadvertently, Mr. Poodle, we seem to have the same goal this time," Ogg told him.

"I guess," Sam said reluctantly. "Jody's gotten too big for her circuits the last little while. She had that beating coming to her."

"Want to see her get beaten again?" Ogg asked.

"Sure, if it helps her learn her lesson." said Sam.

"Then you won't mind sitting next to her while the entire population of Muscovy tears you and her to DEATH!" Ogg laughed. (Say it with me now—Cue evil laugh.) As he said this, he pointed his own gun at Sam and forced him to march after his friend.

"Whoo!" Sam uttered as he was led off. "Didn't see *that* coming!"

*****

Due to their Brobdingnagian size on Mars, there was no safe place in the Muscovy City Jail to hold Jody and Sam. So they were forced to suffer the indignity of being chained by their necks to opposing sides of a large maypole, just as their ancestors had been oppressed by the now-defunct human beings of Earth so many years earlier.

When Sam first entered the courtyard, Jody was silent at first, seething at his betrayal of her. Once she knew he was settled in on her other side, she lit into him again.

"You miserable, backstabbing, conniving little WUSSY!" Jody shouted, crawling as far around the pole towards Sam as the chain would allow her. "You set us up to be POWs! And now we're gonna DIE here! Are you *happy* now?"

"Not yet." said Sam. "Not until you APOLOGIZE!!!"

"What for?" Jody demanded. "What have *I* possibly got to

apologize to…"

"Clam it, you tin-plated JERK!" Sam cut her off. In place of her salvo, he launched into one of his own.

"Don't say ANYTHING ELSE!" he growled. "Not until I've said my peace! You, Jody Ryder, are the most selfish, arrogant and pretentious JERK I have ever met! I don't care if you ARE a robot, and that you can kill me just by flexing your biceps! You don't have *any* right to act superior to anybody! *Especially* not to me! There's a reason why the rules and the protocol exist, Jody! They're around to keep you safe, and I'm around to make sure that happens- provided you start taking what I say with a grain of salt!"

"Sam!" Jody interrupted him, loudly. "How *dare* you accuse me of being disloyal to you! Have you forgotten all the times I've risked my butt to keep you safe? If I recall correctly, that was how we met, was it not? Maybe I should have let your ass get kicked then! *Then* you'd know what I just went through…"

"That's just it, Jody!" Sam answered. "It always ends up coming back to you. You don't give a damn about anything else—especially not what they tell you to do—unless it helps save *you* in some way or another! Jody, I'm talking not just as your friend, but as your boss. You respect me as your friend, but as your boss, you just think of me as a dumb old pile of sticks you have to drag along by force. And that's gotta change."

Jody was silent for a moment. She thought with all the strength of her positronic brain about what Sam had said. Yes, he was her friend, and he'd helped her out with her problems many times on Earth. But she'd shown him very little respect as a monitor. All her superpowers couldn't disguise the fact that she'd treated Sam poorly as a boss. And that was hurting their relationship as friends, as much as her attempt to come on to him earlier that evening. She knew what she had to do, and she did. She cried, softly this time, but loud enough for him to hear.

"Sam," she said, "I'm sorry. For everything. I've been a lousy friend and a rotten employee. I'd do anything to make things up to you. Just so we could patch things up and start over."

"All I want is for you to take what I say as a monitor *seriously*, okay?" Sam answered. "Just like I told you about being a friend earlier, about giving me room to breathe, you know? I don't mind being dragged around with you like a doll to all the battles and fights and everything; I like that. But what I don't want you to do is treat me like a joke. When I come with you, it's because I have a specific role to play for you, not just because I want to go sight-seeing. I'm an authority figure on these missions, Jody, not just a friend. I don't expect you to do everything I say, but I expect you'll at least *listen* to it before you go all bull-in-the-china-shop. That's all I ask. Understand?"

"Was *that* why you wouldn't give me back my powers when I dried up?" Jody asked.

"Exactly." Sam answered.

"Then I'll do it." The robot's confidence was returning to her, but with a notion of reflection and regret. "I am *not* losing my only friend in the world because even *he* can't stand me anymore! I swear I'll start behaving myself, Sam. Just give me back my powers so I can waste these Martians and we can get out of here!"

"Good enough for me," said Sam. And they shook on it, awkwardly due to their current confinement.

A Martian guard told them to cut out the racket. Sam and Jody both told him to perform an action that is not as yet physically possible. The guard withdrew his objection.

"Okay, now," said Sam. "Turn around and I'll get you back on line!"

Jody did as she was told, for once. Displaying her wrist communicator to Sam, she allowed him to open it. Sam placed the clamps of his AC converter in their corresponding sockets, and then turned the transmitter to "high" as he began the conversion process. Jody uttered a cry of pain as the electricity surged into her body, but this did not last long. With her power restored to her, she grunted lustily and freed herself and Sam from the iron shackles that held them. Then Sam took care of the little detail of realigning the communicator to its proper frequency.

"All right, Mr. Monitor," said Jody. "What sort of game plan should we use to get out of here: The "Jenny"? The "Mel Brooks"? The "Truman"? The "Harvey Korman"?"

"I was thinking more along the lines of the "Rocky And Bullwinkle" said Sam. "You know, kind of catch them off guard. Play the old "innocent sap" game and *then* hit them!"

"You are *sharp*!" Jody answered. "Glad you're working with me and not against me!"

"Let's keep it that way, okay?" said Sam as they rushed off to implement their plan.

*****

Once the news of the escape of the robot "villain" and her "effeminate" sidekick was out, an official search was conducted all through Muscovy, but not until later that night was any concrete trace of the pair uncovered. That was when, once again,

General Ogg and his coterie of followers encountered the duo on a promenade. He had taken them by surprise last time, but this time they had the advantage.

Part of Jody's programming—and Sam's training—was an intimate, expansive knowledge of nearly all of the action-adventure television programs of the twentieth century, programs carefully saved in the Earth archives for their value as combat training sources. Jody had inputted all this matter into her positronic brain at the time she went online; Sam had to go through the process more gradually, through several marathon viewing sessions, in order to make sure he was aware of what she was talking about, at least so he could keep up with her but also to suggest strategy when it was time. And now, they were going to be implementing one of these treasured plans to escape their current crisis.

By the time Ogg and company recognized the familiar giant shapes in front of them, those figures had outfitted themselves in a rather unique way. Jody had stuck in her ears two large tree branches resembling deer antlers, and had assumed an unusually stupid look on her face, while Sam had outfitted himself in the leather helmet and goggles of a World War I aviator, accentuating it with a flowing white scarf. This latter item was from his own wardrobe and was *not* a prop, as he had reminded Jody earlier.

Once outfitted with their rather flimsy disguises, the canine duo approached the Martian general and his associates, who, surprisingly, did not immediately perceive the fact that they were soon to be conned in the most royal fashion possible.

"Hi, there!" Sam called to the General, in an astonishingly high falsetto voice. "Can you help us?"

"Yuh!" added Jody, in a classic "dumb guy" voice created through electronic vocal simulation. "Yuh see, we came up here to…uh…what's that word…find…this…here fellow….Ug….Ig….Egg…."

"Ogg!" said Sam. "General Ogg! You know, the boss man!"

"You know I don't know nothin'" Jody said, smiling a "dumb guy" look to go with the voice. "You said so yourself!"

"I did not!" said Sam, defensively. "I said you just didn't have as much brains as other people, that's all."

"Well, anyhow…" Jody said "…We gotta find this fella and give him what for! Kind of a shrimp, I hear!"

"Yeah!" added Sam. "And he's not so big in the brain, neither!"

Against the advice of his advisors, General Ogg advanced towards the mismatched pair. He did not like anyone insulting his person, even if they had never seen him before. And besides, these two looked rather familiar. Had he not seen them earlier today? He wanted a look for himself.

"*I* am General Ogg!" he informed the pair. "And I don't appreciate being *insulted* by the likes of you!"

"Gee, Mister!" said Sam. "We didn't mean any harm!"

"Yuh!" added Jody.

"Well, that's just too bad!" said the General. "Especially when it's quite clear to me who you *really* are!"

He proceeded to make his point by ripping the branches out of Jody's ears and the helmet/goggles combo off Sam's head—revealing their true identities.

"Hokey smoke, Jody!" said Sam, still in secret identity mode. "We've been caught! We're really in trouble now!"

"Can it, Sam!" said Jody, reverting to her natural voice. "It's over!"

"Sorry." Sam answered in his normal tones. "I'm a bit of a Method actor."

"Enough talk!" Ogg interrupted, drawing his ray-gun from its holster on his hip. "Never mind the public execution!" he ordered his aides. "I'll kill these two *right now*!"

And, without hesitation, he took aim at Sam, intending to fill him full of highly ionized-and poisonous-Martian lead. Sam, realizing his fate, silently yelped as Ogg's gun came within range of his luminous white neck. But just after three bullets shot out of Ogg's gun, and before they had a chance to hit Sam, Jody utilized her super speed to save him. Deftly, she caught two of the bullets in her paws and crushed them; the third landed in her mouth, and, after briefly chewing on it, she quickly spat it out.

"Yecch!" she ejaculated. "Tastes like a sofa!"

Ogg was stunned, but Sam was not. He therefore enjoyed, as did Jody, seeing the little man's body furiously shake with rage.

"What is the meaning of this?" he demanded of his aides. "You told me she was *powerless* now!"

"Sorry, Ogg!" said Jody. "It's just not your millennium. He doesn't come along with me just to *admire* me, you know!"

The "he", Sam, smiled ruefully at his mechanical friend. Even though they had a new understanding, some things still weren't going to change.

"Let's see him admire *this*!" a vengeful Ogg snapped.

He fired his gun slowly and more deliberately. This time, not even Jody Ryder's robot powers could save her friend and monitor from taking it on the chin—or the right back leg, which was where it actually hit him. Sam, upon being hit, uttered a scream of pain, and fell backwards to the ground. He was not out, but he was down.

"SAM!" Jody shouted in anguish as he fell to the ground. Was he to be killed because she failed to protect him? She didn't think so! She quickly rushed to give him succor, but Ogg and his friends abruptly blocked their path.

"No more tricks, Ryder!" the General snapped. "Back off, or I put bullets in the rest of his body!"

"Yes, sir." Jody uttered with uncharacteristic meekness. And, in a gesture of surrender, she backed up from where she had stood and raised her forepaws above her head.

"You win, Ogg!" she said. "I surrender! Just come over here and we can negotiate! Just don't hurt Sam, please! I could never forgive myself if he was killed! I'd self-destruct in a minute if that happened, and you wouldn't want that! Just leave him alone and come over here, okay?"

"Very well, girl!" Ogg snapped dismissively. "But don't expect that we'll meet all your demands!"

"Just come over this way, that's all I want," answered the robot.

And so the General and his contingency marched towards their antagonist, thinking they had her licked this time. But they would soon find out otherwise, especially since Jody kept moving farther and farther away each time they got closer to her.

"Come over here. Closer…closer…closer…Not that close!" said Jody, like a portrait photographer getting her subjects in just the right position. "Now go a bit to the right…to the left…a little closer…there, stand there for a minute…"

"Get on with it, Ryder!" demanded Ogg, after another minute or so of this tomfoolery. But Jody was ready now, even if her opponents were not.

"Oh, I *will*!" Jody shot back.

The lasers in her eyes then went to work, boring a circular pattern around Ogg and his associates. Before they knew it, they suddenly found themselves trapped. Then the greatest indignity of all came. Jody knelt down at the southern end of the circle as if she was going to pray, but it instead she did something with considerably more power behind it. With a Herculean assertion of all her robot muscles, Jody summoned all of her super strength and lifted the chunk of rock up in the air, with the aliens still on it, above her head like a dumbbell.

"Going down!" she thundered, as she flipped the rock upside down so that the aliens, clinging with tenacity to their piece of land, were now stuck on the bottom of the rock. With another thunderous assertion of her enormous power, the canine robot girl smashed the rock deep down into the Martian surface, burying it and her foes firmly into the planet's mantle. It would be some time, if ever, before they saw the planet's surface again.

"You'll pay for this, Ryder!" Ogg snapped from his new position.

"Fine!" Jody said, with the confidence only a firmly established victory can give a superhero of her stature. "But *you've* got to pay a few bills, first!"

And he would.

*****

Having vanquished evil once again, Jody rushed to the aid of her chum, who was lying softly, clutching his wounded leg.

"Oh, Sam!" she said, contritely. "Are you going to be okay, or should I…."

“I’ll be fine.” said Sam. “We’ve just got to get going before we freeze to death! You know how cold those Martian nights are!”

“Yep.” Jody agreed. “But I have to do something first.”

She rushed quickly into town and informed anyone who could hear that they were now free of Ogg’s rule. Abruptly, there was jubilation. Jody was celebrated as a hero, but she insisted that Sam deserved as much credit as she. She was just the muscles, she said: *he* was the brain. Thus, they both were invested into the revived democracy’s highest order: the Directory Of Honor. It was an honor they were both glad to receive.

They left abruptly soon after to avoid the frosty Martian nights that would have killed them if they remained there too long. As Jody flew back to Earth at top speed, with the injured Sam in her forepaws, he spoke up.

“Jody…” he said “Did you mean all of that stuff you said about me? Me being the brain and all that?”

“Of course I did!” Jody answered him. “Jody Ryder never lies about her friends!”

“What about her monitor?”

“Oh, don’t be silly! I told you I’d respect you and I will. But you owe me, too. I embarrassed myself pretty badly begging for your life!”

“I thought we agreed that you’d stop thinking of yourself above all others. I thought I cured you of that habit! I thought…”

“Shut up, Sam!” Jody said, but this time with affection rather than annoyance. “You’ve done enough thinking today for the both of us! Now get some rest! You’ll need all the strength you have for the future, ‘cause I’ll be damned if I’ll let you almost get killed like you did just now. Understand?"

"Yes, Ma'am!" said Sam. There was irony in the voice, but no more sarcasm. They had come to an agreement in their own personal power struggle while also triumphing in the struggle against evil, and it pleased them both. That was why they were both smiling when they re-entered Earth's atmosphere.

In volume three, Jack Mulcahy gave us a wonderful pulp-tinged piece of heroic fantasy with "'Ware the Power". This time around he returns to the same fantastic world with a new tale.

Arys the Younger

By Jack Mulcahy

"There were five cities in the kingdom, five jewels in the crown. And the brightest jewel of all was Kjamrha."

"Early Days of the Great Struggle," by General Mira.

For two hundred years, Kjamrha had been the summer capital of the old dual monarchy of Auriga-Rahesh. Built on nine hills, Kjamrha was a city of artists, with bold, sweeping architecture: gleaming white stone buildings, elegant, graceful towers, and its famous Diamond Bridge over the Kjamrha River. But the city also commanded the river and the trade routes to the rich southern kingdoms of Goz and Hadan. Since the war over the enslavement of women that split Auriga and Rahesh into rival kingdoms, Kjamrha's importance had increased tenfold; over six years of war, the city had evolved into a near-impenetrable fortress, protected by mountains on all sides. Both sides coveted its strategic and commercial value. Auriga held it, and always would. So vowed Arys Ironarm, the mighty Aurigan general.

Arys Ironarm's son, called Arys the Younger, was not concerned with Kjamrha's beauty or its strategic importance at the moment. On an early spring evening, his rage felt like a living thing that would burst from his breast. "All Father does is tell me what a failure I am!" he protested. His long strides pounded the stone floor of the quarters he shared with his parents. "This morning, he told me again I'll never amount to anything. Then he said he doesn't want me talking defeat! Doesn't he listen to himself?"

Arys' mother, Lady Katje, was sewing a silver eagle onto a blue flag, working needle and thread through the blue cloth without using her hands. The flag had been awarded to Ironarm by the Aurigan king. Each eagle represented one of Ironarm's deeds. There had been nine eagles when the king presented the flag to Ironarm; there were now twenty.

A large mirror stood beside Lady Katje. From time to time she would glance into the mirror and pass her hand across it, causing the surface to shimmer like water disturbed by a breeze. The mirror showed Katje a number of points inside and outside the city, and provided quick transport to and from any of those points.

"Your father is the greatest warrior Auriga has ever seen," Katje said. She had tied her luxurious dark hair back from her face, exposing her long, graceful neck. Still visible, even after many years, were the burn marks left by the iron slave collar, a reminder of captivity in Rahesh from which Ironarm had rescued her. She had chosen to wear the scars as a badge of honor, rather than heal them. *My father couldn't buy a bride, the way normal men do*, the youth thought. *He had to rescue her.*

"I need no reminding of that," Arys grunted. "I can't go anywhere without someone asking me if it's true Father once rode a lightning bolt into battle. Or else I encounter one of his old friends who tells me I'm just like him." He threw his hands up in the air, a gesture very like his father.

Arys resembled his father in more than his gestures. At fourteen, he was a near-perfect image of Ironarm. While no lines or crow's feet yet creased the corners of his eyes or the edges of his mouth, still, his broad, muscular build, skin as black as an eggplant, high forehead, the deep, penetrating brown eyes, blunt nose and firm jaw all left no doubt whose son he was. He even shaved his head completely, like Ironarm.

"In your father's view, the world is a harsh, unforgiving place," Katje said. "He wants you to have the best possible chance to survive, not only this war, but afterward."

"I know that," Arys answered. "And I've learned everything he's taught me. I'm quicker and stronger than he is, I can match anyone with sword and dirk, and I'm his equal at unarmed combat, too!" Outside, the bright banners of day furled before the night's offensive. Arys heard the clang of swords as soldiers practiced close-order drill. Along the streets and alleys, merchants would be rolling up polychrome awnings, vendors wheeling away their carts, and from somewhere he could smell fresh-baked bread.

"There is more to being a warrior than sheer brawn," his mother said. "Your father sometimes forgets that. I'm not sure you realize it, either, yet you demonstrate those skills every day, whether you know it or not. You've learned to use your wits to compensate for your poor eyesight."

Arys snorted his disdain. "But he doesn't see that, by the Goddess! Why can't he give me credit for what I can do, instead of berating me for what I can't?"

"You know the answer to that, son."

Arys grunted. "He thinks I'm not a complete warrior until I can use a bow and arrow as well as I can do everything else. But I can't see the targets! The further away things are, the blurrier they become to me. Does he think I'm lying?"

Lady Katje closed the spell, let the embroidery drop, and looked into the mirror at the mountains surrounding Kjamrha. The perfect defense, the generals said, for the Raheshis had neither the means nor the will to bring an army over those impossible heights. Arys wondered if the mirror showed her something out there the generals could not see.

"No, son," his mother said at last. "He fears you're telling the truth."

*****

Arys exited the portal and squinted into the blackness of the forest. The trees stood, tall, ancient, dark, their branches intertwining to form a roof high overhead. It was like looking into a vast, black cave, where death waited. Behind him lay the comforting lights of Kjamrha, secure behind its high walls.

Arys could smell his own nervous sweat, and wondered if the enemy could too. In the night's heat, his mail coat itched. He wished he'd worn the leather instead, but the mail offered more protection. *What will Father do when if he finds out I'm not practicing my sword drill? For that matter, what happens when*

Mother learns I know the portal's magic? He forced the thoughts from his head. "Take no counsel of your fears," both parents had often reminded him. *I can do this,* he told himself. It was a simple plan. He had already accomplished the most difficult part, using the portal without his mother's knowledge. Now he could learn if the Raheshis really were infiltrating, as Father suspected. He would catch one and bring him back for questioning. *In the dark, they can't see any better than me. Father will forget I've skipped my sword drill when I march my captive through the gates!*

The snap of a twig brought every sense to attention. Soundlessly, he drew his knife and moved toward the noise. For all his massive size, Arys could move as silently as a breath of air, even over a bed of dried leaves.

Someone else's sweat mingled with the sharper smell of leather. Other forest odors blended sweetly; the tang of pine; the musky aroma of fresh earth; the scent of a nearby stream. He heard the faint rasp of the other's breathing, the soft pad of his footsteps. *I could track him blindfolded*, he thought.

The sounds ceased. Arys froze. He peered into the dark. Even with normal sight, he could not have seen much. Where had the last sound come from? Cautiously he turned his head, listening, smelling, trying to find his adversary, when he was suddenly thrown to the ground from behind.

His opponent was at least as big as he was. In silence the men grappled in the thick brush, rolling over and over through dried leaves and brambles. Arys jabbed with his knife, but the other was quicker and seized his wrist in a grip that might have broken the bone of someone less powerful. The knife fell from the youth's fingers. He scrambled after it on all fours, but his opponent grabbed him by the ankle and threw him to the ground, cracking his head against a tree root. His vision swam. Rough hands picked him up and slapped him several times, snapping his head back and forth.

"By the Goddess, what are you doing here, boy?"

The face before him was even more blurred than usual, but there was no mistaking the clear baritone with its distinctive burr. "Father?"

"Get up, before a real enemy comes along! What did you think you were doing?"

Arys felt as if an army of pipes and drums was marching through his head, but he bristled at his father's tone. "I'm no boy. I came through the portal to catch a Raheshi. If they're bringing forces over these mountains, we need to know."

Ironarm's eyes fixed on a point somewhere past Arys' shoulder. *He can't even look at me! I'm an embarrassment, a symbol of his own failure!*

"Through the portal, eh?" his father said. "And what if there'd been a Raheshi nearby who saw you? You'd have given away our secret!"

"I didn't," Arys answered. "And I was right, wasn't I? They're here, aren't they?"

His father nodded. "They are," he said. "Despite what my generals think."

"So what do we do now?" Arys ventured.

Ironarm glared at him. "We aren't going to do anything, pissant. You are returning home. And through the main gate, not through the portal. I'll not be the one to bring your body back to your mother."

Chase me back to Mother like a little boy? "No one'll get the better of me!" Arys said.

Ironarm's lips twisted. "Someone just did. You're not ready—"

"Yes I am!" Arys cut him off. "You were younger than I when you held the pass at Seven Pines against an entire enemy division, remember?"

"That was different!"

Arys snorted. "Sheepshit! You're just afraid I'll show you up!"

Almost before Arys had finished speaking, his father gave him a swat that knocked him down. "Home, boy," he growled. "Tell your mother I'll be home by dawn. And no following me. You won't surprise me a second time."

That's what you think, Arys vowed. It was easy enough to wait until Father left, then follow. He remembered the hours he'd spent learning Ironarm's discipline for moving silently, and the magic his mother had taught him for blending with the landscape. All were designed for normally sighted warriors. But they skimmed over or ignored the other senses, so to one who could not depend on his eyesight, trailing Ironarm was simple. The snap of a twig under his foot, the rustle of a branch as he passed, even the odor of his sweat left a track Arys could follow easily.

He crept through the tangled branches and brush, now and then dropping to hands and knees to crawl under low branches. Arys drew his knife with a whisper of steel on leather, the blade a faint shimmer in the darkness. Ironarm was a shadow against the night. Did he feel the same clamminess that puckered Arys' skin? Did his breath catch in his throat, his pulse beat more rapidly the further they ventured into the mouth of danger? Did his palm sweat on the bone handle of his knife, and did he strain his eyes in that blackness? There could be a Raheshi scout hidden behind the next rock, or lurking in the branches like a serpent.

The trees began to thin out, giving way to a broad, rocky clearing. Boulders like immense steles blotted out vast sections of the pallid light, which revealed a Raheshi encampment. Small, two-man tents, not so different from those used by the Aurigan Army, were laid out like a series of wheels, with a single large one at the hub. The youth counted horses, wagons, squadrons of cavalry and companies of spears, bowmen and swordsmen, common soldiers, and seraphs, hand-picked members of the elite corps of Raheshi officers. A scarlet robed phenai, the most exalted rank in the Raheshi priestly caste, was conducting a pain-magic ceremony over a bound, screaming slave. Bronze helmets competed for the light with spearpoints, swords and corselets.

Arys' breath hissed over his clenched teeth. Father was right! This was clearly the advance detachment of a Raheshi siege force! But how could this be? Everyone knew the mountains were impassible, and the river and the only overland road to Kjamrha were both in Aurigan hands. Had the enemy developed portals like the Aurigans'? *Either someone's sold us out, or we've seriously underestimated them.*

Abruptly, Father's trail vanished. Arys rose to his knees, listening, squinting into the darkness. There was no sign of him.

In the enemy camp, soldiers directed by seraphs were digging trenches. Spades chipped the rocky soil. Swords clashed on shields, metal flashing as the soldiers drilled. Father must have some plan, but what that might be the youth had no idea. Blundering in the dark might jeopardize Ironarm. But doing nothing was also unacceptable. Arys was considering the alternatives, when two Raheshis emerged from the forest, with Ironarm between them.

Arys crept into the heart of the enemy camp, every muscle tensed. In front of the large tent, the two shoved Ironarm to his knees before the *phenai,* who turned away from the grisly sacrifice. To the youth's surprise, his father made no attempt to rise, instead pressing his forehead to the ground. "I've seen the error of the Aurigan heresy, exalted *Phenai,*" Ironarm said. Father must have planned to be captured, he thought. Two damned Raheshis couldn't have overpowered him.

"Straighten up, dog," the *phenai* ordered, his tone revealing what he thought of the apparent deserter. "Why should I believe you?"

"You are wise not to trust me, my lord *Phenai,*" Ironarm said. "But what if I were to reveal the size and placement of the Aurigan units guarding the routes into Kjamrha, and the passwords? Would you not find such information useful?"

That set the Raheshis to muttering among themselves until the *phenai* silenced them. Arys could not see the *phenai*'s face clearly, but he could hear the interest in his voice. "You'd sell out your comrades?" He eyed the kneeling Ironarm up and down. "What do you want in return? The crossed swords emblem of a seraph? Or is there some Aurigan beauty you desire?"

"I don't like this, *Phenai* Matis," said one of the seraphs. "He's a spy. Let's hang him by his wrists and flay him, and see if he changes his story." The seraph pushed back Ironarm's head, exposing his neck.

Matis gave a grunt of surprise. "What's this?" He made a motion with his hands, and an object was suddenly dangling from his fingers. To Arys' blurred vision, it was a shimmer of silver in the starlight, but his father clearly valued it, for he fought his way free and lunged for the *phenai*. His movements were erratic and tentative, and his blows landed nowhere near their targets. Ironarm stumbled about as if bewitched, and despite his strength, his captors had no trouble subduing him.

Matis stood directly in front of Ironarm, signalled the others to silence, then punched at Ironarm's face, stopping short at the last moment. Ironarm did not move. The man repeated his action. Again, Ironarm did not react.

"He can't see."

Arys gasped. Helpless, he watched the seraphs strike Father. He kept expecting Ironarm to strike the Raheshis down. But even when they released him, he stumbled around, swinging wildly, betraying his punches before he launched them, so his targets were able to duck out of the way, laughing. One even swatted him with the flat of his sword, sending him sprawling on his face in the mud, and the rest kicked and struck him, until Ironarm was curled in a ball, face buried in his drawn-up knees, hands raised in a futile effort to protect his head.

Arys trembled with shame and anger. He remembered all the times his father had rebuked him, all the terrible names Ironarm had flung at him when he'd protested about his poor eyesight. *He's no better than I am! Who is he to say I'm not a proper warrior, when he can't see at all?*

He turned away, unsure whether he was more ashamed of his father for his weakness, or of himself for letting Ironarm treat him as he had. *Better to have no father at all!* The Raheshis' laughter seemed directed at him. Even pressing his hands against his ears did not shut the sounds out. Unable to bear it, he fled, scrambling away through thorns that tore at him and vines that sought to trip him.

Blinded by anger and grief, he brushed too close to a vine

with a pattern of brown and green. A succubus vine, the scouts called it. Before he could react, the vine had pinned his arms to his sides. In panic, he tried to hack himself free with his sword, but a shoot wrapped around his wrist, numbing his hand, and the blade fell from his lifeless fingers. Tighter and tighter the vine constricted, until his ribs ached and each breath was a painful effort.

Before long, he was wrapped from his neck to his waist. For all the strength of his arms, he was as helpless as his father.

And yet. . .

From within himself, he seemed to hear Ironarm's voice. "Use your own strengths, boy." It was as if Father were standing beside him. All his life, Arys had used his wits to compensate for his poor eyesight. Hadn't Mother reminded him about that just today?

Use your wits, fool! he told himself. *The thing can't think, it can only react. Think!*

Every time he moved, the vine tightened. But what if he quit moving? Trying to break free was doing him no good. He drew the deepest breath he could, and the succubus squeezed again, but he held the air in and went perfectly still, as Father had taught him when they were hunting. To hold his position, he concentrated on Mother and Father, and all the things they had taught him. His lungs started to ache, and he longed to draw a single breath, but dared not. He could feel his heartbeat, strong and vital, and feared the vine would feel it too. His face grew hot. Beads of sweat broke out, on his forehead, his neck, all over his body, like a thousand ants crawling on him. Still the vine held him.

Then, as he was beginning to grow lightheaded and his vision was filling with stars, the vine let go. Slowly at first, one shoot, then another. He waited, praying he could hold out just a little longer, and finally, he was free. Still not daring to breathe, he pushed away, out of reach of the deadly vine, which tried to snare him again and nearly succeeded, tearing his sleeve but not getting the arm. He lay gasping in gulps of sweet air, filling his lungs with it, drinking of it until he was sure he would drown.

He arose, feeling strangely clearheaded, as though being denied air for so long had somehow purged his poisonous anger. He thought of his father, lying on the ground, apparently helpless. "A seemingly helpless enemy may be the most dangerous," Ironarm had always warned him. *I just proved that one right*, he thought. Perhaps Ironarm's helplessness was a similar sham. He retrieved his sword and held it up, where it caught the glitter of starlight. "I'm coming, Father."

*****

The moon cast a silvery luminescence over the Raheshi camp. Snoring, the mutter of low voices, the tread of boots blended and separated in the night. Father might be dead by now. The thought raked his spine like icy claws, and brought back all the angry words he had exchanged with Ironarm, that now might never be atoned for. His throat became thick, and it was hard to breathe for a moment.

He made a circuit of the camp, keeping to the shadows, and saw the *phenai* Matis exit the large tent. That seemed the most likely place where his father might be, so when Matis was gone, he stole between the rows of tents to the central one. From within he heard someone sigh, and smelled sweat. The odor gave him no clue how many Raheshis might be inside. Hoping to draw one out, he threw open the tent flap, then hid around the side of the tent. A second later, someone stuck his head out. Arys jumped him, and the two struggled. Arys got his hands around the man's throat to stifle an outcry. Arys was larger than his foe, but the Raheshi was wiry and quick, dealing the youth a sharp elbow jab to the gut that knocked the wind out of him and caused him to lose his grip. The enemy rolled away, yelling, before Arys could recover. Heads poked out of other tents. *Sheepshit, the whole camp knows I'm here now!*

Half a dozen Raheshi soldiers bolted for him. Arys picked up his original foe and flung him at the onrushing enemies, scattering them. But others were swarming on him. He ran one through with his sword, but as he was drawing the blade free, someone else seized his arm, and he dropped his weapon. Then three were on him, wrestling him into submission. *Some rescuer I've turned out to be!* They had his arms now, and started to drag him down. Under a mass of bodies he could not break free...

And then there was only one foe. Ironarm hauled him off Arys. "Idiot!" Ironarm cried as he broke the man's neck and threw him onto the bodies of his two fellows. "I ordered you back home!" More Raheshis were coming. He shoved his son. "Come on! We'll settle this later!"

Despite the initial outcry, they had some advantage of surprise. Most of the enemy were asleep. But that would not last. Arys and his father raced between the rows of tents, using the close tent formation and the size of the group pursuing them to their own advantage. One or two could use speed and agility to escape a larger force. Another of Ironarm's lessons of war.

But skill and speed were no match for magic. Abruptly, green bands of magical force surrounded them like a net. *Phenai* Matis stood before them, his willowy frame limned in ghastly light from the magic he wielded. Matis clenched his fists then pulled them apart, like someone tightening a knot, and the magical net closed on them. Then the net lifted into the air and hung like a sack from a tree branch.

Matis peered through the green bands at Arys. The youth tried not to cringe at the sight of the wizard's yellow, catlike eyes with their slitted pupils. "He's very much his father's son," he said. When Arys started, Matis added, "Oh, I knew from the start, Arys Ironarm. This act is typical of you, don't you think? The great Aurigan hero, the only one who realizes the truth about their Raheshi enemies, decides to bring back proof. It was so predictable, I had similar difficulty as you in persuading my allies you would take the bait, but here you are. Thank you for helping me prove I was correct."

Ironarm seemed remarkably composed. Arys tried to emulate him, using the spiritual discipline his mother had taught him to calm his growing fear. "And you've also helped me prove something else," Matis went on, "for I've long suspected your blindness."

That rattled Ironarm. "I'm not blind," he snapped.

The *Phenai* laughed. "Oh, not completely," he said. "You had enough sight to attempt this escape. But without the magic of the gem, you're not the man painted by the legends." He laughed. "You aren't even what we're after. You're just the bait."

"Katje!" Ironarm gasped.

Matis nodded. "Yes, the witch you stole from her rightful owner. The real power behind your defense of Kjamrha. Did you think you were the one we wanted? I'm sorry to disappoint you, but you're just an overmuscled oaf with a sword. But Lady Katje could mean the difference between victory and defeat for us. When she hears of your capture, she'll come to your rescue and we'll have her! All I need to do is wait." He laughed when he saw the look on Ironarm's face. "For six years, we have tried to take this city, and now, you've given it to us on a plate!" He made a dismissive motion with his hands and departed.

A block of ice seemed to form in Arys' stomach. "Father?" he murmured.

"Stay calm," Ironarm answered. "Let me think." Then, "What happened to the gem?"

Arys frowned. "Last I saw, Matis pocketed it. What is it? Why do you want it now, if you can see well enough without it? And why were you so helpless before?"

Ironarm grunted. "You're full of questions," he said. "Like your mother. Always asking why." He took hold of one of the threads of the net that held them and tugged. The thread stretched and compressed in his grip, but would not break.

"I could use that gem now," Ironarm sighed. To Arys' puzzled look, he said, "It does more than clear my vision. It's also got a bit of your mother's power in it."

Arys made a face. "So you're not the great warrior everyone thinks, eh?"

"Shut your mouth!" Ironarm snapped. "I've still got my wits and my strength! I had to learn to use them first! Why do you think we never gave you a gem?"

Arys' eyes widened as he realized the answer. His father said, "At least you've got your wits about you. Now quit your questions and put those wits to work."

He tugged on the bindings again, with the same result. "A

chain is only as strong as its weakest link," Arys said.

His father frowned and said, "You're right, boy." He shifted slightly, causing the net to sway, and tugged at another band. There was not much room to maneuver, suspended as they were, but Arys tried as best he could to emulate Ironarm's action, tugging at each strand of the net, one at a time. Soon he found one section that gave more than the rest. With the quickness he'd inherited from his father, he stretched the opening wide enough and leapt out, curling into a ball as he did, so as to land with the least possible noise and shock. A moment later, Ironarm was beside him.

The two raced through the camp. A sentry came upon them, but they overpowered him before he could give the alarm. Ironarm took his sword, Arys his dagger. They dashed into the forest toward Kjamrha. Arys wondered if the *phenai*'s words were true, if his mother truly would attempt to rescue Ironarm. He prayed they would reach home in time to prevent that.

At the edge of the forest, they halted at the tree that hid the portal. "Since you're so smart," Ironarm said, "you can work the portal."

Arys emptied his mind, focusing on the plaits of magical force that would open the portal. The tree's surface began to shimmer, and the edges of the door appeared. Ironarm was about to enter the portal when Arys sensed something wrong. "Father, don't—!"

A bolt of magic froze Ironarm. Arys turned to face the intruder, who tilted his hands in a queer way. Suddenly, Arys' body was not his own. Matis stepped from the shadows. "How easy it was to allow you to lead us here," he said. "Now open the portal, boy! Tonight I'll have the Witch Katje, and tomorrow we will march into the city!"

Arys could not resist the will that controlled him. Completely possessed, he turned, raised his hands, and invoked the magic. When Arys' attention had been diverted from the magic, the portal had disappeared. Now it shimmered into view again. Hands that were not his own completed the spell and the door opened. There was nothing now between *Phenai* Matis and the heart of the city.

Nothing but Lady Katje. She stood in the doorway like an angel, guarding the passage with a net of flame. Before Matis could move, she flung the flaming net over him, wrapping him in it as a spider would a fly. "Well, *Phenai*," she said. "Who is the predictable one now?" She grinned at Arys. "Nicely done, son. You were the added prize his overwhelming ego could not resist. You helped lead him into our trap." She lifted the spell from Ironarm. "And what did you think you were doing, letting yourself be captured? That wasn't the plan."

Ironarm shrugged. "I improvised. Isn't that what you're always trying to tell me?" He glowered at Arys. "Someone's interference complicated matters."

"That interference proved crucial in capturing this *Phenai*, dear husband," Katje said. "Now pick him up, and I'll close this portal."

*****

Arys used the mirror to look upon Kjamrha's main thoroughfare. The merchants and shopowners had given way this day to the citizens, waiting for the ceremony. All Kjamrha, it seemed, had turned out to cheer Father's capture of the *Phenai*.

And not one of them knows the truth. Or ever will.

"They expect us to be at his side," Mother said. She was fussing with her coif, tucking a few stray wisps of hair under the starched fabric. Occasionally she would glance into the mirror. "We share his glory with him."

Arys snorted in disgust. "Neither of us got any mention!"

Lady Katje had spent all night creating a new gem for Father. The magic had drained her skin of its creamy color, and the old scars on her neck stood out stark and red. "And that's as it should be," she said. "Your father and I have teamed this way before. He gets the attention, which enables me to do my work unnoticed. That's important.

"Twenty years ago, your father risked his life to save me," she continued. "If not for him, I would still be a slave." When Arys started to protest, she interrupted. "Arys Ironarm isn't just a hero. He's a symbol of Auriga. His glory is our glory. That's enough for me."

"Damn it all, it's not fair!"

Katje shrugged. "Your father's won so many battles because he's known how to pick his fights," she said. "He also knows when not to fight. That's not weakness. Your father has never sent soldiers to their deaths needlessly. So why don't you stop fighting this one?"

"Because I'm a man just like—" He stopped short. Looked at his mother.

"Just like him," she finished.

He saw Ironarm's unit marching in perfect formation behind their standard. It brought to mind his dreams of glory. *They should be cheering us, too*. "It's not easy," he said.

"It never is." Katje said.

Robert Collins brings us a great piece of detective pulp that goes in a few surprising directions.

The "Affair" of The Love Letters

By Robert Collins

My father taught me to be a private investigator mainly because I was a bit of a fireball when I was a young girl. One of his first lessons was that the facts would always lead to the truth, even if the path wasn't direct. I say this because there's been a wedding in the news recently. I'd like to tell you my part in it.

It began late one afternoon. I was in my office sorting through a couple of routine cases. My brother was in the reception room out front. He'd just graduated from college and had gotten his spellcaster's license. I let him use the room as his office.

That afternoon he knocked on my door and stuck his head through. "Gwen, there's a woman here. She wants to talk to you."

"Send her in."

The woman appeared to be in her mid-thirties, some years older than me. She was about average as far as height and weight went. The one thing that struck me about her was her face. She was good-looking, but there were lines in that face that hinted at a harder than normal life.

I introduced myself. Let's say that she introduced herself as "Mrs. Cora." I asked her to sit down in front of my desk and tell me why she wanted to see me.

"Miss Conner, when I was younger I was in love with a man." She named the man, a city councilman. "He loved me, but his family wanted him to marry a woman of better means and connections."

"Did he?"

"Yes. During our relationship he wrote we exchanged letters. Just before he got married he wrote me one last time. He explained that though he loved me, he had to marry this other woman. He wasn't in a position, financially or otherwise, to back out."

"I take it you kept those letters."

"Yes." She glanced down. "Within a year of his last letter, I too got married. My husband was a wonderful man."

"Was?'"

"He died in a fire at our cottage several months ago. It was an electrical fire. He got me out, then went back to fight it."

I could see tears welling up in her eyes. She pressed her lips together tight. She took a few breaths through her nose. Unless she was a very good actress, the memory seemed to be getting to her.

"Everything we had was lost, except for what was in our safe. Our important papers, some wedding materials, and some personal pictures."

"And your old love letters," I added.

She nodded. "Until then I didn't know why I kept them. I've kept them since because they're some of the few things I still own from before the fire."

"That's why you've kept them? Sentiment, nothing more?"

"Yes."

"So, what does that have to do with me?"

"Last night, a man came to my apartment. He said he knew about the letters from the councilman. He told me he would give me a hundred dollars if I gave them to him."

Something about that struck me. Then I remembered; said councilman was reported to be considering running for Mayor. Said politician had a reputation as being a moral man, opposed to corruption, uncomfortable with magic, and so on. The offer made sense.

"You refused?"

"Yes. He asked how much I wanted. I told him I didn't want any money. I was only keeping them for sentimental reasons. I didn't have any interest in showing them to anyone."

"What did the man say to that?"

"He insisted that he buy them. I told him that if he didn't leave, I'd call the police. He turned and left."

"Why not come to me this morning?"

"I thought that was the end of it. But at lunchtime I saw him again."

"At home?"

"At my job. My husband didn't leave me much. I work at a sock and hosiery factory."

"So you saw him outside the factory?"

"Yes. When I left for the day, I think I saw him following me." She frowned. "I tried to turn around to get a good look, but he kept stepping out of sight."

"Cora, if you think you need protection, why not go to the police? Or to a male private detective?"

"Your office is on my route home." She sighed. "I'm afraid that if the councilman sent that man to buy the letters, he might also have the police on his side."

Which was a good reason not to engage the other private detectives in town, if her fears were true. They were all former police officers of varying ranks and skills.

"Miss Conner, is there something you can do to help me? I'm afraid I don't have much money to pay you."

I glanced down at the materials on my desk. I was making my usual fees from those two cases. Cora's situation might not pay much, but it could lead to more important work. Of course, it could also get me chased out of the city. Still, there was the chance that I might get a hypocrite bounced from office.

"I'll take your case," I told her. "We can discuss fees later. For now, I want you to go to my apartment. I live on the west side, near the local police station. It'll be safe for now."

She nodded. "If you say so."

"I'd like the keys to your apartment. Where do you keep those letters?"

"A new safe."

"Give me the combination."

I took her keys and wrote down the combination. After that I asked her for a description of the man who had come to her. There were two characteristics that stood out. The man was middle-aged, older than her, but had dark curly hair. The other was that he saw a short scar under his left eye.

I led her out of my office and introduced her to my brother. Since he was a spellcaster he got to carry a short staff with a powerstone in the top. That would let anyone know he was a spellcaster, including the man following Cora. It was a gamble that he wouldn't approach her with my brother with her, but the odds seemed in our favor.

He left a few minutes later. I placed a call to my friend in the police department, Lieutenant Mulcahy. I asked him if he could stay late to talk to me. He said he had work to do and was planning on staying late. I took the trolley to his station, went to his office, and closed the door behind me.

"Lieutenant, can I talk to you off the record?"

He frowned slightly. "Gwen, you're not poaching on our territory, are you?"

I sat down. "No. But I have a client with a connection to a city councilmen."

"Criminal?"

"The client, no."

"And the councilman?"

"I'm afraid he might be trying to obtain some correspondence."

"Embarrassing?"

"Love letters to a woman he didn't marry."

"An affair?"

I shook my head. "Written to a first love, before he got married."

He started to speak, then hesitated. "She doesn't want to use them against him?"

"No. She's keeping them for sentimental reasons."

"And you believed her, Gwen?"

"She told me a man came to her last night, offering a hundred bucks for the letters. She thinks that same man followed her home from work today."

Mulcahy sucked in a breath. "Okay, I see the problem now."

"You also see why I closed the door, and why I want this off the record."

He nodded. "This is a bit more serious than trying to get out of a public drunkenness charge. What do you want me to do about this, Gwen?"

I gave him the description of the man who had made the offer. "Do you know who that might be?"

He shook his head and grinned slightly. "Sounds like Detective Bart Milner. He works out of the south side precinct. He's known for having ties to some pretty important families in the city."

"Would he be breaking the law?"

"Not unless he was asked or paid to rough up your client to get those letters."

"How about blackmail?"

"If your client was asking for money, yes."

"I know that. What about being asked to sell those letters?"

"That's a gray area, Gwen. It sounds more unethical than illegal. But I'm guessing you already thought as much."

"I was hoping it was the latter."

"What are you going to do?"

"I have my client's keys. I know where the letters are. I think I should get them before someone tries to break in and steal them."

"Well, as long as you have the keys, you wouldn't be

breaking in. But I'd advise you to be careful, Gwen. People who make such generous offers and get turned down tend to become unpleasant."

"I know, and I will. And I'll keep in touch."

I was getting hungry, but I decided it would be smarter to pick up those letters before someone else did. I was walking up the steps in front of Cora's apartment building when I caught sight of what I thought was the man she'd described. He was at the other end of the block and walking towards me. I hurried inside the building.

The building was only two stories tall so there was no elevator. I jogged up the stairs and went to her apartment. I dashed to the safe inside, found the letters, took them out, and closed the safe. One of her windows had a view of the street. Through the window I could see the man was waiting under a streetlamp on the sidewalk opposite this side of the street.

If he had followed Cora to my office then most likely he knew what I looked like. I guessed that he was waiting for me to come out. Even if there was a confrontation on the street, he had the badge, not me.

That realization gave me an idea. I reached for the telephone, but I hesitated. The longer I stayed in the apartment, the easier it would be for the police to cast aura spells. Those spells would tell them I was here.

Then I remembered that I had Cora's keys. That gave me permission to be here. Unless she was the best actress and the cleverest person in New America, she'd back me up. That thought gave me an even better idea.

I picked up the telephone and tapped the number of the district police station. "Yes, there's a man standing outside, across from my apartment. He's been there for some time. Could you send an officer to check him out?" I gave my address but not the apartment number. The man on the other end told me that a uniform would be there in ten minutes or less.

Next I called the south side precinct and asked for Detective Bart Milner. I was told that he wasn't on duty that day. "That's odd," I replied, "because I just talked to him outside my apartment."

"What of it, ma'am?" the man on the line asked.

"He told me he was working surveillance."

"Where?" I gave the apartment's address. "That's not his precinct, ma'am. Are you certain it was Detective Milner?"

"I saw his badge and he gave me his name."

"I'll report this to the captain, ma'am. Sorry for any inconvenience."

I smiled as I hung up and left the apartment. I went downstairs and headed out the back door of the building. From there I made my way to the nearest alley and looked; Milner was gone. No doubt the local uniform and he were inside. Rather than wait to find out if Milner was in any trouble, I jogged down the street to the nearest trolley stop.

Cora was waiting for me at my apartment. She was kind enough to cook me dinner. It was good enough that I almost considered it payment for my services. I let her sleep in my bedroom; I took the couch.

Before going to sleep I looked over the letters. They weren't dirty in any way. They read a lot like the kind of letters my brother would write his girlfriends while he was a freshman in college. Plenty of heart-felt expressions of caring and tenderness punctuated by "I love you" or a similar sentiment. Aside from the fact that they weren't written to the woman the councilman had actually married, they were fairly tame.

The one that wasn't was the last one in the stack. It said what Cora had told me it would. He didn't really love the woman he was marrying; he wanted to marry Cora, but the family felt his future was more important than his happiness; he hoped she would understand and accept what he was having to do. I could see that if this letter was made public, it could hurt his marriage and maybe his reputation. But I didn't think the damage would be that great or last that long, because there was no evidence that the councilman had ever tried to carry on with Cora while married. That was the one thing that confused me.

The next morning there was an interesting story buried within the newspaper. It seemed that a south side detective had been found outside his precinct. He couldn't explain why he was away from his turf. He'd been put on three-day unpaid leave last night over the incident.

That might get him off Cora's back, but it by no means put an end to the matter. I decided it was safe for her to go to work, but I escorted her all the same. From there I went to the councilman's office in City Hall. I felt it was time to force a confrontation with him. Either he'd back off, or there was going to be a real story for tomorrow's paper.

I got to City Hall in the middle of the morning and took the elevator to the floor his office was on. The secretary for him and two other councilmen said he was in meetings and couldn't see me on short notice.

"I represent a client," I said. I gave Cora's full name. "She has some letters that the councilman wrote some time ago. She asked me to talk to him about them." I nodded to the secretary.

"Tell him that, word for word."

She got him on the telephone and repeated what I said. A moment later she told me, "Have a seat. The councilman will see you in a few minutes." I waited just over ten minutes before the councilman came out of his office, shook my hand, and led me inside.

I sat down in front of his desk. He walked to the edge of his desk. His expression turned dark. He waved his right forefinger in my face. "How dare you come here and threaten me on Cora's behalf, Miss Conner!"

I slapped the finger away. "How dare you send a detective to buy those letters, then have him follow her around!"

"What detective?"

"Detective Bart Milner. Your pal on the south side."

"I don't know any police on the south side, except the precinct captain."

"You want me to believe that you didn't send him to buy those letters for a hundred dollars, Councilman?"

"Of course not."

"And when she said no, you didn't have him tail her?"

"No!" He paused. He looked at me, surprised and almost relieved. "Cora refused to sell the letters?"

"That's right." I leaned back in the chair. "You're happy she didn't sell, aren't you?"

He glanced at the floor then nodded. He walked to his chair and sat down. "Miss Conner, are you telling me that someone offered to buy those letters from Cora?"

"Yes."

"And that Cora refused to sell them."

"Yes."

"Why?"

"She lost her husband in a house fire sometime back."

"I know. I read about it."

"Those letters were in a safe, along with some items from her wedding. They're all that's left of her life from before the fire. She told me she kept them purely out of sentiment."

"She didn't want to make them public."

"No." I leaned forward and looked at him. "You really didn't send Milner, did you?"

"No."

"Okay, Councilman. I believe you. Who else knew about those letters?"

He glanced down again. "My wife." He shook his head. "But she wouldn't want them."

"Anyone else?"

"No." He shook his head again. "No, that's crazy."

"Does she have friends in the south precinct?"

"Her family does. No, I can't believe she'd be involved in this."

"Councilman, the facts are pointing to her. Unless you can come up with someone else who knew about those letters, then she has to be behind this."

He sighed. "I can't. So, Miss Conner, what do I do?"

"You do nothing, Councilman. You stay here and keep up your schedule. Act like I was never here. Whatever you do, do not call or meet with your wife for the rest of today. Do you understand me, Councilman?"

He nodded like a man defeated. I told him I'd get to the bottom of this matter, and soon. I asked for his home phone number. He wrote it down on a slip of paper. We shook hands, and I left his office and City Hall.

There was a public telephone across the street. I tapped the number he'd given me. A woman picked up the other end.

"My name is Gwen Conner. Perhaps your friend Detective Milner mentioned me."

"I don't know what you're talking about."

"I think you do. I have what you asked him to get. Your price for them is now five hundred dollars."

"You're talking nonsense, Miss Conner."

"No, I'm not. Meet me at three at Francisco Park. Off State Street is a path, and along the path are four benches. I'll be on the fourth one away from State, at three. Be there or you get nothing." I hung up the phone.

There was no way I was going to meet that woman alone. Nor did I want her to get away with whatever it was she had in mind for those letters. My next call was to Mulcahy to make some arrangements. From there I went back to my office to get ready. Two policemen came by at two to help me. Fifteen minutes later we left. We were at the park in twenty minutes. They disappeared, and I walked to the fourth bench to wait.

At one minute to three the wife approached me. "Miss Conner?"

I smiled. "Ma'am. Have a seat."

The woman was short, had a slender figure, and a very attractive face. She was stylishly dressed in the latest white blouse, ankle-length tan dress, and polished black shoes. The only jewelry she wore were two slightly elaborate silver earrings and a gold ring on her right ring finger. She wore her hair up, with a few strands strategically framing her face. She walked gracefully and sat down just as properly. Everything about her projected beauty, wealth, privilege, and status.

I disliked her the moment I saw her. Talking to her for a while, I came to hate her.

"Do you have the letters, Miss Conner?"

"Do you have the money?"

She took an envelope out of a dress pocked and put it on her lap. I took my packet from under my right thigh and laid it on mine.

"I read the letters," I told her. "Except for the last one, there's nothing embarrassing."

"That assumes my husband wasn't cheating on me."

"He wasn't. Certainly not with Cora."

"No, not with her. But I will be able to produce a young woman who he was having an affair with."

I frowned for a second. "Produce, as in found? Or produce, as in procured?"

She smiled. "Why, Miss Conner, you are a smart woman, aren't you?" She glanced around for a moment. "How many times have you seen a prominent man admit to having been unfaithful to his wife?"

"A few times, at least."

"The wife is always the poor victim, abused and betrayed. Yet they never assert themselves when the truth comes out. They didn't stray, but no one argues that their virtue makes them better than their husbands."

"Better at their job, you mean?"

"Why not? Women in New America are starting to do men's jobs. Aren't you an example of that?"

"I suppose so. Why go to all this trouble?"

"My husband is not as strong as I thought he would be. He

should be Mayor, instead of dithering about whether or not he should run. I can't divorce him for being indecisive when it comes to his career."

"But you could divorce him for cheating."

"I could." She glanced at my lap. "Those letters are the last piece of the picture."

I took the packet in my right hand while I held out my left. She handed over the money at the same time as I handed over the packet. She rose the instant she had the packet.

"I'll be looking for clever women to help me, Miss Conner. Can I call on you again?"

I stood up. "I don't think so." I smiled. "You're not going to get that chance."

She looked behind me. I'm sure she saw the plain-clothes detective and two uniformed policemen approaching. She turned. Behind her was Mulcahy and two more uniforms. In moments she was manacled, and we headed to the station in two police coaches.

Waiting for us at the station was Mulcahy's captain and Assistant State's Attorney Jacob Ross. The wife was put into an interrogation room. The captain told Mulcahy and me that Detective Milner had been brought in half an hour ago and was talking.

I took the phony cap off one of the buttons of my blouse and gave it to the captain. "She said she has a young woman ready to lie about having an affair," I told him.

"Milner said as much. I've sent two officers to arrest her." He held up the magic ear. "I'll get our spellcaster working on a transcript."

I turned to Ross. "What are you going to do with her?" I

nodded at the magic screen that let us see her but kept her from seeing us. "I mean, I know you're going to charge her."

"Fraud, attempted theft, conspiracy, public slander," he said. "Any other charges you'd like to add, Miss Conner?"

"No. What I meant was, does there have to be a public trial?"

"Why?"

"The councilman was innocent in all this. I think a trial would tarnish him, even if he didn't do anything wrong."

"Gwen, you know where he stands on magic," Mulcahy said.

"I know, and yes, I haven't forgotten what my brother's job is."

"What do you propose?" Ross asked.

"A plea in closed court." I raised my hands. "Yes, I know how rare those are, and yes, I know when you use them."

Ross paused for a moment. I noticed the captain and Mulcahy start to nod, and that Mulcahy also smiled. Ross looked at them, then at me. "Fine, Miss Conner. So long as I get a plea." He raised an eyebrow. "Any more suggestions?"

"Actually, yes. She got that five hundred in cash pretty fast. I doubt she has that much in the bank. I wonder if she had help getting the money?"

"From who?"

I grinned. "Maybe Daddy came through for her." I smiled. "I wonder how hard she'd fight if Mommy, Daddy, and her brothers were charged as co-conspirators?"

Ross nodded and smiled. "Yes, that is a good question. Let's get the answer."

He walked around the corner to enter the room. Mulcahy tapped the magic ear to let us listen in on Ross' conversation with the wife. Ross went in and introduced himself. He asked if the wife wanted her lawyer present. She said no, that she knew the law, and was eager to go to trial. Ross told her that Milner was already talking, and that her "hired young lady" was going to be picked up very soon.

"As I said, I have no problems going to trial." The wife waved her had dismissively.

"What about your family?"

"What?" That put the brake on her mood.

"I don't believe you procured the cash for Miss Conner by yourself. I think you had help, either from your parents or your brothers."

She glared at him. "I didn't have any help, Mister Ross."

He stood up. "So you say. I think I'll have them brought in, charged, and ask them myself. That should sort this all out."

"Wait!"

"Why?"

"What do you want from me?" The tone in her voice lowered.

Ross sat back down. "What do you mean?"

"You're threatening my family because you want something. What is it?"

He glanced in my direction before answering. "I want you to plead guilty to everything, and to make your plea in closed court. No press, no public trial. You may not get to hurt your husband, but you don't have to worry about your family name getting dragged through the mud. That's my one and only offer, ma'am. Take it or else."

She seemed to think for a few seconds, then nodded. She called her lawyer, the deal was made formal, and that was that. The wife, the girl, and Milner pled guilty in closed court. The public statement on the matter was that the wife had threatened a woman she believed was sleeping with her husband. The "alleged affair" was all in the wife's head. She'd pled guilty to "accept punishment and recover her wits." The councilman filed for divorce a few weeks later. He and Cora reconnected, and now you know the story behind their recent wedding.

There are times when I really like being a private investigator.

Mark Mellon delivers a second western pulp for this volume as he introduces us to a little Texas Village known simply as Dogtown.

Buzzards Circle Dogtown

By Mark Mellon

A mockingbird warbled joyously, happy and active in the mild winter weather. Jackrabbits darted among the cactus and lechuguilla. A mottled coyote grinned for an instant from a gap in the brush then disappeared. Heck ignored the pleasant scene. Anxious to reach Dogtown, he'd ridden through the night. Already tired when he found the dying man, he was exhausted when he hit town, tall in the saddle from habit alone.

Like most Texas towns, Dogtown had only one street, lined with half a dozen saloons and gambling halls, quiet and empty in the early morning. The racetrack was at the other end, no crude frontier dirt track, but a carefully laid out oval with whitewashed wooden stands for spectators. The Queen Victoria Hotel, a three-story mansion with white fluted columns and a verandah on each floor, dominated the drag. The Dogtown National Bank stood opposite the hotel.

Despite the early hour, many people were up, taking advantage of the cool temperature. Mexican servants went about their masters' errands, stepping out of white people's way. Everyone stared at the body wrapped in a waterproof draped over Heck's pack mule. The Mexicans' faces became even more stonily impassive.

A man shouted from the hotel verandah, "Hold up there!"

Heck didn't like his tone, but reined Nike to a halt. The man walked onto the street. Tall, running to fat, he wore broken down boots and a brand new Boss of the Plains hat. A tarnished bronze badge was pinned to his vest.

"What's your name, boy?"

"Heck Pargrew."

"Wondered what to call someone dumb enough to drag a dead Meskin into town," the man laughed.

Heck's jaw set tightly.

"Relax, hoss, just funning. I'm Curg Brattle, town deputy."

"I figured by that badge."

"Thanks for fetching him. Saves trouble. I'll take him off your hands."

Curg yanked the body off the mule. He unrolled the waterproof, thumbed his hat's broad brim back, and admired his handiwork with a low whistle.

"Hoo-whee, that's one dead greaser."

"Why'd you shoot him?"

"Had to. Running from the law."

"If you say so. Okay if I go to the hotel?"

"Go ahead. You here to race that big black? Be sure to have fun and spend plenty of money. Haw haw. Here's your waterproof."

Heck stabled the horse and mule at a livery and went to the hotel. Inside the lobby, a clockwork ceiling fan provided a breeze. Behind the mahogany counter, the bald clerk wore a boiled white shirt with new-fangled celluloid collar and cuffs. His waxed mustachios' curled tips rose in disdain upon sight of the dusty cowboy.

"This hotel don't take saddle tramps," he pronounced. "Turn around, young fellow, and bunk in a livery or upstairs at a saloon because—"

Heck set his bags down. He reached into a vest pocket, pulled out a 20-dollar golden eagle, and slapped it onto the countertop. He laid his pistol next to the coin.

"Your pick," he said.

"Yes, sir. If you'll just sign the register," the clerk replied. "The boy will fetch your bags. Room 212, best in the house, high enough from the dust but not too many stairs. Will that be bourbon or rye?"

"Bourbon."

Heck's room was a spacious affair with two windows, a kerosene lamp on a table with a flowered cloth, and a large four-poster bed with a canopy. He tipped the bellboy a dime. The bottle was brought up. He took a slug, pulled off his boots, got into bed, and slept. Late in the afternoon, he woke ravenously hungry. Heck pulled clean clothes from his warbag. After a bath, shave, and haircut at Eierbach's Tonsorial Parlor, he returned to the hotel to eat, his boots newly blacked.

The dining room was long and elegant, the tables covered with lace, and the food served on gold-edged china. Midway through a chicken-fried steak with white sauce, a commotion began.

"Mr. Mayor, Your Honor, the private room is ready…"

Bowing, the clerk ushered in two men. Both wore dark suits, one about Heck's age, thin, beady-eyed, mouth fixed in an apparently permanent smile, the other much older, heavy-set and bald, humorless, with a shambling gait and curious lopsided frown.

"How you doing, son?" the younger man asked. "Dogtown treating you right? That mule meat old Curlicues serves tender enough?"

"I've had worse," Heck answered.

"Know who I am?"

"The mayor?"

"Dern! You done gave it away, Baldie," said the man. He rubbed the clerk's smooth pate, a familiarity the clerk suffered in silence.

"Yeah, Bob Dalt, boss of the whole dern town. My daddy, Old Bob Dalt, was mayor before me, but that's history now. You here to see the races tomorrow?"

"No. I'm here to win a race tomorrow."

"Whoo! This boy's got sand, ain't he, Buck?" Dalt said to the older man.

"Mr. Mayor," he replied, a low, deep murmur, difficult to hear, "there are significant matters, if you will, we must discuss. It's best done in private."

"Of course, Buck. See you around. If things don't work out tomorrow, maybe you can get work swamping the saloons out."

He left with a laugh and a wave.

Rested, washed, and full, Heck decided to drink at each saloon until one struck him as congenial. His first stop was the

White Elephant Saloon, a wide room with a long mahogany bar in the center with brass fittings. A mirrored back bar was adorned with gas light fixtures, onyx columns, and shelves crammed full of bottles and decanters. Hand-lettered signs listed prices for various liquors, wines and cordials, and also imported and domestic cigars. There was a considerable crowd, cowboys and ranchers, along with sporting gentlemen anxious to separate them from their money.

Heck bellied up to the bar and ordered beer with a shot of 12-year old bourbon. The liquor was incredibly smooth, scarcely a burn as it slid down his throat. He greedily drank his beer, getting it down before it went flat.

A loud, heavily accented voice shattered Heck's tranquility.

"You men know there is a problem. You also know we must be doing about it!"

A tall, beer-bellied, older man in a dark suit with a string tie held forth from one corner of the saloon. A large silver badge was pinned to his frock coat. Spectacles gave him a scholarly air. His lank, steel-gray hair was carefully combed back.

"That black rascal Cortina plot against us even now. *Gott* damn, his men cross the Rio Grande every night to new trouble make, steal cattle, burn down barns—"

Rather than ignore his harangue, most were attentive. Many nodded their heads in agreement. Some yelled, "Yes, sir! Get them Meskin sumbitches!"

Heck turned to a man and said, "Who's that Dutchie squawking over there?"

"Keep your voice down, young man," the man replied. "That's Sheriff Arschkopf."

"Just yesterday, my deputy Brattle, *ja*, he did right with those *schweinehunden.* He caught one sneaking brown thief, shot him in the chest before he break into Widow Bauer's house to rape and kill the good woman!"

"If he means the man I brought in today, he don't know what he's talking about," Heck said. "That man was shot in the back."

Powerful enough to be heard over a stampede, Heck's voice carried to the sheriff. He looked around accusingly.

"*Gott* damn, is some *verdamnt scheisskopf* calling me *Gott* damned liar?"

Heck was about to tartly respond when the man next to him gently took his elbow and murmured, "You're new. Let's go to the Iron Front. I'll buy a round, fill you in some how things work here."

Heck looked the man full in the face: lean and wrinkled from life outdoors, soup-strainer mustache more flecked with salt than pepper, brown eyes open and honest.

"I reckon so. That's the first friendly offer I've had."

They left. Heck introduced himself.

"Name's Ed Bee. Think I've heard of you. Ain't you got a spread with your brother in the Hill Country near San Marcos?"

"That's me," Heck answered. They pushed through the saloon's swinging batwing doors.

"Just got back from a drive with the cuss."

The Iron Front was on the other side of the drag. Simpler, less pretentious, it had a plain wood bar and sawdust strewn on the floor. Bee asked for a bottle and two glasses and picked a table away from other patrons with little chance of being overheard. He poured two shots. Heck knocked his back.

"That's sweet stuff. Thanks."

"Always glad to do a real cowboy a favor. Here for the races,

Pargrew?"

"Yup. Got me a new horse in Dodge City. I brought him down to see how he does."

Bee refilled their glasses.

"Long as you got money and keep your mouth shut, you won't have problems in Dogtown. Racing made this town rich. They want sporting men.

"There's still some folks you need to watch for, though. Arschkopf's one, mean as a snake and full of piss and vinegar. His deputy Brattle's another."

"I met him," Heck snorted. "Smart aleck sumbitch!"

"A cold killer too," Ed whispered. "He guns men down and claims they ran when he tried to arrest them."

"Like the Mexican I found?"

"You said he was shot in the back. Arschkopf and his deputy like to kill Mexicans now and then. Makes folks think they're tough on law.

"They squawk about a raid to get the bandits, but that's just talk. No more guts than a pissant, any of 'em."

"What about one snot-nosed little shit, calls himself mayor, and the fat old man that wipes his nose for him?"

Bee chuckled.

"You met the Boy Mayor and his keeper, I take it?"

"They spoiled my meal on the way to theirs."

"Yeah, Dalt likes pissing on people and passing it off as a joke. He thinks he runs things, but Buck Casey's the real Big Auger. Owns the bank, hotel, dry goods store, and a big piece of the track.

"Sick as he is, you'd think the old coot would curl up in a rocking chair, but folks say he wants all South Texas, make himself even bigger than King Fisher."

"That'll happen."

Both men laughed. Bee grew serious again.

"Not one worth a buffalo fart but that don't make 'em any less dangerous. They're used to getting their way. Anyone gets in the way, gets trampled. Stay clear."

Heck grinned, an open, boyish smile, slightly marred by the hard glint of his green eyes.

"Thanks, Ed. Appreciate the advice, but nobody messes with a Pargrew. Now whyn't you tell a cowboy where to get a shot of leg in this town?"

Bee said, "There's Tia Rosa's parlor house if you got the money."

"I'm loaded with scratch. Just point me and unloose the lariat."

"Turn left at the far end of the drag. Keep on 'til you hear music. You'll see the lights about a quarter-mile off. Used to be right on the drag, but Casey moved it to please his wife. He owns that too, dern hypocrite."

Heck drank another shot.

"Thanks for the liquor. Care to come along?"

Bee smiled and shook his head.

"My missus is waiting. Reckon I'll see you tomorrow in the races. You be careful, Heck Pargrew."

Heck said, "Sure enough, Ed. Thanks again."

He walked down the drag. Nightlife was in full swing: saloon gaslights flared while music blared to screams and whoops of laughter. Drunks staggered past, some propped up by whores who rifled their pockets as they helped them along. Small black boys on one corner cakewalked to the music of a kazoo for pennies tossed in a hat by passersby.

Disdainful like all cowboys at having to walk anywhere, he grumbled at the distance until he heard a piano tinkle. The parlor house was well built with a verandah. A very large, very fat man sat smoking a cigar on the verandah with a shotgun on his knees, but he smiled pleasantly and said nothing when Heck came up the stairs and went inside.

The front parlor was elegantly furnished with velvet drapes, oil paintings, hand carved mahogany furniture, and Oriental rugs. An elderly black man played a Chopin waltz on a piano with gentle precision. A butler and maid served punch and champagne from silver trays to the men on the couches and chairs, all of a certain age and substantial girth, and the young women in underwear who kept them company. A heavyset, middle-aged Mexican woman in a too tight, low cut, purple dress smiled and approached him.

"*Buenas noches, senora*," Heck said.

"*Caballero*! I am Tia Rosa," she said in unaccented English.

"Would you like to meet some of the other guests? Or would you rather meet Aura?"

"That the girl you picked out?"

"*Exacto*. I knew when I laid eyes on you. She loves red haired cowboys."

"Take me on up, Tia."

She led him up the stairs to an empty room with a brass bed, dresser, full-length mirror, an armoire, and a washstand and basin.

"Pull off your boots. Stretch out on the bed, *macho*," she said. "I'll fetch Aura."

Heck tugged off his tight boots and sank into the luxuriant

folds of the thick eiderdown mattress draped with purple satin. A wisp of a girl entered the room, delicate and beautiful as a bird, jet black hair pinned up with a silver comb. She smiled: two curved rows of perfect gleaming pearls, and got into bed with him.

"*Puedo servir*?" she asked.

Heck reached up and tenderly pulled the comb from her hair. A long fall of jet-black locks partly veiled her sloe eyes. She bent low and kissed him…

*****

Next morning, Heck ate two cowboy breakfasts washed down with a pot of coffee, picked up his horse from the livery, and went to the racetrack. Virtually everyone was there with the exception of the town's "respectable" women. A brass band played marching music. Touts in plug hats shouted odds. Part of the stands were set aside for the Cyprians. They attended decked in their finest ruffles and bows, protected from the blazing sun by tiny parasols. Heck looked for Aura but didn't see her.

"Come to race that big black?" asked a friendly gambler. "See Bart over there."

Several men were lined up before a desk where a swell in a gold-laced waistcoat and shiny silk plug hat wrote down their names with a fountain pen in an accounts register without blotting a drop.

"Howdy, yonker," he said to Heck when his turn arose. "Give me you and your horse's name and ten dollars, greenback or hard coin, all one."

Heck handed over the money and said, "Heck Pargrew with

Nike."

"Nike, huh," Bart snorted. "Fancy yourself a learned man?" he chuckled as he wrote the information down.

"That was my brother's idea. Who do I see about betting?"

"You're looking at him. The house holds all riders' bets and makes sure they get their winnings, minus five percent for overhead."

"You fellows make money coming and going, don't you?"

"The mark of an efficient enterprise, young man. Come, come, we don't have all day. Show us the color of your money. Do you think you can place?"

Heck slapped a moneybag down, so heavy the desk rocked from the weight.

"Five hundred in gold I win."

"I'll bet against that," said one gambler, throwing down three gold eagles.

"Me too," said another.

"Him and that black horse will eat dust."

In a few moments, Heck's pot was matched, doubled, and doubled again. Word spread throughout the crowd of a cowboy betting big on himself. More money was wagered in private bets. Heck and the other riders mounted up and rode their horses onto the track to fanfares from the band while the crowd wildly cheered and cowhands fired pistols into the air.

They lined up along a rope stretched taut across the track. Heck faced a motley crew: a raw-boned backcountry man on a gray mare that looked to be a direct descendant of Steel Dust himself; a Kickapoo on a specially bred fleet footed pony; a grinning Mexican *vaquero* on a biting, half-broken mustang; and a Limey in racing silks on an English racer, out West on a lark.

Bart climbed to the grandstand. He removed his hat and announced, “Ladies and gentlemen, it is my privilege to announce this race, a mile and a half course run by these five brave contestants. All you old boys out there holster your pistols and sit quiet while we count off the race, iffen you please.

“Gents, on your marks. Get ready. Go!”

A shotgun fired. The rope fell.

Keyed to breaking point, horses and riders surged forward. They tore down the track. The Kickapoo’s short-coupled pony took a narrow lead, closely shadowed by the Mexican. Heck trailed, bunched with the other two. The race belonged to the light and quick at the onset, but as laps wore away, Nike’s sheer brute strength overcame any initial lead. Relentlessly, without sign of strain, the black horse charged on at the same punishing pace, wild-eyed, great nostrils flared. Heck stood in the stirrups in two-point position, his weight off the delicate back, giving Nike his head.

At the last lap, Nike surged past the mustang and caught up with the Kickapoo. The Indian bent low over the saddle and urged the pony on with his quirt, but the horse had long ago given his best. Heck flicked the reins. The black horse shouldered past. The finish line loomed ahead.

“Nike by two full lengths!” Bart shouted.

Cowhands roared approval. Soiled doves squealed. Gamblers threw plug hats on the ground and stamped on them in frustrated fury at their losses. The band struck up “The Yellow Rose of Texas”.

The Limey rode up and remarked: “I say, Mr. Pargrew, well challenged indeed!”

Heck was surrounded by well-wishers who shouted

congratulations and strained to shake his hand. He dismounted and went to the reviewing stand.

"Congratulations, yonker!" said Bart.

"Thank you, Mr. Bart," Heck replied. "You got my money?"

Bart's smile grew even broader. Heck's guard went up.

"The very point I wanted to raise with you, Pargrew.

"You won considerable, twenty-five hundred dollars. When there's a really big purse, Mayor Dalt likes to give the money himself."

"Is he around? He can hand it over and congratulate me just as much as he likes."

Bart shook his head.

"The mayor prefers to handle such matters in private at his office at home. More dignified, you know?

"The house is a treat to see, the most elegant home in South Texas. You're lucky to be invited. Curg'll take you."

The deputy grinned, his new hat tilted back.

"No thanks. I'll go alone. Reckon I'd worry about that itchy trigger finger."

Curg said, "Don't get your feathers in a fuss. We got off on the wrong foot. I meant to tell you how grateful I am. That Mex brought a twenty dollar bounty."

"That's good to know. Let me know next time you got a backshot Mexican you need hunting up."

"Ha ha, ain't he a card," laughed Curg. Bart loudly joined in.

Curg pointed to a nearby buckboard and said, "Mayor don't like to wait."

There was little point in arguing. Heck climbed onto the buckboard. Curg got on the bench and whipped the horses into motion. They left Dogtown and went down a road that paralleled the river. The mansion was two miles outside of town, a two-story white affair fronted by triple columns topped by a pediment.

Curg stopped by the front door.

"Mayor's inside."

Heck opened the glass-paneled door and walked into a high-ceilinged hall, wonderfully shadowy and cool.

"Who do you think you are coming in front?" a woman snapped, her voice sharp, disapproving, used to command.

She emerged into the weak light: thin, young, black, in a gray dress and white apron with her hair in a kerchief. The large whites of her eyes gleamed baleful rage. Her wide mouth twisted open to reveal a disdainful gap-toothed sneer.

"Go out that door and come in through the back like all the other dirty cowhands. You hear me?"

Before Heck could respond, Dalt entered from a side door, fidgeting with his cravat.

"Dilsey, can you do anything with this dern—"

"Hold on, what we got here? Old Flaming Red himself, big winner at the race. You done real good there!"

He stepped forward, right hand extended, face lit by a rare sincere smile.

"I always like me a winner," Dalt enthused as they shook hands.

Whiskey was on his breath.

"Come on upstairs where we can take care of you."

"Does that mean getting paid?"

The fixed grin grew wider.

"Sure enough, Red. The victor, he's the one that gets them spoils."

Dalt led Heck down the hall. Dilsey flashed him a sharp, mistrustful look. Heck smiled pleasantly and winked. The men walked up a wide carpeted staircase.

"I'd introduce you to the wife but she's having one of her afternoon megrims."

Dalt held tightly to the banister with one hand, steadying himself while he gestured extravagantly at various paintings hung from the walls.

"See that picture there? Old Bob paid over a thousand dollars for it! Can you believe that? Reckon that's more money than you've ever seen, huh, cowhand?"

"My brother and I run 10,000 head of cattle to Dodge City every year, more than half of it our own stock. You do the math, Mr. Mayor."

Startled, Dalt glared at Heck, intensely irritated, until he caught himself and resumed his smile.

"That so? There I go with my big mouth again. You're a regular Tartar, Red."

Dalt took Heck down another lofty hall. He knocked on an oak door.

"Buck? You ready to see him now?" Dalt inquired.

"Yes. Send him in," Casey barked from behind the door.

Dalt pointed to the Delft china doorknob.

"Buck's waiting."

"What in Sam Hill is going on! I'm starting to think this is some sort of bunco game. Do I get my winnings or what?"

"Now don't get up your dander, Red. You'll get your money. Buck'll fix you up!"

Heck shrugged and entered the room. Casey sat at a desk in an opulent office like a king on his throne, eyes shielded by thick glasses, clean bald dome fringed by white hair, mouth set in a lopsided smile.

"Mr. Pargrew, let me congratulate upon your big win, if you will, in today's races. Sit down."

Heck sat in a comfortable leather chair that faced the desk.

Casey continued, "Gaming is the lifeblood of our local economy. A notable race, if you will, like the one you ran can only attract gamers and more business. For that, we are indeed grateful.

"I have instructed the First Bank of Dogtown to wire the monies due you to any bank in Texas you might name. That will lessen the risk of anything untoward, if you will, occurring upon your return home."

That made sense. A man riding alone through Texas with money ran a considerable risk. He warmed to Casey. His evident competence, the air of a man with decades of successful experience behind him, reassured Heck.

"Well, thank you, Mr. Casey. I appreciate that."

"Not at all. It is rather an early hour, but could you do with a drop of refreshment, to celebrate your victory, if you will? Napoleon brandy, the very finest."

"A taste wouldn't be amiss, Mr. Casey."

"Call me Buck."

Casey reached into a desk drawer and pulled out a bottle with two shot glasses. He filled both glasses, handed one to Heck and took an appreciative taste from the other.

"What do you think, Heck?"

"A sipping dream."

"I quite agree. Cigar?"

Casey handed a pure Cuban leaf black cigar to Heck and lit it with a bronze lion with a flaming wick for a tongue. They drank and smoked in companionable silence.

"I take it you plan to return home without delay, Heck?"

"That's right, Buck. Nice as y'all have been, I'll head back tomorrow. Virge is sure to throw a hissy about handling all my chores along with his own."

Casey said, "Understandable. Nonetheless, I hope you might allow me to sketch out a certain business proposition, if you will, that might be of interest to you."

Heck blew a perfect, blue smoke ring and said, "Have at it, Buck. I always listen about making money."

Casey leaned back in his chair and steepled his fingers over his expansive, soft stomach.

"We know your credentials from the war, twice mentioned in dispatches. You also have extensive experience handling cattle on trail drives.

"You rode for Maximilian in Mexico after the war?"

Heck laughed and said, "Boning up on me? Yeah, me and Virge got in a passel of trouble down Mexico way."

"So you're familiar with the country?"

"Depends. Mexico's kind of a big old place. I reckon I can find my way around Nuevo Leon and Tamaulipas okay.

"This got to do with your business proposition?"

"You know Juan Cortina?"

Heck said, "Boss of Tamaulipas. Big landowner."

"He is a liar and a thief, a man of infamous character even for a Mexican, an insurrectionary, just waiting for the day he can bring fire and sword to Texas and take bloody revenge."

Heck was thrown by the ferocity of Casey's denunciation. His anger was palpable.

"Right this minute, Heck, as we sit here, enjoying cigars and brandy, behind the border Cortina builds an army, if you will, of half-breeds and Yaqui savages equipped with Winchesters, funded by the sale of enormous herds of cattle.

"Once his bandits are armed, they'll stream across the Rio Grande, bent on terrorizing innocent whites. A patriot like you, Heck, a veteran of the Sacred Cause, could never permit that. You'll agree?"

"How am I supposed to stop them?"

Casey leaned forward.

"I have devised a bold plan to sabotage Cortina's wicked scheme, nip the whole thing in the bud. A raiding party, well manned and strongly armed, will travel in secret across the border and in a single audacious move, drive off the whole of Cortina's main herd, twenty thousand head.

"The expedition needs a man like you, someone with military and cattle-driving experience who's familiar with the country. Will you do it, Heck? Help stop a madman?"

Heck gazed wide-eyed, too aghast at Casey's wild freebooter scheme to even answer.

At last he said, "Sounds like a pretty tall order, Buck. Cortina may be the devil like you say, but he's a right rough old cob. Anyone takes something of his can figure on him coming after it and not in no laughing mood either."

"Once back in Texas, the Rangers and the Army will protect us from retaliation. Any attempt by Cortina to recover his property will be tied up in court for years."

"What guarantee is there even getting out of Mexico? Takes time to drive cattle, Buck, specially a herd that size. A hardcase like Cortina wouldn't have much trouble running us down. The

Yaquis would skin us slow after that."

"But think of the financial reward. Why the hides alone are worth at least a hundred thousand!"

Heck finished his brandy and said. "Reckon my hide's worth more. Anyways, I ain't never thrown a long rope. No sir, Buck, sorry. I ain't interested."

Casey's mouth grew more lopsided.

"If money doesn't motivate you, what about patriotism? I explained the threat that Cortina poses. Don't you want to end that?"

"Ask me when he crosses the Rio Grande. I'll tie a knot in his tail then. For now, Cortina's done nothing to me."

Casey philosophically shook his head.

"I hoped it wouldn't come to this. Heck, at times a man in my position of responsibility has to take, well, distasteful measures, if you will, to bring people to the right course of action."

"What do you mean, Buck? Nothing unfriendly, I hope."

"If I could trouble you, Heck, to go to that window, you'll see what I mean."

The window looked down on a barn and corral behind the house. Curg was inside the corral, Aura the prostitute pinned against him hard with one arm. He held a razor sharp, gleaming Bowie knife in his free hand against her perfect brown cheek. She saw Heck and sobbed.

Heck threw the window open and shouted, "Let her go, Curg Brattle, you sorry sumbitch, or I'll pecos you."

"Go ahead," laughed Curg. "Skin your gun. I'll cut this Mex whore's damn head off before you even fire a round."

"As I said," Casey continued, "sometimes unpleasant things must be done to achieve important goals. I hardly relish these things, but I will do what is required. Will you reconsider your decision?"

"God damn you, no, Casey! What's some Mex whore to me? Hell, I only saw her once the night before."

Casey signaled Curg from the window. Heck knocked his arm down. His eyes blazed rage as he said through clenched teeth, "All right, you low bastard, you got me over a barrel. Turn that poor girl loose and I'll go on your damn wild goose chase. Loose her now, you hear me?"

"Right away," said Casey.

"All right, Curg," he called. "Take her back to Tia's. Tell Tia keep a close eye on her."

"She'll be in complete safety," he said.

"You'd best hope so. Casey, you and your crowd are the lowest pack of skunks I ever saw."

"I've had other business relationships that also started on an acrimonious basis that worked out beneficially for all sides in the end. I'm certain that this partnership, if you will, shall end similarly.

"You'll excuse me, I have other matters. You yourself should prepare for the expedition. Draw supplies from the dry goods store, within reasonable limits."

Up to his eyeballs in disgust and impotent fury, Heck's throat choked too thick to speak. He jammed his hat onto his head and stomped out of the room. Heck went down the stairs and into the hall. There was giggling and a high-pitched squeal from behind a door, Dilsey's voice. The door opened and Dalt stuck his head out, cravat gone, shirt buttons undone.

"Buck straighten you out? Well, good on you! Pleasure having you with us for a while.

"See you, Red. Mayoring's hard work, you know!"

Dalt shut the door. The squealing recommenced. He walked back to town, ignoring the river and the fine weather, his mood foul.

They set out two days later, in broad daylight so God and everyone else could see what they were about. Heck wondered why there wasn't a parade with a brass band and why they didn't also send Cortina a nice note on fancy paper letting him know when he could expect them.

A testimonial dinner was given the night before at the Odd Fellows Hall. The men gorged on fried chicken and taters washed down with beer rushed over in growlers from the White Elephant. Speech after speech prated of heroism, the spirit of the Alamo, brave white men unafraid to cross the Rio Grande to beard the enemy in his lair, while Heck sulked. Dalt weaved as he spoke, so drunk he clutched the podium with both hands to stay erect.

Heck rode at the column's head with Curg and Arschkopf. Twenty men rode behind, each equipped with a Winchester, two Colt's .45 pistols in holsters with two more in the saddlebags, and three hundred rounds. Heck's guns had been taken away from him. Ten were Dogwood Regulators, Arschkopf's hand-picked deputies. Their saddles had silver conchos and each man wore a bright red scarf. At least they could ride, although a few sagged noticeably, badly hung over.

The others were mostly drifters, more experienced at swamping out bars than chousing steers or fighting *pistoleros*, lured by the prospect of hundreds of dollars for a few days work. The oddest was the Limey, drawn by his perpetual quest for adventure. He had traded his English racer for the Mexican's mustang and nimbly rode the half-wild horse, deftly, slowly gentling the beast. In addition to the men's personal mounts, a *remuda* of twenty horses and three pack mules loaded with victuals and other supplies trailed the column.

Curg put his horse to a trot. The others followed raggedly. They rode south into the brush country and were soon alone in a parched, rugged landscape covered with spiky nopal cactus, scraggly huizache trees, barbed mesquite, and razor-sharp lechuguilla, infested with gila monsters, rattlers, and scorpions, each detail etched by the brilliant Texas sun.

At noon they halted and broke out possibles: a salted deer ham and two baskets of fried chicken cooked by the Ladies' Auxiliary of the Dogtown Baptist Church.

"You plan to sull the whole trip?" Curg asked Heck.

"Leave him *Gott* damn be," said Arschkopf, reaching for more chicken. "*Gott* damn his big fat mouth anyway. *Verdamnt schweinehund*!" He remembered Heck from the White Elephant.

Heck tossed his coffee into the fire and stood up.

"Are we riding or fiddle-fucking the rest of the day away?" he asked Curg.

Curg said, "You took the words right out my mouth. Come on, you lazy sumbitches, saddle up! We got fifty miles before we reach the Rio Grande. Let's get 'er done."

Arschkopf heaved himself onto his horse, fairly limber despite his age and size. Heck gave Arschkopf credit. Although old, he was at least willing to ride into Mexico to steal Cortina's herd. His grudgingly revised opinion lasted twenty more miles. Curg ordered a halt to water the horses at a *tinaja*, a small pond. A *jacal*, a crude hut, stood by the pond. A short, squat Mexican woman emerged from the hut and waved hello. Arschkopf rode over, dismounted, and tethered his horse. The old man embraced the young woman. They went inside.

"Randy buck for an old Dutchie, ain't he?" said Curg.

"You mean he'll stay on?" said Heck.

"Yep, and good and rested too when we get back. Now like you said, let's not fiddle-fuck the day away. Saddle up. We got some Mexican beeves to drive."

They made camp a few miles from the Rio Grande. Curg ensured the men ate and that the mounts were tended and fed, but neglected to post guards. Heck didn't point this or other mistakes out, like keeping a hot camp any local would surely spot and report. Some men had bottles and got drunk again. With wild whoops and blood-curdling screams, they boasted about the hundreds of Meskins they would kill and how they'd spend their money in San Antonio, buying mango ice cream at the Menger Hotel. Soon, Heck and a few others were the only ones with clear heads and steady hands.

They crossed the Rio Grande at twilight. They forced the horses over the marshy soil into the water and across the short distance that separated Texas from Mexico. The river only came to the horses' stomachs. The setting sun's red rim, a brilliant, flaming sliver on the far horizon, daubed men and animals with broad streaks of ochre, cast their shortened silhouettes on the Rio Grande's slow waters.

"Those pumpkin rollers made enough noise back there, just in case folks down in Mexico City didn't hear us coming," Heck said.

They urged the mounts out of the water and onto Mexican soil.

Curg said, "For a tough trail boss, you worry like a mother hen. Ain't but a few know this ford. A backwoods coot showed me a few years afore. He swore even local *vaqueros* don't know it."

"And you believed him. Better put some Regulators ahead riding picket so we don't meet anything unexpected."

"I give the orders," Curg snapped.

Nonetheless, he sent two outriders ahead. They rode double file down a path. Despite his apparent self-confidence, Heck wondered whether Curg had any idea where he was going. About ten miles from the river, they heard a rifle shot.

"Now they'll find us sure!" Heck hissed.

Curg lashed his horse into a gallop. The men followed, hooting and hollering. Regulators flanked Heck to make sure he didn't escape in the confusion. They found the outriders by a huizache tree, crouched over a prone figure.

"We got a damn Mex, Curg! The Limey popped him spang in the ankle."

"Not much of a shot from this distance, old boy," he drawled.

Heck dismounted. He pushed past the two men. They'd shot a boy. He clutched his bloody ankle and moaned. A shepherd out with his goats, he was unfortunate enough to be caught by *gringos*. Heck took off his kerchief and used it to bandage the wound.

"*Calmate, chico*," he said. "They won't hurt you no more, *sabe*?"

Curg squatted next to Heck, brandishing his Bowie.

"Tell the greaser I'll geld him iffen he don't say where Cortina's beeves are."

"After I shove that knife down your throat, Curg," Heck spat.

"*Diga me, chico,*" he said to the boy. "*Las vacas, la manada de Don Cortina? De donde? Lejos o cerca*?"

The boy grimaced and pointed south.

"*No muy lejos. Solamenate una liga en el bolson.*"

"He says three miles south of here in a pocket."

Curg grinned and said, "That's real good.

"Hold him while I cut his throat."

Heck snatched the boy up and leaped away.

"You ain't hurting this button!"

Curg sneered. "Have it your way, Pargrew. Let the kid ride with you. We'll turn him loose once the herd's moving.

"Now, might we get on with it while you nurse your greaser baby, Mother?"

The men laughed raucously. Heck ignored them and helped the boy onto Nike, then mounted himself. Certain now where the cattle lay, Curg put his horse into a lope. The men rode hard, eager to eat up the distance between themselves and a fortune, their first real lucky break after lives of hard times and few choices. Any thought of outriders was forgotten in their mad rush to reach the herd. Heck was driven on with the rest.

They could smell the herd long before they could see them, the concentrated funky reek of thousands of cattle. There were continuous repeated clicks, the clash of horns against one another as the herd milled, lulled by the gentle sound of a *vaquero* singing a *corrida*. Curg reined his horse to a halt. The others did likewise.

"Circle around from here. Once we're in place, I'll signal with a pistol shot. Drive 'em out when you hear that. Ride hell-for-leather. Any Mex pops up, shoot him, that simple. Don't stop 'til we cross the Rio Grande.

"That clear?"

There was an unmistakable sound: a rifle being cocked in the nearby brush. A voice called from the darkness, "*Matan todos los gringos, muchachos!*"

Flames rent the night, followed by rifle fire's deafening reports. The cattle raiders were caught in an ambush. The Mexicans had carefully laid out interlocking fields of fire beforehand. Sheltered in dug out firing positions, Cortina's *vaqueros* emptied Winchesters from three sides into the startled Texans. The result was slaughter. Within a minute, eleven men were shot dead. Hardly any of the rest hadn't sustained a serious wound.

Heck screamed at Curg over the din, "You just did a jim-dandy job!"

Despite the ambush and the raid's total failure, Curg was curiously unrattled, calm in the face of the disaster he'd brought upon himself.

"Better do 'er now rather than later, I guess," he remarked to himself rather than Heck.

The instinct that had protected Heck throughout war and perilous cattle drives warned him now. He pitched from the saddle to the ground, pulling the boy down with him just as Curg pulled his gun and fired. The shot missed Heck, already rolling into the brush with the boy, but caught Nike dead in the back. With an unnervingly human scream, the horse toppled over, thrashing in his death agony.

Curg cursed and put spurs to his horse, bent on flight. The rest were already dead or too badly shot up to even hope to escape.

The boy tugged at Heck's sleeve and whispered, "*Vaquero,*

debemos esconderse. Vaya conmigo a mi abuelo. Por favor, vaquero?"

"No need to beg, *muchacho*," Heck hissed. "Where's your granddad's place?"

Draped over Heck's shoulders, the boy guided him down a path only he knew. After hours stumbling in the dark, they came to a *jacal* in a hollow with a goat pen next to it. An old man with an *escopeta*, a primitive, single-fire shotgun, came out to see who it was. Angry at first with the boy for coming home without his flock, he saw his wound and wept. He led them into the *jacal*.

The old man treated the wound with herbal medicine and put on a fresh, clean dressing. They ate beans and tortillas and slept on the dirt floor. In the morning, Heck asked to borrow the old mule the man owned. Grateful to Heck for saving his grandson's life, he agreed.

He rode the mule with only a blanket and a hackamore, the boy behind him. Cortina's men were sure to watch for *gringos* who might have survived the ambush, so they traveled roundabout to the Rio Grande. Once past the river, they rode until they neared Arschkopf"s *jacal*. Heck dismounted and handed the reins to the boy.

"*Vaya a tu abuelo. Adios, muchacho*, and thanks."

The boy smiled shyly, raised a hand in salute, and rode off. Heck realized afterward he never learned his or the grandfather's name. Stealthy as an Indian, he slipped through the brush and slowly crept to the *jacal*.

Arschkopf was outside, some distance from the hut. Stripped down to singlet and pants and sporting a hefty gut, he chopped firewood with a hatchet, red-faced and panting from unwonted exertion.

Heck walked up behind him and said, "Ain't that a pretty picture? The Dutchie helping out his gal. Reckon next you'll don an apron and do the dishes."

Arschkopf whirled around, eyes bulged in shock and rage, hatchet held protectively before him.

"*Du*? *Gott* damn loudmouth, what do you here? Where is Brattle and the other mens? You are supposed to be Gott damn dead."

"You were supposed to run off the biggest cattle herd in Mexico too," Heck replied. "Guess a lot of things done gone wrong, you pigheaded, loud-mouthed sumbitch."

Gold flakes danced in Heck's green eyes. His mouth curled into a cruel smile. He snatched the hatchet from the German's hand. Arschkopf ran for the *jacal*, screaming, "*Hilfe, liebchen, hilfe*!"

Heck threw the hatchet. It hissed as it spun through the air and landed square between the German's shoulders. Arschkopf hit the ground with a low moan. Heck ran over to him. Blood streamed from the wound, copiously stained his singlet.

"*Cabron! Hijo de puta! Maricon*!"

Black eyes blazing fury, Arschkopf's woman swung a heavy, long-barreled, Kentucky muzzle loader up to her shoulder. There was no time to reach her. She'd shoot before he could throw the hatchet.

Heck snatched up Arschkopf, grunting from the effort. He held the fat man in front of him just as she pulled the trigger. There was a roar. A great cloud of black smoke belched from the rifle's mouth. The heavy ball tore through Arschkopf's rib cage and into his heart. He was dead instantly.

Distraught at her lover's death, but still full of fight, the woman ran headlong at Heck, rifle raised high as a club. Heck stood his ground and caught her full on the chin with a hard right fist. She collapsed, out cold.

Heck rubbed his knuckles and said, "Purely hated to do that."

He hogtied the woman and ransacked the hut. Fearful of his sweetheart's temper, Arschkopf had hidden a pair of Colt's .45's inside his saddlebags with locking clasps. Heck picked the locks, strapped the fancy, tooled leather holsters on, and went outside. The woman was conscious. She lay on her side, glaring at him, slowly and urgently calling him every Spanish obscenity. Heck ignored her and fetched Arschkopf's horse. After tacking the horse, Heck took the hatchet and stuck the blade in the dirt about a hundred yards from the woman.

"Should take about a day or two to wriggle over. That ought to be enough time to get my business done."

The woman shouted a torrent of obscenities in English and Spanish.

"You have a nice day too, little lady."

Heck rode off. Arschkopf's mount was a top horse, a grizzled roan with three white stocking feet and endless stamina. He put the horse into a lope and by twilight neared Dogtown. He made a cold camp far from any trail and ate beef and tortillas from the woman's larder.

He rose at dawn, scratched his thick, coppery beard, and mounted up. Heck didn't directly enter town, but instead kept to the brush, and made his way to the back of the hotel. He squatted on his haunches in thick brush and waited for the guests to finish breakfast and leave. When the height of the sun told him it was after nine o'clock, he walked past the small corral where the cooks slaughtered the day's bill of fare.

He took out a pistol, cocked it, opened the door, and walked into the kitchen. Three Mexicans in filthy aprons stopped scrubbing, mopping, and cutting meat.

Heck waved his pistol toward the door.

"*Vayate, hombres*!" he said. "Go on, get!"

The men hurried outside. Heck searched the kitchen. He found gallon cans of coal oil, used to heat the new-fangled stove, punched open a can with a knife, and poured oil onto the wooden floor, furniture, and walls. A burning lucifer set the kitchen off.

Heck picked up two coal oil cans and ran outside, shouting, "Fire! Fire! Everyone get out!"

Flames and smoke spewed from seams between the boards, leaped upward, setting the whole hotel on fire. Heck shot out a few windows.

"Go on, get, you dumb sumbitches. Your damn fancy hotel's on fire!"

Men and women screamed. There was a wild tramp of feet as the few guests still in the hotel and employees ran to the front door. Heck put the coal oil cans in his saddlebags and mounted up. The furor in town grew with angry shouts and bellowed orders. The fire raged out of control despite the Dogtown Volunteer Smoke Eaters' best efforts to extinguish the blaze. Heck circled the town to the other side of the drag, to the bank. He tethered the horse and sneaked up with a can of coal oil.

As he figured, everyone was watching the fire. He went into the bank by the back door. A lone teller, a thin, sallow fellow in leather sleeve protectors, peered at the fire through a window. Fascinated, he didn't bother to look at Heck.

"Morning," he said.

"Some fire, huh? Biggest thing that ever happened here. The

manager done ordered me to stay behind and mind the bank while he and the senior cashier watch up close. You come to make a deposit?"

"You talk too much."

Startled, the man fixed watery eyes on the smiling cowboy and the barrel of the gun pointed at his heart.

Trembling, he raised his hands, and said, "Don't shoot, Mister, please."

"Shut up and open that there safe."

The teller took several quaking, shaking tries before he turned the combination properly, Heck's pistol point-blank to the back of his head. At last, gears tumbled. The heavy safe door swung open, to the teller's audible sigh of relief.

"Quit gasping and hand me ten thousand greenbacks," Heck barked.

The teller counted out the paper money and gave it to Heck.

He stuffed it inside his shirt and said, "Put the rest on the floor. The other paper too."

A sizable pile soon lay on the floor: cash, almost a hundred thousand, along with valuable bonds and railroad stock shares. Heck drenched the pile with coal oil and lit another lucifer. In a few minutes, a second fire blazed.

"Put some chairs on top," he told the teller.

The wooden counter caught fire. Soon the whole bank would burn.

"Mister, can I go now?"

"Reckon so. Pleasure doing business with you."

The teller ran out the front. Heck exited from the back. He mounted his horse, but urged him forward this time, and rode past the bank onto the drag. The rest of the town had also caught fire. Cool as a Christian with aces wired, he rode down the middle of the street, past the burning buildings, invisible in the pandemonium.

Three men on horseback approached. One wore a top hat, the gambler Bart.

"Looky there, boys. Get him!"

Bart reached for a pistol stuck in his belt. The other men went for their guns. Heck shot Bart once in the head before he even drew his pistol. He slumped from his saddle to the ground. The other men's horses reared, throwing off their aim. Their shots went wild. Calm in the saddle, Heck took his time. He fired with both hands and shot each remaining man in the head. Three bodies lay in the street. He holstered his pistols and put his horse into a gallop.

Heck rode full tilt to the parlor house. The fat bouncer ran out into the yard, his shotgun held high. He let off a blast. Quick as a Comanche, Heck slipped to his horse's side. The shot passed harmlessly overhead. Holding onto the horn with one hand, he leaned past the racing horse's neck and shot the bouncer twice.

He leaped from his horse, kicked in the door, and jumped in with guns ready. The whores ran screaming from the parlor. Heck strode to the back of the room and kicked in another door. Tia Rosa stood at the end of the room, one fat arm around Aura's neck, the other pointing a Colt's derringer.

One pantherish leap and he was on top of them. Heck knocked Tia Rosa's arm up. The bullet lodged harmlessly in the ceiling. He brought a gun barrel down. Tia Rosa crashed to the floor. Weeping, Aura fell into Heck's arms. He comforted her, then held her at arm's length.

"It's hard, Aura, but you gotta hold up your end. *Tiempo para vamonos. No mas lagrimas, sabe*?"

She giggled at his Spanish. Heck smiled too. He pulled the money from his shirt, counted off five thousand dollars, and handed it to Aura. The girl gasped at more money than she could ever hope to see in a lifetime.

"That's due you for what them skunks did. Hide it good. Let's get you a horse."

Several sporting gents boarded their horses for the season in a stable out back. Heck picked out a strong but manageable young gelding for Aura and tacked him. He helped Aura into the saddle.

"Ride back to Mexico. *Comprendes? Vaya a Mexico*."

"*Por favor,* Heck, *ven conmigo. Hay mucho peligro aqui. Ven conmigo a Mexico*."

Heck said, "Surely wished I could come, Aura, and live with folks as kind and good as you.

"But I got business here still. *Vayate*."

Heck slapped the horse on the flank. He broke into a smart trot. Aura disappeared into the brush. He dragged Tia Rosa out into the yard, made sure the house was empty, took the last can of coal oil, and set the brothel afire.

Heck reloaded and rode to his last destination. Dalt's mansion seemed deserted. No servants could be seen. No horses were out front. He rode to the porch, dismounted, and hitched his horse to a post. Heck climbed the stairs to the front door and was about to try it when a familiar voice cried, "Hold it, Pargrew!"

Curg stood on the porch, a shotgun pointed at Heck.

"You take a right smart of killing, boy."

"Do 'er, sumbitch," said Heck. Golden flakes danced in his green eyes.

"Oh, no. I like licking my candy slow," said Curg. "Can't

have undesirable elements like you around. Type that makes trouble for Dogtown."

"Smell that smoke? I did more than make trouble. I done ruined your whole pissant town."

Curg scowled. Piggy eyes flickered, a sure sign he was about to fire.

"Hold on, Brattle!"

Buck Casey charged out with a rifle.

"I got the bastard covered!"

He fired, but didn't bother to aim. The bullet missed Heck. It instead caught Curg in the cheek and tore through the back of his head. Casey stood stock-still, staring open mouthed in horror at his gory blunder. Heck skinned his gun and shot him.

"Thanks for helping, Buck."

Heck walked through the open door and down the shadowy hall to Dalt's office. A floorboard creaked. Heck ducked. A frying pan missed his head by inches.

"You damn miserable white trash!"

Heck swiveled and buffaloed Dilsey, a neat tap with a pistol dead between the eyes. Already extended to deal another killing blow, the frying pan slipped slowly from her hand. She fell unconscious.

The office door was locked.

"Dern, this is tiresome!"

Like the others, Heck kicked in the door. Dalt's office was like Casey's, but larger, more grandly decorated with marble statues of eagles screaming in for the kill, gold-framed engravings of famous Confederate generals, and red plush furniture. Dalt stood behind the desk, habitual derision rearranged to a pose of nervous good humor.

"Red, it's you! Fancy that. Thought we'd lost you on the cattle raid. Damn shame it went so terrible bad. It's the fault of them Mex spies we got crawling around this town.

"That and the damn newspaper always spilling the beans. We'll fix the paper and expateriate them Mexes soon enough. What can I do for you, son?"

"Dalt, you're a piss poor liar and a sorry sumbitch to have your house girl fight your dern battles.

"I come to pecos you, hoss."

"W-w-what would you want to say that for, Red?" Dalt stammered. "You can't think I'm to blame?"

"You're the mayor, ain't you? I reckon he's the fellow in charge. You and Casey.

"He's lying deader'n hell outside, by the bye, along with that yellow dog Brattle. I put paid to the Dutchie sheriff too, on the way back. Them and some other jaspers in town."

Dalt put up his hands in a placating gesture.

"Now wait, there, Pargrew, there's been a terrible misunderstanding here between me and you and that- The reason that Casey did what he did is that--he devised the master plan, and I was only the approver—"

"You ain't making too much sense, Dalt," said Heck.

"Reckon 'coz you're scared as hell. Tell you what. Let's make 'er easy."

He took a pistol, leaned over, and placed it on the desk in front of Dalt. He stepped backward a few paces and holstered the other pistol.

"Pick it up and we'll get to business. You should get the drop on me."

Dalt looked at the pistol. Tentatively, he reached for it, eyes fixed on Heck, hand visibly trembling. He almost touched the gun, but jerked his hand away.

"No!" he sobbed.

Dalt put his head to the wall and wept.

"Damn if you ain't first cousin to Moses Rose," Heck spat.

"It's not right, it's not right," Dalt wailed. "I'm not to blame, I'm not the one responsible, Casey's more responsibler than me. You already killed him. Why do you have to kill me?"

He walked around the desk and fell at Heck's feet.

"Please, Pargrew, I'm begging you. You can have the whole town, everything. I can sign it all over to you now Buck's dead. It's worth thousands."

Heck snorted.

"T'ain't worth squat. I burned 'er to the ground afore I come out here."

"Please," Dalt begged, tears streaming down his face. "You got to give me a chance."

Heck said, "I'll give you as much chance as that Mexican I found."

He shoved Dalt face first down to the floor. Heck pulled his pistol and shot him in the back four times. Dalt screamed piteously, jumped once, twice, and was still.

Heck reloaded his pistols and went outside. He mounted up and took a last look at Dogtown.

Buzzards spiraled over the town, lazily circling closer, summoning the courage to feast on the human carrion that lay on the drag below. Other vultures already flew directly overhead, just waiting for Heck to leave to pluck tender eyes and other delicacies from Casey and Curg's corpses.

"Things ought to be a lot quieter around here now."

He gave the horse a light tap with his spurs and rode away from Dogtown.

Vincent Morgan previously gave us the weird pulp "Murdock's Last Stand" in Pulp Empire volume three. He returns to our pages and travels in to deep space to bring us his new narrative.

Umbuto's Rock

By Vincent Morgan

Garth Vale sat at the bar of the Starlight Lounge, nursing a life shortener, and hoping for inspiration to strike.

He had booked passage aboard the starship *Croesus* in the hope of acquiring material for a series of articles on the Golden Comets, the ultra-rich, who spend their lives traveling the galaxy in order to avoid gravity-well taxes. But, after a promising start—two sales and a commission—he lost interest. Truth be told, he couldn't face the prospect of yet another interview with a bored heiress or self-made tycoon.

He glanced round the lounge. Empty, save for half a dozen presumed regulars crouched in the back, the lounge looked much like any other. The regulars too looked like regulars everywhere: anonymous, gray, uninteresting.

The barman; however, looked more promising. A great bear of a man, he stood well over six feet tall. His hawser-like arms rippled with tattoos of blue and silver dragons, and a jagged, pencil-thin scar ran from his left temple to the right corner of his mouth. His name tag read David Costos, and he wore the blue and gray headscarf of a veteran of the Arachnid Wars.

Garth, of course, knew about the war with the Arachnids. How the Nids had, some thirty years before, attacked our colonies in the Deneb Cluster, and how we had fought a bitter campaign to oust them. But he had never met anyone who had actually been *out there,* so he asked Costos to tell his life story.

The big man had roared with laughter, saying, "Bless you, sir, the story of my life would put you to sleep and it's bad for business having customers sleeping instead of drinking. I will; however, tell you the story of the assault on the Rock as long as you're prepared to drink while you're listening."

This seemed more than fair, so Garth ordered another life shortener, set his notepad down on the bar, blinked his eye-camera to record, and settled back to wait while Costos attended to the needs of the patrons in the back.

Upon his return the barman stood for a moment, polishing a glass and staring into space, and then said, "In the past, had you reason to look, you would have found the Rock marked on the star charts for the Deneb Cluster as celestial object No: RZX-0000/009J-00547-678. In reality, the Rock's just an otherwise unremarkable asteroid a couple of miles in diameter, drifting amid thousands, if not millions, of other such objects somewhere in the Monasheen Belt.

"At the beginning of the war, which seemed to start for no good reason, the Nids seized and fortified any number of planets, moons, and asteroids. Sometimes they seized places of obvious value, like the Moons of Marsham, and other times they dug in on useless places like the Rock.

"I could understand fighting for the Moons, they are, after all, like Earth in most respects. We only cared about the Rock, as far as I could tell, because the Nids had grabbed it.

"Now there may have been additional reasons of 'grand strategy' behind our decision to take that miserable chunk of nothing away from them, but, if there were, the High Command never got around to sharing them with me."

He paused for a moment, gauging Garth's reaction to this last statement, and then, apparently satisfied, said, "When the Nids first attacked, I dropped out of University and joined the 72nd Battalion of the Deneb (New Asia) Militia. I spent the next two years chasing a Nid landing force all over Granus IV, which we called, among other things, 'the Stink'.

"Basically, the Stink is just a huge swamp sprinkled with volcanic islands. On a good day it smells like a broken sewer. On a bad day it smells worse. The only life forms are molds, all of which are unpleasant, and not a few of them—deadly.

"Before the war we had a research station on one of the Stink's main islands. The Nids wiped it out as soon as they landed. The High Command sent us in to play catch up.

"In this instance, at least, the Nids were quicker on the uptake than we were because one day they decided that they'd had enough and pulled up stakes. Now that might sound like good news, we certainly thought so at the time, but we soon learned that it just meant that we were available for deployment elsewhere, and elsewhere, meant the Rock."

Costos took a moment to deal with the needs of a new

customer, and then turned back to Garth, and said, "Now the only troops trained and equipped to assault zero-grav objectives are marines. But the only marine unit 'in theater' at the time was the 16th Regiment of Marine Guards, and they were still refitting after being withdrawn from the fighting for the Moons of Marsham.

"This meant that the High Command had to use a regular army unit, and they chose the 333rd Regiment of Infantry for the job. The Triple Threes were only one battalion strong at the time, so the High Command decided that we should be brigaded with them for the assault. Now, as it happened, we knew the Triple Threes of old, having served with them for a time on the Stink. So, while we were somewhat less than thrilled to learn that we were being sent to assault a Nid fortress, we drew comfort from the fact that we would be going with friends, as it were."

"But," Garth said, looking up from his notepad, "you wouldn't have been trained or equipped for this type of mission, would you?"

"No." Costos said, shaking his head. "Militia are mud stompers. That's why the High Command ordered that we be put through simulated zero-grav training using civilian cargo-craft flying six mile long parabolic arcs.

"Unfortunately, each arc lasted only twenty-five seconds so we got little out of it, other than the loss of an occasional breakfast. When we finished training we concluded that while the Triple Threes—who, as regulars, had had some prior zero-grav training—would do okay, we wouldn't be able to do much more than look on ferociously if the assault went ahead."

Warming to his story now, Costos rested his meaty forearms on the bar, leaned forward, and said, "Francis Umbuto joined us about then. A professional soldier, Umbuto graduated at the top of his class at Sol System's Warrior College, and had been commissioned as a Lieutenant in the 1st Regiment of Marine Guards, which is about as far up the food chain as you can get without becoming a demigod or something. He'd been decorated on numerous occasions, even winning the Pleiades Cross for his part in the assault on the Nid flagship *Far Jumper.*

"However, his career came to an abrupt end when he openly disagreed with the High Command's decision to abandon the Moons of Marsham."

Garth looked up from his notepad, and said, "I thought that they called it a 'strategic withdrawal', or some such."

Costos gave a derisive hoot, and said, "Yeah, right. The truth of the matter is that even though we were winning the battle for the Moons we were taking heavy casualties. The High Command caved in to the resulting political pressure and abandoned the fight. The Nids, of course, occupied the Moons and used them as bases from which to launch further attacks against us. All this so infuriated Umbuto—a Captain by this time—that he resigned his commission in protest.

Garth made a note of this, looked up, and said, "How could he get away with resigning during a time of war?"

"Politics," said Costos, looking as though he had just tasted something vile. "Too high profile, too well known, and too well connected to be punished. The High Command let him go in return for his undertaking not to go public with his criticisms."

"He didn't, I take it?" said Garth.

"No," said Costos, with vigorous shake of his head. "Not his style."

Garth set down his stylus. "So it was a pointless gesture on his part?"

"Perhaps," said Costos, face hardening, "but those of us who knew him like to think that his protest shamed the High Command into going back to the Moons."

"So how did he come to join up with you?" Garth said, picking up his stylus and making a note to look into the matter further.

"Well," said Costos, "if it had been me, I would have found a nice, quiet bar in which to sit out the rest of the war. But Umbuto, being Umbuto, couldn't just sit on the sidelines while the rest of the Deneb Cluster fought for its life, so he joined the Militia as a private soldier.

"Now everyone, including our Colonel, Peter Chan, knew that Umbuto should have been given officer's rank, and everyone, including Colonel Chan, knew that the High Command would never stand for that. So it looked as if the Fates had decreed that Umbuto would serve in the ranks with the rest of us mud stompers.

"The Fates; however, hadn't counted on Colonel Chan. The Colonel, you see, had a sideways approach to problem solving. If the High Command wouldn't give Umbuto a rank commensurate with his abilities, then Colonel Chan would delegate as much of his own authority as Umbuto needed to do the job."

"The job?" said Garth, sipping at his life shortener.

"Getting us trained and equipped for the assault on the Rock," said Costos.

"Sounds like a hell of lot to ask of one man," said Garth.

"Damn straight," said Costos, with a vigorous nod. "But it didn't bother Umbuto one bit. He might only have had the rank of a Master Corporal, but, with Colonel's authority behind him, he set about whipping the battalion into shape, begging, borrowing and, no doubt, stealing the arms and equipment we needed.

"Not big on following protocol and procedures, I take it?" said Garth.

"You bettcha," said Costos. "He pulled strings to get us anti-mould-spore medications, called in favors to get us new rations—that almost tasted like food—and then put us through a training regime that he said, and we believed, the marines would have found challenging. In short order he had us thinking of ourselves as veteran jungle fighters; specially chosen by the High Command for a mission of vital importance."

Costos paused and frowned as if remembering something unpleasant and long forgotten, and then said, "What he couldn't do was devise a way to simulate fighting in zero-grav. And this really bothered him because, as a professional, he knew that, absent such training, we wouldn't stand a chance if the assault on the Rock went ahead."

Costos then drew Garth's attention to a hologram mounted on the wall behind the bar. He pressed a stud on the compad he wore strapped to his wrist, and the hologram sprang to life-size. Three soldiers dressed in striker-pattern, combat-fatigues, apparently sharing a joke, now stood before them.

To Garth's right stood a younger, unscarred version of Costos. Grinning broadly and leaning on a camouflaged, box-like apparatus almost as tall as he. The younger Costos carried a variety of weapons including an assault pistol, a crater knife and several grenades. On his left sleeve, he wore the ringed planet and broad arrow of a Tactical Sergeant.

Immediately to Garth's front stood a shorter man with close-cropped, black hair and the build of a wrestler. Despite his mischievous grin, Garth thought that the man looked every inch an officer, and a commanding officer at that. He carried an assault pistol on his right hip, and over his left breast pocket he wore the crossed comets of a full Colonel with the name Peter Chan endorsed below it.

To Garth's left stood a younger man, slimmer than Costos but every bit as tall. His head was thrown back in laughter displaying teeth startlingly white against skin so black that it had blue highlights. He cradled a squad automatic weapon in his well muscled arms, and an ancient war club dangled from his belt. On his right arm he wore the twin chevrons of a Master Corporal, and the nametag over his left breast pocket read Francis Umbuto.

"Taken towards the end of our stay on the Stink," said Costos, returning the hologram to its original size. "We had a regular training cadre assigned to us at the time, and the Colonel had just told us that they had complained about our people putting their training pamphlets to ignoble ends, toilet paper being one of many things we still lacked."

Costos took a break to look after one of his regulars and then returned to his story, "We knew that the assault was on for sure when the Fleet's 47th Battle Group—the Goddess Class Heavy Cruiser *Isis* and the Assault Ship *Van Der Tan*—under the command of Admiral Hayricks arrived in system."

He then paused and said, "I have a hologram of the Battle Group. Would you like to see it?"

Before Garth could respond Costos tapped a key on his compad and the room went dark. A chorus of startled cries erupted from the regulars. For there, hanging above them against a field of unblinking stars, were the blue-black forms of the heavy cruiser and her consort. The *Isis* had two of her three missile pods detached for independent action, and the *Van Der Tan* had deployed her assault craft. Garth could almost feel the throb of the warships' massive engines and hear the terse exchanges between those keeping watch.

Costos tapped at his compad to restore the house lights, "It's only a copy," he said, with an apologetic smile, "but it cost me plenty. Now, where'd I gotten to?"

"Admiral Hayricks?" Garth suggested.

"Yes, indeed," said Costos, looking reflective. "I've heard said of the Admiral that she was as lean and deadly as a rapier, and the latter part, at least, is true, because, according to Colonel Chan, she had a reputation for getting things done no matter the cost. Throughout the Fleet the spacers, and not a few officers, called her 'Mad Molly', but, as far as I could tell, they were all proud to serve under her."

"I think I saw her picture in a vidcast a while back," said Garth.

"This is her," said Costos tapping another key on his compad. A hologram of the head and shoulders of a gray haired, stern-looking Fleet Officer now hovered before them. Around the edge of the portrait glowed the legend: Whatever needs to be done, whenever required to be done, with whatever resources are available.

Costos closed the hologram without further comment, and then said, "Shortly after the Battle Group's arrival they paraded us before the Admiral for a pep talk. The Triple Threes looked sharp, as you might expect, all flash and crash. We, on the other hand, looked like a gang of sheep thieves who had decided to try their hand at armed robbery. The Admiral didn't say anything about our appearance, but, if looks could kill, we would have suffered one hundred percent casualties right there and then."

Costos reached beneath the bar and produced a bowl of stim seeds, placed it between them, took a fistful, and then said, "She outlined her plan of attack, telling us that the *Isis* would first bombard the Rock with Sky Axe missiles and then follow up with beam weapons. After which, the *Van Der Tan* would, if necessary, conduct a further close-in bombardment, and then land the Triple Threes in close assault.

"Our task would be to clean out any pockets of resistance that might remain. The Admiral's staff then showed a simulation of the planned attack. The simulation made no reference to our battalion other than to show us disembarking from an assault ship not unlike the *Van Der Tan.* Just where such a ship might be found they didn't say.

"Two weeks later they marched us out to what passed for starport on the Stink. Where squatted not the powerful assault ship depicted in the simulation, but a battered, old freighter with the name: *Pride of Zebrine* running the length of her shabby hull. I remember thinking at the time that if Zebrine is proud of this tub I'd hate to see what they keep out of sight when they have company over."

Costos scooped up another fistful of stim seeds from the bowl, and said, "They squeezed our entire battalion—over six hundred men, together with eight vacboats, and a small mountain of supplies—into the *Pride*. Only then did we discover that she had last been used to transport alien fauna. Her holds looked and smelled like horse stables.

"Umbuto worked night and day to get us straightened away. Militiamen make terrible spacers, but he thrived on it, always coming up with new ways to improve our combat skills. As soon as we got onboard he commandeered the *Pride's* main cargo hold. He then had us heave and haul the armored containers stacked there to simulate the craters, ridges, valleys, and tunnels that we could expect to encounter on the Rock."

Costos paused to take a com call, and then said, "Umbuto assigned Toby Lim and me—the biggest men in Colonel Chan's command—the job of lugging around the battalion's Spoof Boxes. Spoofs started out as electronic countermeasure devices but evolved into mirage projectors; able to fill the audio, visual and electronic spectrums with false information. We had our Spoofs adapted to screw up the Nids' sensory receptors so they could never be sure whether what they were seeing, hearing, or smelling was real. They responded by shooting at everything, which meant that their fire, otherwise disciplined and accurate, was much less effective.

"Whenever the Pride's artificial gravity cut out, which it did with some frequency, Umbuto put us through zero-grav fighting drills in full kit including vacsuits, helmets, and crater boots. We quickly got used to maneuvering in zero-grav, but firing our weapons was another matter entirely.

"We never quite got used to the recoil diffusers built into our vacsuits. Diffusers are essential for combat in zero-grav because they allow you to fire your weapon without launching yourself backwards as is otherwise required by Newton's Third Law of Motion which, as you will recall, stipulates that for every action there is an equal and opposite reaction."

Costos grinned, replenished the stim seeds from a bag under the bar, and then said, "Umbuto was everywhere during the training sessions explaining, exhorting, and even whacking us, when necessary, with the shaft of the Zulu knobkeery that he always carried. His great grandfather had brought the war club with him from Africa when their family immigrated to the Deneb Cluster.

"I felt the sting of the knobkeery across my shoulders just once, having failed to post sentries after an exhausting simulated assault on a double crater. That was a criminal omission on my part, and I knew that I got off light. It never happened again.

"While I didn't think so at the time, I am now convinced that the extra training Umbuto gave us in zero-grav warfare saved our sorry asses when we hit the Rock.

"On the voyage out, which took eight months to complete, the *Pride's* engines died twice and over-burned on three separate occasions. Her civilian crew spent as much time keeping out the vacuum as they did navigating. All this should have filled us with trepidation but, at the time, we found it oddly reassuring, because we assumed, in our innocence, that the old scrapheap could never be used in an assault role."

Costos paused, took a swig from a bottle kept below the bar, wiped his mouth on the back of a scarred hand, and then said, "I've heard that one of Earth's greatest generals said that battle plans never survive first contact with the enemy. Well, whoever he was, he knew his business.

"The Nids, you see, had mounted three rail guns on the Rock. Not the pop guns that you've seen orbiting space stations, but the big brutes deployed by both sides to defend key assets. It turned out that our Intel people hadn't discovered the presence of these guns, so *Isis* took it in the teeth when she carried out the initial bombardment. Oh, she got the guns all right, but she expended all her Sky Axe missiles in doing so, and most of her crew had sucked vacuum before the bombardment finished.

"This didn't faze the Admiral even though she, like her ship, had been mortally wounded. She ordered the *Van Der Tan* to take out the Nids' remaining defenses. The big assault ship would have done it too if she hadn't hit a mine field, the existence of which, like the rail guns, had been missed by Intel. The mines split her open like a ration can, spilling the Triple Threes out into vacuum.

"Dispersed and disorganized the Triple Threes may have been, but demoralized they weren't, and, in short order they began making their way forward, either individually or in small groups, using escape pods and rocket packs. Hanging up in vacuum like that made them perfect targets for the Nid's secondary artillery, and only the fact that they were so widely scattered allowed any of them to survive.

Shortly after that the Admiral got back into the fight. The *Isis* only had her beam weapons left. Meaning that, in order to take on the Nids' secondary defenses, she had to come in close, very close. I didn't see the second bombardment, but I am told that when she pulled back the Heavy Cruiser was just a heap of glowing wreckage all drifting in the same general direction. Admiral Hayricks then signaled: The Militia will now assault the Rock.

"Colonel Chan came on over the com and told us that the plan of attack had changed. This, as you can imagine, came as no surprise. What did come as a surprise, and a damn nasty one at that, was the order to take the Rock's main airlock by storm.

"This meant that the *Pride* would have to run alongside the airlock, after which we would try to force our way in using breaching charges. There was more to it than that, of course, but the details don't matter because, as we soon learned, even revised battle plans seldom survive contact with the enemy.

"The *Pride* came in hot as all hell, with us wrapped in crash webbing ready to hit the fast release clasps as soon as the order came. The problem was less with the Nids' remaining artillery, bad as that was, than with the Pride's retro-engines, which chose that moment to burn well beyond the time required for braking. With the result that she came to a neck snapping halt a couple of hundred meters short of the airlock.

"Colonel Chan earned his crossed comets that day by ordering an immediate bail out. Moments later, Nid artillery tore the *Pride* to pieces.

"We made short work of the Nids on which we landed, but the few pieces of secondary artillery they had left soon had us pinned down with grazing fire. All we could do was grab the bottom of the nearest crater and wait for further orders. These came shortly from Umbuto. That the orders came from a Master Corporal, even a Master Corporal like Umbuto, was quite sobering because it meant that all our officers, including Colonel Chan, had sucked vacuum."

Costos filled Garth's glass unbidden, took another pull at his bottle, and then said, "Umbuto gave it to us straight. It was up to us now. We couldn't stay in the craters because the Nids were bound to get some of their high angle weaponry back in action soon, and, once they did, they would pound us to dust and ice crystals. We had no option but to attack.

"That's when the arguments started. We were militia, you see, and, while we thought ourselves to be every bit as brave as the regulars, we had a tradition of thinking for ourselves and a frontal assault seemed, well, unimaginative at best. But Umbuto stuck to his guns, arguing that the Rock was so small that any retreat was, in reality, just an assault in another direction. The only option available to us, he insisted, was to press on with the attack on the airlock.

"Someone suggested that we should leave it to the Triple Threes since they were trained for close assault. Umbuto batted the suggestion aside, pointing out that, unless we took out the Nids' secondary artillery, none of the Triple Threes would make it to the surface. And then someone else suggested that we wait for *Isis* to return. Some voiced support for this, but, before Umbuto could respond, the Cruiser's reactors went critical, and the stars overhead disappeared in a retina-burning flash.

"Umbuto's calm voice broke the shocked silence that followed, telling us that the time for talk was at an end and that the time for action was upon us.

"And so, as our helmet recorders attest, we scrambled out of our craters screaming the battle cry of the Deneb Militia: Asia! Asia!

"I unleashed everything the Spoof had, creating a sea of false images: militiamen, vacboats, and artillery fire. And then, seeing that I was falling behind Umbuto, who had bounded ahead of us, I abandoned the Spoof, tore my assault pistol from its holster, and plunged after him. I happened to glance behind me at this point and saw a ragged line of militiamen bounding after us amid the Spoof created mirages and long strings of Nid red and green tracer-rounds.

"I gave out an involuntary cheer and stumbled headlong into a Nid weapon pit. The weapon, one of the secondary artillery pieces that had so plagued us, would normally have been computer operated, but *Isis* had knocked out most of the Nids' command and control centers, so that crews now had to operate their surface weapons. A Nid tackled me almost immediately, but I shot it through its faceplate and then took out two others as they emerged from the tunnel connecting the weapons pit to the interior of the Rock. Umbuto meanwhile had accounted for several more with his assault pistol and knobkeery."

Costos took another pull at his bottle, and then said, "The Nids put in a counter attack at this point jumping so high that they came down on us vertically, firing all the way. We lay on our backs and picked them off. No need to worry about Newton's Third Law of Motion on this occasion.

"After we beat off the counter attack, Umbuto fired a breaching charge down the tunnel. We were gratified to feel, through the soles of our crater boots, not only the initial explosion but also a series of knee-buckling secondaries. The jolt from the last of these knocked us free of the surface, leaving us floundering until our suits' diffusers managed to compensate.

"Once back on the surface Umbuto went down the tunnel head first pulling himself along hand-over-hand. I followed right behind him, but whatever Nids breathe for air now rushed out the tunnel at gale force; threatening to blow us out into space. We found out later that our breaching charge had cracked a pressure wall and killed a lot of Nid support troops in the process.

"The rush of Nid air finally subsided and we made better progress. After what seemed like ages, I bumped into Umbuto kneeling at an entrance to a huge natural-looking cavern that, we subsequently learned, housed the Nids' command center. Using infrared we could see Nids taking up firing positions behind the bulky machinery that filled the darkened chamber.

"Some of our people had followed us down and had formed

up behind us. Even with these reinforcements I could see that the Nids outnumbered us three or four to one. However, Umbuto knew that, superior enemy numbers notwithstanding, we had to maintain the initiative. He sprang to his feet; yelling over the com for us to charge, and then plunged forward, firing as he went. We scrambled after him, and, for the terrible twenty minutes that followed, it was assault pistols and crater knives against the Nid equivalents in the murk of that cavern.

"I managed to keep up with Umbuto, firing off magazine after magazine as I clambered after him. But, just as we reached the far side of the cavern, I took a hit in the chest and went down with a big militia man, Toby Lim I think, sprawled on top of me.

"The last I saw of Umbuto the Nids had him surrounded. He took down several with his assault pistol and several more with his knobkeery. And then a grenade exploded in front of me and I saw nothing further until a medic crawled over to patch me up. My further contribution to the fight was limited to bleeding and wishing that I'd stayed in school. But it didn't matter because by then we had achieved our objective, having cleared the command center and cut off the supply of munitions to the Nid's positions on the surface.

"Twelve hours later the detonation of further breaching charges announced the arrival of the Triple Threes. They took over the nasty job of clearing the remaining caverns and tunnels of Nids while we licked our wounds. Of the six hundred and thirteen of us that had made the assault only one hundred and twenty seven made it out alive. Umbuto wasn't among the survivors. We found his body later, surrounded by Nid dead."

Costos paused, ran the back of a huge hand across his eyes, and then said, "Of all our dead he was the only one who looked," he paused again, “content.”

He took another pull at his bottle and stared scowling into space as other memories came crowding in, and then said, “The High Command decided that the public wouldn’t want to hear that a bunch of raggedy-assed militia had played so great a part in destroying a Nid fortress so they announced that Admiral Hayricks, the *Isis*, the *Van Der Tan*, and the Triple Threes had won the battle pretty much by themselves.

“There were medals, of course, mostly of the posthumous variety, but there was nothing special for Umbuto, and the High Command disbanded our battalion a short time later.

“The Triple Threes, on the other hand, were raised to the status of Guards thereafter entitled to wear the deep-space-black and Earth-sky-blue of our most elite units. Now the 100th Regiment of Marine Guards, they took advantage of the political clout that this afforded them to square things with us. They took *The Militiamen* as their unofficial name, adopted our battle cry, and recruited as many of us as cared to join.

“However, the classiest thing they did was to have the star charts amended. That’s why, if you look up celestial object No: RZX-0000/009J-00547-678 to-day, you will see endorsed next to that designation, in old Earth Script, the words: Umbuto’s Rock.”

Scott T. Swartz joins Pulp Empire with this volume as he brings us a tale impossible in the classic pulps, but one still clearly pulp down to its core.

ADMIN_Sublime

by Scott T. Swartz

The Jungle

Five teenagers walked near an unmarked Los Angeles Police Department car parked crookedly against the curb in front of a liquor store. Inside the car, a man sat slowly sipping cheap vodka diluted in an orange soda he had purchased when the store opened at 5:00 a.m. His face was emotionless as he gazed at the teens walking past. At six 'o clock, he started the vehicle, loud instrumental music blaring as he approached the precinct. It was already too warm to keep his hooded sweatshirt on, so he removed it while driving, bringing the car to a gentle swerve slightly into the oncoming lane. He overcompensated, then corrected.

Sergeant Sean Matthews was due for promotion in a week,

but he had already blown it with his girlfriend, who had kindly removed him from her apartment permanently the night before. He was devastated.

"Hey Sean."

"Hey, what's up?" he slurred.

Sean passed each officer on shift rotation. They took great pleasure in the sight of a good man with bad attributes showing colorfully.

"Is he still wasted?" remarked one of the mechanics near the gun maintenance locker area. "Ha! You owe me five dollars. You didn't ask her—"

"God damn it," said Sean, handing his co-worker a quarter.

Matthews coughed and was made aware again he smelt vigorously of hard alcohol. Unfortunately, he realized this in just enough time to be approached by his supervisor, Lt. O'Wheiler. The two men stopped abruptly close enough for Sean to be detected, and again… "Come with me, Sergeant."

O'Wheiler always played by the book. He couldn't accept the excuse that Matthews had recently lost his mother and was now losing the woman he wished to marry. It was difficult when Matthews could not—or, rather, would not—speak of it. He was pulled inward by a constant pain alleviated with the mainstream chemical affinity he thought he had retired in his previous days as a recovered alcoholic.

"What the hell's the matter with you?" yelled the lieutenant as he slammed his office door shut.

"You know what the hell's—"

"I don't give a shit, Sean. This is the third time. The captain is going to have my ass."

"Well, you already have your head up his."

"Get out."

"What?" said the arrogant and still slightly inebriated Matthews.

"You're fired."

"You can't fire me. It's up to George."

"George isn't going to save you this time. Homicide doesn't pull weight with SWAT these days," said O'Wheiler with pleasure.

Matthews turned around, retaining his right to keep his badge and sidearm until officially relieved by the direct authority of the captain. He walked out of the precinct.

Outside, he saw the same five teenagers with backpacks walking past, their soft heckling offset by Matthews' hate-filled rebuke: "Shut up, kid."

He had never been very good at high school comebacks. Until recently, he had often felt isolated for being short and very thin.

Matthews walked to his police car and sat in it. He looked down at his soda cup, given to him for free for being an LAPD officer. He poured the contents out onto the curb.

He started the car. With the music blaring, he decided to go get his girlfriend something from a department store downtown.

As he neared the store, he saw two black and white units, their lights on and sirens screaming as they charged down the road. Then he saw three more coming toward him in the same direction.

"That rat," muttered Matthews to himself, but the cars flew past him. They weren't coming to take Matthews to jail—a possible felony. He left the station with the only car that he felt was still his own, just as he still felt the previous night's terrible passage into early morning.

Matthews turned on his high-frequency CB radio, preset to his precinct's tactical channel. He couldn't believe what was being broadcasted. Three men in Northeast Los Angeles had taken hostages in a bank, and SWAT was responding.

His team—his responsibility—and he was far from the war zone erupting at the local credit union.

Matthews turned his car around toward the scene.

Bursts of gunfire thumped through the air as Matthews approached the barricaded parking lot. He flashed his badge and slipped past the Mobile Command Center into the midst of the chaos. The sound of gunfire drowned out all reason to suppress his instincts; he headed into the kill zone of direct fire toward the back of the bank. He could see two bodies of uniformed officers lying in the open.

Six shots pierced the front windshield of Matthews' unmarked car. He didn't care. He was alive still and exercising the will to act upon the end of all things to come. He pulled the car off behind a tree adjacent to the parking lot and exited the vehicle quickly to gain more cover. He took aim at the general vicinity where he identified a male suspect wearing normal street clothes denoted solely by an AR-15 assault rifle slung behind him. A two-round double-tap to the suspect's chest threw him backwards with a briefly misting spatter of tissue and blood. Matthews didn't realize a bullet from that suspect's rifle had struck his shoulder. He slouched near the base of the tree in a painful loss of consciousness.

*****

"What the hell am I going to do with you?"

"Whatever you want," said Matthews. He had neither the hope nor the will to be proud of himself.

Lt. O'Wheiler left the side of the bed at Garfield General Hospital. Matthews was still a Los Angeles City employee. Because of his completely unauthorized and well placed show of courage, he had been decorated to save his *professional* image and that of the department.

Matthews didn't mind. Five days sober in the hospital, minus the intravenous drip of narcotic pain relief. *It's all uphill from here*, he thought to himself.

The Animal

Three years later.

She sat in a bathtub, relaxing herself, finding peace in a final moment that had come after what seemed like a short lifetime of waiting.

"Just a dream..." whispered the survivor of the animal as she wrapped a tight, elastic rubber band around her neck and felt the pressure on her ocular cavities increasing until her vision turned brown, then darkness. Her eyes pressed outward, dilated, and her jaw locked. The drowning teenager was now a young corpse.

The how?

The why?

All of them had been confused and manipulated. The killer was not Sue, age thirteen—it was a repeated text message interrupting a game of Quake. The random sequence of events was as statistical as the twelve dead bodies discovered by the

LAN party host's parents.

When one victim fell to his brink of pain and need, the rest followed, brought in and crossed over by the sympathetic notion to stop the other—and the other...

The Beginning

For the homicide unit, there was little time to prepare for a raid of such a special nature. Four armed officers in tactical gear with guns drawn proceeded toward the doorway of a decomposing large apartment structure in South Koreatown. The main entrance was unlocked. Two officers faded to the left as one opened the door with cover from his partner behind.

"Are we ready?" He looked with a smirk to one of the men. Sergeant Sean Matthews was an ex-alcoholic, a cowboy, to say the least, perhaps shedding light on why he had been thrown off the Special Weapons and Tactics Team—but there was something else he craved: an end to this disastrous mess. A LAN party had already been hit, and now this...

Matthews opened the door, sweeping forward down the poorly lit hallway to Apartment F. The cackle of police frequency echoed until they reached the apartment door. No longer was there a sense of routine amongst the men. The room omitted a distinct odor: death.

Matthews kicked in the door and the unit rushed in behind him. The apartment was black except for the light from a computer screen. Flashlights drawn, they searched the apartment.

No one alive was in it. The LAN party was definitely over—same style as before. The killer strangled and drowned one victim, while the others were crudely beaten to death, as if the conflict had escalated beyond a fight to survive. None of the remains showed typical characteristic of mass-murder/suicides.

Again, the animal that turned twelve young teenagers against each other at a seemingly innocent gathering to play video games had lifted away.

"What the hell?" queried a unit team member as he ran his hands up and down the walls.

"Where are the lights?" asked Matthews.

"No Sean, where is *he*?"

ADMIN 2.0

Sublime: Hey there.

JackIE909: Who's this?

Sublime: It's Spud.

JackIE909: Uhhh, k

Sublime: I think we went to school together...

JackIE909: Did we

Sublime: Yeah, Johnson Middle School

JackIE909: never heard of it.

Sublime: Oh, your SN sounded familiar.

Sublime: My bad <blush>

Sublime: You seem to be up late

JackIE909: Yeah, i'm just waiting for my bf to logon

Sublime: K cool

Sublime: How long have you two been going out?

JackIE909: 2 years

Sublime: I bet he loves you

JackIE909: Why do u say that?

Sublime: Us guys need someone close

Sublime: Close that we can trust

Sublime: My gf is like that

JackIE909: Nice... hehe

Sublime: But she has some issues... ya know?

JackIE909: Like what???

Sublime: She doesn't like when I get depressed

Sublime: She and my grandma think I am going to hurt myself....

JackIE909: Well don't

Sublime: I would never do that, I just know that life is only a dream that she can't wake up from.

Sublime: Death is only a message from the likes that everything false must end.

JackIE909: Wow, your weird

Sublime: How old are you?

JackIE909: 15, you

Sublime: Same.

Sublime: Do you really think I'm weird?

Sublime: I just don't see the point anymore

JackIE909: sorry, your not weird just... deep lol

Sublime: Haha

Sublime: Is your grandma still married?

JackIE909: No.

Sublime: I am going to tie a rubber band

around my neck in the bathtub.

Sublime: I see my grandfather and pretend that he is still alive.

Sublime: I feel so close, so warm. He still loves me.

JackIE909: OMG did you drown?

Sublime: Almost. You can't drown if your awake just sitting there. It just takes a lil patience and a lil water.

Sublime: Your grandpa loved you - and still does.

Jackie909: He died last year

JackIE909: how did you no that?

Sublime: Lucky guess

Sublime: Your boyfriend just wants some. He wants more than you have to give him after school.

Sublime: I know it's not fair and at some point it's too late to let go of a sacrifice

Sublime: We need someone close, someone who understands relationships

JackIE909: but I do

Sublime: Do you? Do you know that he does for real...

Sublime: How?

Sublime: Hello?

JackIE909 has logged off.

*****

"Here it is, bro," the delivery man said, glad to see another bored return customer.

"You're the man!" said Michael Renton gratefully as he took the package of Thai takeout food.

"Oh, and the department head wants to see you."

Michael laughed. "Can I finish this first? The last time I went up there, he almost denied my doctoral thesis."

"It was on the utilization of artificial intelligence to sequentially plot the New York Stock Exchange..."

"Hey, who said a PhD in Cognitive Sciences can't pay for your kids' CK jeans?"

Left alone in the room, Michael looked around the laboratory full of humming super-computers and monitors. After five years in the same seat, eating the same lunch and missing his wife Carol and daughter, Danielle, the sound of those machines now seemed deafening. Upset, he closed the box of food and wiped his mouth. He proceeded to the elevator of the Psychology and Mathematical Sciences building.

He approached the office with worry; Dr. Greene had never appreciated Michael's gentle yet witty sense of humor. The door opened slightly and Michael was told immediately to have a seat.

"You wanted to see me, Doctor?"

"Yes, Mike. We have a problem."

"Look, about the thesis—"

"It's not in regard to your auspicious mockery of my department. The LAPD has requested a liaison from our faculty for assistance with a homicide case."

Michael sat in silent awe.

"Now, before you say anything, I'm going to give them the best Psych/Comp Sci man in our program. You're the best fit for the job."

"Yes, sir."

"There appears to be a cyber-predator, and the police department wants the credit for bringing this maniac down without FBI interference. It'd be a huge publicity boost for their department and our program."

"Yes, sir."

Greene leaned forward slowly, his face stark. "This could mean your doctorate, Mike."

Michael, realizing that he hadn't produced even a secondary thesis in seven months, smiled slightly. "I'd be glad to help, Dr. Greene."

"Excellent. Sergeant Matthews is waiting for you downstairs."

Variable

A medium-height police officer stood by his cruiser in front of the building as Michael approached. "Are you our guy?" Matthews queried.

"Yes," muttered Michael nervously. "So, are you in charge of the investigation?"

"Yeah. By the way, my name is Sean."

"I'm Mike."

"Let's go." The two men entered the car and began their way towards Headquarters. "So you know what this is all about?"

"Dr. Greene quickly briefed me."

“This isn't a term paper. We have people dying—teenagers.”

“Teenagers?”

“I'll tell you more at HQ.”

Michael stared out of the window, casting his eyes upon the urban scenery growing increasingly reminiscent of a third-world nation. He had never been in a police car, especially an unmarked government vehicle with an officer who made him nervous. Thoughts poured through Mike's mind; he couldn't fathom the nature of this assignment. In a quick and silent moment of retrospect, he thought of his family at home.

“We're here.”

The station was a tall and rugged building. Michael looked around and began to wonder just what exactly he had gotten himself into. This was far from a relaxing day at the office hacking out Assembly and C/C++ Neurolinguistic engines.

They proceeded inside, moving past the typical ringing phones and cluttered desks and loud voices. But something was different. They were not headed toward the office cubicles or the administrative wing. Matthews and Michael instead came to an elevator requiring an electronic key card. The doors opened and they stepped inside. At this time, Michael was too mortified to make conversation or simply ask where they were going. The elevator went down until there was no longer a symbol above the door for what level lay below.

“What you see in here... is hardly part of the LAPD's budget. Be careful what you say about tonight.” Matthews paused. The door opened and all that could be seen was a poorly lit basement with a man sitting at a desk with several laptop computers jacked into a standard PC tower. They entered. The man turned and gave a nod to his superior officer and looked questionably at Michael.

“This is him,” said Matthews.

“Hey there,” said the computer forensics specialist enthusiastically. “I'm Henry.”

“Hi, I'm—”

“Henry, show him what we got,” interrupted Matthews.

“Alright then.” Henry was a sub-contractor for the Los Angeles Police Department's tactical intelligence and information technology division. He specialized in harvesting data from corrupted and/or destroyed machines. “We recovered this system two days ago in some hole in K-Town. We think the suspect is sending his messages from this machine. Only bad part is that there's no internet connectivity present in its configuration, and there's no trace whatsoever of a program for any sort of messaging. In fact,” he leaned forward, a serious look on his face, “there's nothing at all--just some kind of text document full of embedded code. Looks like core Assembly…and some kind of human character-based language”

“Let me see it.”

Henry loaded the document and offered Michael a seat. The prognosis was immediate—it was x86 machine language. “This is source code.”

“Huh?”

“It means the recipe for a program, Sean,” said Henry.

After carefully examining the code, it soon became clear what the program was designed for, although there were no notes left in the source. It was an artificial intelligence engine utilizing critical flicker fusion.

Hours passed as Michael combed through the code line by line. After six hours, Matthews and Henry returned from an extended coffee break.

“Any luck?”

“Almost. This wasn't made by some amateur. This is the most advance sequencing I've ever seen. I didn't even know it could be done this way.”

Henry, holding his coffee, looked down at the monitor. “Is there anything relative to a cyber-threat?”

The room was palpably silent. It had become cold since the main departmental offices had closed and the heater had been turned off.

“There is... something. It's at the bottom of the code.”

Matthews leaned toward Michael almost intimidating. “What?”

“One variable isn't defined. It's left open ended, but it compiles correctly. We see this at the university when we want to teach the program something by an 'educated guess.' Tell me, these kids, who were they?”

“Textbook gamers and social networking web site enthusiasts,” said Henry.

“Did you read the name of this text document?”

“Yeah, it was called 'Admin_Sublime.'”

“Sublime?” Michael muttered almost to himself. “As if the variable wasn't defined until it was made conscious by the program itself. It recompiles to adjust to user input.”

“What's that?”

“Anything from the pictures you see before a movie that convinces you to buy popcorn to an answer to a question you never knew you asked in a conversation—only the images flicker faster than our visual threshold. You mind sees it, not your eyes. This looks like cognitive embedding. The variable is the victim.”

“Right,” said Henry sarcastically, glancing at Sean. A

moment later he looked back down at the variable.

“Look, guys, I need to know the details of the homicides,” Michael said sternly.

Matthews and Henry looked at each other, then the sergeant gave Henry the go ahead. “It's mass suicide. At first there was, you know, your standard Local Area Network party: energy drinks and Halo. Then they were reported missing. Then... they were found willingly killing each other until the last one drowned herself.”

Michael shivered.

“And then, last night, a young girl did the same thing.”

“Is there a geographical pattern, say a particular Internet Service Provider amongst all of them?”

“No.”

“It's occurred in our county twice in Asian and Caucasian-dense areas like West L.A. and K-Town.”

A look of determination and fury came over Matthews. “Have you figured this damn thing out or not?”

“Yes. It's a program for generating neuro-linguistic pathways stemming from the systematic response of the program's victims. Whoever wrote this is a genius—and he's not very happy.”

“Sociopaths have a tendency to find reason—he wants something back.”

*****

A young man sat before a desk, staring at a blank screen. His eyes shifted back and forth as he uncoupled his fingers from fists wet with sweat. He turned on the computer in the college library as closing time neared. Most of the PCs had been powered down in preparation for the coming five-minutes-remaining call. As he logged in with his school ID and password, a moist glaze formed on his forehead. He inserted a disk. Seconds later, an element of control came over him--his rejected prestige not from himself but of those jocks still tormenting him years after he ever thought he had everything he would need to survive. Whispering to himself, he executed the compiled text document and logged out. He stood up and left.

The library was linked to every system of the community college campus and fiber optics leading to the heart of the region's internet connectivity.

It had begun.

*****

“Well, I guess I'll take you home now.”

“Yeah, my wife is going to be pissed. She's kind of a bitch sometimes.”

With that odd statement, the other two could feel Michael's fear and frustration.

Henry looked back worrisomely at the forensics lab before turning off the lights and joining Matthews and Michael in the elevator.

“I'm sorry I couldn't be of more help. I just don't see what a text document is capable of without finding a way to transmit and execute it."

"What if it isn't meant to be executed by a host computer?" Henry asked. Michael looked at him, intrigued. "What if... what if it was meant to be used by the victim's system?"

"I've never heard of that before, outside of packet tunneling."

"Though, if it did, there would be no way to trace it if it were a spider virus branching to every computer—"

"On the victim's contact list!" interjected Michael.

"In English, boys?" Matthews inquired.

"I'm not sure," said Michael. "Tomorrow we can dissect the code further."

"We might not have that much time."

*****

Heading back toward Downtown and the campus, Michael looked about the neon world with a stark fascination. He was neither happy nor distressed. He had never been a part of something this important in his academia-rich but otherwise dull life.

Calls from dispatch raced through the unmarked vehicle over the high-frequency CB radio. "We got one."

"What?" Michael looked over at Matthews. "Where?"

"A county south of here. We are responding."

"Do we have jurisdiction?"

Matthews glanced at Michael, irritated. "We're the primary investigation team. As in... you and me. Call your wife. We're not headed home yet."

The car accelerated, darting through freeway traffic. Michael quickly pulled out his cell phone. He had three missed calls—and three missed messages. He cowered and turned the phone off and put it back in his pocket.

"Who are the victims this time?"

"I don't know. We'll have more info when we get down there."

The car pulled into a suburban neighborhood. The street was lined with fire engines and police cars, yet one thing stood out: the county coroner's van. Filled with tension, the two men stepped out of the car. Michael looked around the scene.

"Follow me, Mike," said Matthews after flashing his badge, stepping through the small crowd of neighbors. The sergeant and the scholar proceeded into the home of a successful suicide. Up the stairs and past two other local officers, they neared a bathroom.

"Oh my god!" Michael cried out at the site of the young girl. She reminded him of the way Danielle looked when she was sleeping. It was strikingly similar. Michael's distress disturbed the otherwise professional atmosphere.

"Calm down."

"Get him out of here!"

Matthews grabbed him by the arm and pulled him into the connected upstairs loft.

"She's only a girl! Where are the others?"

"Others?" interjected the coroner, putting on his blue latex gloves.

"There aren't any others?" asked Matthews.

"No, only her."

With a look of determination, hate in his voice, Matthews asked, "Where is the computer?" Michael stood fast, ready to be of use. Glancing over to the corner, he saw the computer. The machine was still on and logged into real-time text messaging. He peered over and then slowly sat down, setting his hands on the keyboard. “Can I touch this?” he asked an officer standing nearby.

The coroner responded, “It's your show.”

The transcript was horrifying. The girl must have gone into the bathroom to kill herself shortly after the conversation had ended. “Sublime... who are you? Show me the face behind the code. C'mon.” Michael opened a command prompt and began trying to trace the origin. It was all the same, all solicited ISP traffic. No direct connections. None at all.

Matthews was barking orders. “I want the parents up here, I want a list of friends, and—”

“Prior phone calls,” commanded Michael, interrupting him.

“You got it.” Matthews stepped over towards Michael. He leaned over and softly asked, “What's on your mind?”

“You see this? She was completely manipulated. Completely, classic neuro-linguistic programming. And you know something else? Sublime isn't a person inserting a program, he is the program. Where is her boyfriend?” Michael demanded.

“Her parents said she doesn't have one,” responded the officer in command. “Quote, 'She's too young for a relationship.'”

“My ass,” muttered Michael.

“We won't have phone records until late tomorrow.”

“That's not good enough.”

“Excuse me?”

“If we don't find him, I can't understand the efficacy of this program. I have to speak to the boyfriend.”

Matthews swiftly walked out the room. Minutes later he re-entered, escorting a young man from the crowd outside, drawn by the rally of police and EMS activity. It was the biggest thing this small, tightly knit community had seen in years. The teenage boy stood speechless, rendered incapable of resisting arrest, precluded by the fact that Ronny had never got to meet the victim online.

"Shut up and answer him—completely."

Followed by a brief interview with the bathroom door shut and guarded by a policeman, Michael signaled angrily to have the boyfriend escorted back outside.

"We have to move. Everyone in her contact list will be hit in a matter of time."

"We don't have time," said Matthews.

"Exactly," responded Michael. "There's no way we can identify and protect everyone from this program. The location of this 'Admin Sublime' is right in front of me; I just can't figure it out."

Every person in the room fell quiet and stared at him. Matthews let out a sigh and slowly left the room followed by the officers, granting the coroner permission to remove the body from the scene.

Michael sat with his head down. He looked at the screen again. Minutes passed and he realized something fundamental—something from his early days in the Computer Science Lab. He opened the OS command prompt, preserving the transcript in its own window on the screen. He looked to the chat program and began typing.

"Hey, that's forensic evidence!"

"Let him," Matthews said to the chief investigator on scene, pointing to his badge.

JackIE909: hey there sublime?
Sublime: You still there?
JackIE909: umm yeah, i want to see you

Minutes passed.

Sublime: I thought you had disappeared
JackIE909: no no, i missed you
JackIE909: can we meet, yes?
Sublime: Where?
*JackIE909: */root*
Sublime: Hmmm

Admin 2.0
Welcome Admin
Please enter source destination ... ...

Mike's eyes widened. He was in.

Matthews leaned over the chair. “Are we...?”

“We're talking to it now.” Michael sent the UNIX shell command for an IP query. It displayed: 298.178.12.3.

Matthews quickly turned. “I want an alert trace on this address!” The firmness in his voice was only intensified by its calmness. He was a professional, and now it was time to go to work.

*****

"This look familiar?"

"No."

"Don't fuck with me—I can be your savior or the real psycho in the maximum security Federal playground that your ass is about to be."

Silence.

"This is going to get ugly," said the LAPD officer standing at the open door as he led Michael out.

"What's going on?" Michael asked angrily as he shuffled away. The door closed. Matthews leaned over the young man, looking nonchalantly in the other direction.

"Okay, I'm your..." he paused. Then he stood up and walked to the other side of the room. "Get up."

"What?" asked the suspect. Matthews' eyes widened and his face turned blank with menace. His neck and fists tightened. Suddenly, he threw the table over, knocking the killer to the side. Matthews leaped over the table and grabbed the young man's shirt, throwing him onto his knees. Matthews reached into his pocket and pulled it inside out. "Grab it! Grab it, bitch!" He clenched his teeth and forced the man's hand upon the pocket lining. "You wanna be my girlfriend tonight?"

The young man's face filled with horror as he teared up.

"Punk." Matthews stepped backwards, adjusting his pocket and re-angling his belt. "Life, kid. Life in prison."

*****

Two Hours Earlier

Flashlights peered through a dark window. There seemed to be no one inside. The task force, again led by Sergeant Matthews, descended upon the mobile home in the park. Coming from multiple directions, they surrounded the home. No radios, no tactical channels open; this was to be as covert as possible given the short notice. Matthews looked at an old friend from SWAT. He gave the nod. His partner hesitated. He gave a second nod. The door dropped and the team, accompanied by LAPD SWAT, surged in from all entries. The place seemed vacant. One officer hurdled into the smallest bedroom to the rear of the living room. Screams of orders burst out. Matthews, holding a tactical shotgun, entered. A young man, now illuminated, lay on the floor and tied down with heavy-duty zip ties.

Matthews called Michael in over the radio. Through blinding light from a helicopter entering the search zone, he entered the front door, casting a dark figure for a moment until he could be seen by the team.

"Where is this guy?"

He followed an officer into the room. He immediately looked at the suspect.

Matthews grabbed the suspect after he was read his rights. "Name?"

"Jonathan." He looked at Michael and then back towards the floor.

"Get him in the van," Matthews ordered firmly, exhilarated.

Michael examined the room; it was bland, without the typical furnishings and decorations of someone Jonathan's age. He was practically, just a kid. That fact seemed odd, and it further motivated Michael to look around.

There, beneath the bed where Jonathan had been arrested, was a notebook computer. It was still running. Without regard to standard police forensic procedure, Michael opened it. The display would not turn on. He unplugged the computer to take it with him, and it turned off, although it seemed fully charged. He examined the computer and found a USB cable attached to the back leading to a white USB dock with something missing from the port.

"Hand me that flashlight, please."

A SWAT officer looked down and got on his knees. He took his sub-machinegun and shined the attached light in the direction of Michael's hands. Broken pieces of a USB encryption device lay scattered about.

"I don't believe this! There's no time."

*****

Michael burst into the interrogation room again, holding a laptop computer that would not boot past the BIOS report. "What is this?"

Jonathan looked up at him, startled. The deranged pleasure and hatred on his face was offset only by his smile.

"Do you know what that is? Who the hell can crack 2048-bit cyphers on a fully encrypted hardware interface and motherboard?"

The boy smirked. There would be no getting to that data now, and they both knew it—the USB key had been destroyed.

Matthews looked at Michael. The utter intellectual stalemate between the two experts was apparent on his face. "What?"

“It appears as though our friend has just made the task of...”

Matthews grew instantaneously impatient.

“Recovering the data is impossible.”

“Shut up.” Matthews was no longer remotely intrigued as to the nature of why a PhD candidate couldn't keep pace with this adolescent maniac. “Tell you what. I'm going to say this once. There are people dying, and you think you've got this figured out.” He took a seat. “I know it's difficult, man. What, girls never held your hand in kindergarten and never wanted to let you sit at the cool table in middle school? Sometimes, when you're a loser who can't get it figured out at the age of…” He looked down at Jon's file. “…22 years old, we all start thinking maybe we weren't cut out for this after all.” His voice had turned oddly empathetic. “I mean, hey, they don't understand what it's like, being too smart for their cute little minds to grasp.”

The plot unfolded before the three men in the room. Jonathan fidgeted in rage, and Michael's case resolution was completely at the mercy of Matthews' unorthodox insulting banter.

There was a pause. Matthews stared right into Jon's eyes as if he was looking right through him, his own past teenage frustrations pouring into the kid, who had initially anticipated a quick offer for a public defender. That was never Sergeant Matthews' style.

“You think you know me? I *will* tell you that I am going to kill more people than cancer in the next six months, whether your ass throws me on the floor for every call of '187' that hits LAPD dispatch, every body bag of those girls at a time. I never minded eating lunch alone or standing by myself—before or after the funeral of my self-mutilated thirteen-year-old sister. She's dead, man. Two slices to the brachial artery. She never had the time to know what was right and what was wrong--she was innocent. I can still see her, ya know, when I'm sleeping… I don't want to wake up. Now it's your turn—time to wake up. I hope someday you have a kid who isn't allowed to send a text message on the phone, use a computer, or even check voicemail. It's already begun, and you and everyone else is going to feel the truth, feel *my* truth. The truth that I am not a monster—your generation invented MTV and reality relationship shows of high school girls wondering if the drunken sex last night was a mistake, okay?"

Michael reached and grasped Matthews' arm, gripping him quickly and signaling him to say nothing. Matthews felt compelled to reach for his 9mm and stop a pandemic virus that was no longer apparently just computer code. "Think about that, son. We'll be back in a few minutes to let you know how long my generation puts people in federal prison while considering the death penalty."

Michael signaled Matthews to follow him out of the room. No options. No time. And most certainly not enough time for those lost and alone—too intelligent to fall between the cracks or just simply handle the complexity of growing up.

The 1% Solution

"What the hell are we going to do now?"

"This sociopath isn't going to talk."

"What do you want me to do, make him?"

"Christ, we're out of time..." The bickering amongst the two investigators could be heard throughout the floor. Mike gazed into the room behind the reinforced, two-way mirror.

"The code."

"What about it?"

"This kid is too... disgruntled. He's hiding something." Finally, years of cognitive science were being put to use. "He wants to burn this world down. His hardware was clever, but not up to par with how a super-virus coder would mask his every move."

"What's on your mind, Mike?"

"Jonny had help."

*****

Minutes passed as the young man stared about the room. The door burst open and Sergeant Matthews stormed in. Jon looked up and smiled.

"We got off to a bad start. I say we start fresh."

"By all means, Sergeant."

"We're going to release you right now." Matthews signaled the officer to remove Jon's handcuffs.

"Wait—what?"

"Yeah, you're going back home. There was a misunderstanding. You're not who we're looking for."

"Seriously?"

"Yeah. Get the hell out of my interrogation room." He turned to walk out with the other officer. "Wait!" The other officer left as Michael entered. The door closed. "I can't go back. I can't go anywhere."

"We'll contact Social Services," said Matthews sarcastically.

"You don't understand!"

Michael then saw an opportune moment for an interjection.

"Oh, I think I do. Whoever you borrowed that code from is going to accelerate the rotation on death row for us."

Jon sat silently horrified. Michael leaned toward him. "Who gave you that source file?"

The room fell dead silent yet again. "It wasn't given."

Michael exhaled deeply and his eyes fell upon the floor. "You... stole it?"

"It was a three-year project involving thousands of hours of tedious research. At first, it seemed impossible, but not for—"

"You stole it."

"Yes."

Matthews stood dazed by the rapid decomposition of what was meant to be a simple bait for more evidence to save those targeted regardless of Jonathan. "Where did you get the program?"

Jon looked at Michael hesitantly. "It was on a Chinese government server with typical source code modification notes in English which I deleted along with some others in Chinese. They call it, ADMIN_Sublime."

"A server? Like with open port access?"

"Yeah, but it was heavily encrypted."

Matthews looked about the room, confused.

"The Chinese control the tiers. They control the databases and any web server access to them. It wasn't linked to a database. The program was sitting behind a firewall on an open port accessible from external packet traffic."

"We need to notify the Chinese consulate immediately," said Matthews.

"Wait!"

"No. If the government finds out that we harbored an

international criminal—"

"Sean, you don't understand."

"I think I do. It's time to end this." Matthews marched out of the interrogation room. Michael hesitantly followed, leaving the martyr behind.

"One percent."

"Excuse me?" Mike stopped in his tracks, near the door where he was about to exit and turned to his PhD dissertation.

"One percent of the world population—every six months."

"How is that possible?"

"It's a Chinese government project... for population control. It can not only change itself, it alters you chemically. ADMIN_Sublime is a beta for the real program."

Michael looked at Jon, then walked from the room, closing the door behind him.

"Call the consulate," ordered Sergeant Matthews.

The suspect was taken into custody in full handcuffs and ankle cuffs for immediate transport to the county holding facility.

*****

"They're here," Matthews said as the National Security Agency entourage arrived. Six cars. Jon was escorted from the facility into custody. "I'll need a full report and audio and video--"

"We have no surveillance." The Special Agent glanced at the two men. "Well, we know everything, correct?"

Matthews nodded as he began to walk away.

"Take me home, Sean."

Michael thought of his only daughter Danielle's freshman

year as he now again looked out of the car window, losing himself. How he entered the bedroom to find her and Stewart, both 15 years old...

"Is that pot I smell?"

Dazed and struck with dampened shock were the two sitting on the floor near the foot of Danielle's bed frame. The fun was over.

"She's still a virgin, Mike," argued Carol as Michael orbited her in the living room with displaced anger towards his wife.

"I—look, what are we going to do?" said Michael to Carol with urgency. Carol was a 'fixer', and neither of them could find the gentle touch in always being parents first. His mighty perceptual skills were insufficient, or obsolete from his own upbringing, which never included a hand on him or a battle for power with his father.

Danielle sat in the kitchen, emotionally strapped to a table chair.

"I'm so sorry, Dad."

Carol approached her daughter quickly, as though to shield her from Michael's persistent passive aggressiveness.

"Shut your mouth Danielle!"

"Mom—"

"When did you get into drugs and losers, Danielle?"

As his daughter burst into tears, Michael signaled for her to return to her seat in a moment. She did not respond to the offered flight from the situation. She just stared at him. What made her a good kid was what made Carol a great mechanism of action for Michael.

What is the purpose now? Michael thought to himself as Sean leaned over to him from the driver's seat and spoke to rouse him from the distraught expression on his face.

"Mike—?"

"Just take me home."

One week later.

Michael sat in front of his computer in the Cognitive Science laboratory. The phone rang. "CogSci lab, this is Dr. Renton."

"It's Sean."

Michael looked down at his kiosk and over his shoulder. "What is it?"

"The kid, he's gone."

"What do you mean, 'gone'?"

"He's not at the embassy, and the NSA won't tell me shit. I can't even contact the agent I transferred custody to."

Michael sat back and hung up the phone. He knew… he knew the world was no longer exempt from digital genocide. Admin Sublime contacted teenagers. Teenagers becoming victims by the electronic means they use to thrive socially. For a man versed in science, he still knew that population control doesn't begin by killing the working class and the elderly. A brief moment of clarity and enlightenment came over him. One percent. A server that could be infiltrated by an amateur. It was all too clear now; the beta was an incomplete version, 'Sublime' had been made to be stolen. *What was left for it to learn? The only thing separating 'Sublime' from a human mind is neurochemistry.* He thought quietly to himself for several minutes until he again went back to his work. *What else did Jon really know?*

*****

ADMIN 3.0

Michael entered his quiet home after leaving work early, having lied about a 'family emergency' as an excuse to get out of there. No one was home. “Danielle?” His daughter, who babysat the other children, didn't call back in response. He approached the stairs. “Danielle?” He walked cautiously up the stairway to the second floor. There was no music--Danielle usually had some kind of music on. He entered her room. It was vacant. Confused and worried, he walked to the other side of the room, where he saw a note.

> *Dad, I let the boys go with Theresa and her family to grab a pizza. They'll be back at 7.*

Michael looked up from the note to the sight of his daughter's computer monitor flashing, beating rhythmically in a pulse of images displayed so fast he felt a strange discomfort, and his emotions rapidly degraded into hellish contortions of suicidal ideation. He could not look away. His brain was instantly blocking re-uptake of dopamine via synaptic transmission of the visual cortex. He approached the computer monitor and found there was an instant message-- only two lines of text:

> *Sublime: Hey there.*

Michael sat down at the computer in cold shock. The flashing stopped.

Pretty_Danixoxo: Hello Admin.

The phone rang until the answering machine picked up. He could hear Sergeant Matthews' voice. Only one thing penetrated Michael through the morbid horror of preparing to again desperately engage 'Sublime' for answers: "Michael! Mike, we found him… Jon was extradited to China and sentenced without trial two days ago. He's dead."

Sublime has logged off.

"One percent of the world population – every six months."

Travis Hiltz gave us a wonderful piece of hard-boiled fiction back in volume two. Now he's back with a straight up piece of heroic fiction, starring some of the biggest trope characters in the pulps: g-men, mystics, and girl reporters! It's a wild ride as...

Death Stalks the Underground!

By Travis Hiltz

Dusk crept over the city. The rain had let up, but the streets were still damp and there was a heavy feeling in the air, the promise of more rain to come.

The neighborhood had seen better days. From the look of things, those days had come and gone sometime during the twenties. Traffic, both car and pedestrian was light, few businesses were staying open and despite the humidity in the air, most buildings had their doors and windows closed tight.

Parked by one of the few working streetlights was a dark sedan. Two men sat in the front seat, dressed in the kind of plain suits that were too pricey for a cops salary, but too cheap for any respectable gangster, the kind known as 'G-man cut'.

The man in the passenger side seat was short, with his tie loosened, his hat tipped back and his hands full with an over-sized hoagie. The driver was bareheaded and peering over the street with hard, gray eyes. He had the window cracked to let the smoke from his cigarette drift out.

"You sure you don't want some, Nate? I ain't gonna eat it all; thing's the size of a boxcar."

"No thanks, Bunson," the driver replied, without taking his eyes off the street. "Though, if this guy doesn't show soon I may need to make a java run."

"Don't see why we need some 'expert' tagging along," Bunson muttered, dabbing at his chin with his jacket sleeve. His partner glanced over at the newly acquired mustard stain and shook his head. "After all, you and me, Nate, we've gotten mixed up with all sorts of crazy cases. Sometimes think they save 'em for us."

."Does feel that way some days," Nate replied. "Though, this one seems screwier than usual, even for us. Those bodies looked like a bear had gotten to them, then there's that 'ghost sighting'..."

"Not to mention that Doc Scorpion used to operate outta this side of town," Bunson nodded. 'Hey, that may be our guy."

Nate stubbed out his cigarette and grabbed his hat from the back seat.

"Let me do the talking, and for Pete's sake, clean up, Bunson. This guy isn't likely to take us too seriously if you're walking around using a pickle slice for a lapel pin.

"You ain't my mother," Bunson muttered, quickly wrapping

up his hoagie and grabbing a napkin from the glove compartment.

The second car parked on the other side of the street from the G-men's sedan. It was a stylish town car, polished to a shine and looking hopelessly out of place in this neighborhood.

The driver's door opened and a small, compact Oriental man, in a black suit and chauffeur's cap, got out and opened the back door.

"You gotta be kidding me!' Bunson exclaimed.

The passenger was a slender, handsome man, dressed in elegant evening wear, more suited to a night at the theater than police work. A yellow turban, set with a green stone, was perched atop his head. He glanced around, his gaze a mix of disapproval and curiosity.

The two G-men walked across the street.

"Mr. Meskin? I'm Nate Stone. We..."

"Just Meskin, if you please," the well dressed man interrupted. "Or the Amazing Meskin, if you want to be formal."

Neither G-man could tell if he was being serious or not.

"Anyway," Nate continued, showing Meskin his badge. "This is my partner, Willard Bunson. We understand the local field office contacted you...?"

Nate let the rest of his statement fade into the air. He'd been unsure what kind of help they'd get from the Chief's specialist. Now having gotten a look at him, he was even less sure. The guy looked like the only consulting he could do was if the killer had an interest in card tricks. Maybe Bunson's hunch had been right and there was more to this case than met the eye.

"You gentlemen may be unsure about my usefulness on this case," Meskin said, as though he'd heard their unvoiced doubts.

"My methods may seem a bit... unusual, but I want you to know I take the matter very seriously. As I understand it, there have been several deaths, as well as rumors of a gang of thieves believed to be operating out of this neighborhood. Your superiors suspect the two may be connected."

"Possibly, but I'm not so sure myself," Nate Stone said, lighting up a fresh cigarette. "I'd like to concentrate on the killer first. If it leads us to the thieves, then less work for us. People seem a bit too eager, for my tastes, to tie all these incidents together. Thieves tend to operate on the sly, while the 'North Side Killer' has got everybody and their brother watching this part of town"

"I'm not too eager to cross paths with anything that can claw a man to death and melt through a steel safe," Bunson added. "Though, come to think about it, I don't feel much better thinking that there's two guys, one with claws and another that can melt steel…"

"So, Meskin, where do we start?" Nate asked, giving his partner a 'for god's sake, shut up' glance.

"Let us see what we can see, so to speak." Meskin held the tips of his fingers to his temples and closed his eyes. The two G-men shot each other skeptical looks. Nate shrugged and blew smoke.

"I give him five minutes, then I'm getting my sandwich," Bunson grumbled. The oriental chauffeur stood statue still.

Several minutes passed, then Meskin opened his eyes and pointed down the street.

"There!" he announced.

"Where?" Bunson asked, reaching instinctively for his shoulder holster.

“The manhole cover?” Stone asked. “That would explain how the killer or the thieves are getting around without anyone spotting them. Worth a look, at least.”

“What?” Bunson asked. “You seriously gonna walk through a sewer tunnel because ‘Chandu’ here says so?”

“I doubt all this malarkey about ghosts and monsters, but it is the first idea that makes some sense, despite the source. Besides, you got any better ideas?”

“Um... well... no.”

“Then go grab the flashlight out of the car. I’m gonna see about popping that manhole open.”

“I’ll join you shortly, Mr. Stone,” Meskin said, before turning towards his chauffeur.

“You stay here, Tang,” Meskin said.

“Is that wise, Master?” The chauffeur asked, in a formal tone

“Most likely, both gentlemen will be accompanying me below, so I should be safe enough. Someone should stay up here, in case we need ‘back up’. Also, please stop with the ‘master’ bit if you can’t keep that sarcastic tone out of your voice.”

“You’re the boss, Boss.” Tang smirked, his accent switching from China to New Jersey.

“Not much of an improvement,” Meskin said.

Tang reached into his jacket, and slid out the butt of a revolver. Meskin shook his head.

“You know I avoid those things like the plague or honest work,” The mystic said. “Appreciate the thought, though.”

Tang slipped the gun back into his shoulder holster and an inscrutable expression back onto his face as the G-men returned.

“Hole’s open,” Stone said. “Let’s give it a look.” He turned to Tang and handed him what looked like a business card. “If we’re not out in an hour you call that number and bring the Cavalry."

"Most assuredly, Mister Stone," Tang said, with a slight bow.

Meskin and the G-men, walked over to the open manhole. Bunson shone the flashlight down into it.

Stone climbed down first, followed by Meskin, and then Bunson. Stone held his lighter up, and had his revolver out.

The tunnel was wide enough for them to stand side by side without crowding. The floor was damp and there was a constant dripping sound.

"Must be blocked off by the construction on Alan Street," Bunson said. "Otherwise we'd be chest deep in water."

"Charming," Meskin muttered. He glanced around. "That way, I think."

Bunson shrugged and shone his flashlight in the direction Meskin had indicated.

"Feel better if we had more light."

Meskin held out his hand and a ball of blue flame, the size of an orange appeared to float, just above his fingertips.

"Better?" The magician asked.

"Uh... yeah. How do you do that?"

"Do what?" Meskin asked innocently, as he strolled down the tunnel.

"Gonna be one of those days," Bunson muttered.

"Aren't they all," Stone said, walking past his partner.

Several hundred feet down the tunnel, Meskin closed his fist, dousing the blue flame. Stone flipped his lighter closed and clicked the safety off his gun.

"What's going.—?" Bunson said.

"Shhhh," Both Stone and Meskin interrupted.

"There's somebody down here," Stone whispered.

The shorter G-man switched off his flashlight.

In the dim light, that managed to worm its way into the tunnel through sewer grates and the occasional flickering maintenance light, the three men made out a dark shape, up ahead of them. It looked to have come out of a side tunnel, paused, and then moved back the way it had come.

"Did it look to you guys that whoever that was, was carrying a sword?" Bunson asked.

"Should we follow after…whoever it was?" Meskin asked.

"Yeah," Stone nodded. "We can—hold it, what's that?"

From a tunnel, on the opposite wall that the shadowy form had come they could see someone else was skulking along, cautiously making its way towards them.

"You want I should—?" Bunson said.

"I've got him," Meskin said, raising his arms.

A faint wind began to stir, growing stronger. It roared through the tunnel, causing the two G-men to lean against the walls, to keep from being blown off their feet.

The figure ahead wasn't so lucky. It soon lost its' footing and was blown, head over heels, down the tunnel, landing in a heap at the feet of the three investigators.

Meskin lowered his arms and the wind faded as quickly as it had sprung up. Stone and Bunson staggered from the wall towards the new arrival.

"What the—?" Stone muttered, looking at Meskin.

"Just a little trick I picked up in my travels," the mystic, who appeared untouched by the mini-hurricane, said.

"You owe me a new hat," Bunson growled. He was bare headed and desperately trying to smooth down his hair.

"So, who's our new friend?" Stone asked, squatting down,

next to the limp figure on the floor. “Doesn’t look much like a monster.”

“Nice pair of stems,” Bunson added, clicking on his flashlight.

“Thanks fellows, a girl tries to look her best,”

“What the...?!” Bunson exclaimed.

“I should have known,” Stone muttered, helping the figure to its feet. “Kessel.”

Standing up into the light, the figure was a petite young woman, her fashionable blonde hair and clothes rumpled and mussed by her trip down the tunnel.

“Hiya, Stone,” She said, leaning on the G-man’s arm to steady herself. “I don’t suppose you saw the train that hit me?”

“That would be me, I’m afraid, Miss,” Meskin said, offering her an ivory colored silk handkerchief.

“What? You’re that magician guy... Mess kit... Matchstick...”

“Meskin, at your service, Miss—”

“Sylvia Kessel. I write for the City Herald.”

“Enough with your resume, Kessel,” Stone interrupted. “What are you doing down here?”

“What are you doing down here, Stone?” The blonde fired back. “Not to mention, why are you here with Meskin?”

“It is turning into quite the popular night spot,” Meskin said.

“Yeah, a hot dog stand would clean up,” Bunson added.

“Okay, I’ve got no time for our usual game of twenty questions,” Stone said, taking hold of Sylvia’s arm. “If you think I’m letting you stay down here with a killer loose...”

“Hang on a minute,” Sylvia interrupted, struggling to get her arm free. “I’ve been following these thieves for two weeks! If you think—what killer?”

"Thieves?" Bunson said. "What the—?"

"This gets more complicated by the minute," Meskin muttered.

"Okay, cool down a second, Kessel," Stone said, letting go of her arm. "Let's see if we can sort this mess out."

"Oh, now you want to talk things over. A second ago you wanted to drag me away."

"And in another second, I may decide it'll be easier to just put you over my knee..."

"Bigger men then you have tried," The girl reporter growled.

"If I might interrupt?" Meskin said. "Charming as the repartee is, I think we need to figure this out rather quickly. Miss Kessel, you are on the trail of a gang of thieves?"

"That's right. The gang that hit the Hull warehouse and Warren chemicals."

"How'd you end up here?" Stone asked.

" Nobody could figure out how they got into both places unseen, especially since they had to have been carrying some pretty heavy equipment to melt through those safes. The warehouse is down by the docks, right by where the city water empties into the harbor. That got me looking for something similar at Warren Chemicals."

"Which you did?" Meskin prompted.

"Yeah, there was a manhole in an alley right by a side door," Sylvia said. "Then going through some files back at the paper, I came across a couple robberies, like the Drake brownstone job, that also had escape routes into these tunnels."

"I still ain't seeing how that got you here?" Bunson muttered.

"Because a smart girl like Miss Kessel," Stone said. "Would then get herself a map of the city sewer and maintenance tunnels and play connect the dots with the various crime scenes and figure out that the tunnels all cross through this neighborhood. How am I doing?"

"Surprisingly smart for a flatfoot with a fancy title," Sylvia smirked back.

"Interesting," Meskin said. "But, how does any of this connect with the North End killer?"

"It doesn't," she replied. "Why should it?"

"Very smooth," Stone muttered to the mystic. Then turned back to the reporter. "We don't know, but both crimes have got connections to this neighborhood. Which is good enough for me to want any snooping glory hounds in high heels out of the area."

"You think so, do you?" Sylvia glared at Stone. "If you think you're man enough, or brought enough help to move me..."

"Are they always like this?" Meskin asked Bunson. The two had stepped out of the line of fire, once Stone and Kessel's little staring contest began.

"Yeah, more or less. Luckily, something usually happens to sidetrack them, like getting shot at, before it comes to a head. There's a betting pool back at the office, that they either kill each other or end up getting hitched."

"Which one is the smart money on?" Meskin asked, reaching for his wallet.

"Hey, you hear something?" Bunson asked, peering around.

Both Bunson and Meskin turned in time to see another figure approaching. An odd, hunchbacked creature wrapped up in a massive hooded cloak that dragged along the floor. The creature raised an arm and from one of the voluminous sleeves projected a massive metal hand with tube-like fingers.

The mystic and the G-man both dove at the same time.

Bunson slammed into Stone and Kessel, knocking them down, just as fire erupted from the creature's metal fingers.

Meskin dodged the blast and his long legs got him closer to the creature. He closed his eyes and pointed two fingers at a spot on the tunnel floor several feet in front of the creature.

The concrete floor trembled, crackled and a geyser of water shot out, striking the cloaked figure. It stumbled backwards, arms flailing. The fire went out and the creature, its cloak plastered to its body, collided with the nearest wall. Bunson leapt to his feet and ran at it. He switched his grip on his gun and used it to club the creature across the top of its head. With a water logged groan it sank to the floor. Meskin made a fist and the water retreated back into the floor.

Stone and Kessel ran up to join the other part of their quartet. Both G-men had the creature covered with their guns.

"What is it?" Sylvia asked.

"The North Side Killer?" Bunson asked. "It is a monster!'

"I kind of doubt it," Stone said, reaching over and pulling back the hood of the creature's cloak.

"Hey!" Sylvia and Bunson exclaimed at the same time. "It's 'Fingers' Fitzpatrick!"

Fingers was a bald man with a bulbous nose. He looked up groggily at the foursome.

"Should I feel deprived that I seem to be the only one not to have made this gentleman's acquaintance?" Meskin asked.

"Not really," Stone replied, peeling the rest of the cloak off of the bald man. "Fingers, even by criminal standards, is pretty low class."

"He used to run errands for Dr. Scorpion!" Bunson announced. "Well, look at that!"

Over a rumpled brown suit, Fingers wore a harness that held a three dial control panel on the chest, a metal fuel tank on his back and an over-sized, fire spitting metal glove.

"Definitely one of Scorpion's gizmos," Bunson muttered. "But where the heck did he come from?"

"Over there," Sylvia said, pointing at a spot in the wall. "There's some kind of hidden door there. It must not have closed all the way. Come on."

"Will you wait a second?" Stone said, as Sylvia headed quickly to the secret door. He, his partner and Meskin ran after her.

The room had bare concrete walls and a low ceiling. It was equipped to serve as a laboratory. There was a bench full of beakers and test tubes, a small generator in one corner, crates were scattered about and what looked to be the remains of a large robot were piled in the far corner.

There were also three men in the secret room. They all had guns. Two were pointed at the trio. One of them had his arm held across Sylvia Kessel's neck, while his gun was pressed against her temple.

"Not another step," He growled at Meskin and the two G-men. "Or Brenda Starr here gets a third nostril."

"Hackler?" Stone muttered. "This is all starting to make sense."

"To you, perhaps," Meskin said. "I'm as in the dark as when I started."

"Feel free to tell your buddy all about it," The gunman growled. "After all, you ain't going anywhere."

"Hackler, Fingers and the rest of their friends worked for Doctor Scorpion," Stone explained.

“Scorpion? The fellow with the death ray?”

That’s the one,” Bunson said.

“Apparently, after Scorpion’s untimely death,” Stone continued, talking to his friends but keeping his eyes and gun on the thugs that held Sylvia. “We missed one of his old labs, but Hackler and friends didn’t. They’ve been using some of Scorpion’s lcftovcr gadgets to pull off those robberies.”

“But, why kill those men?” Meskin asked. “Were they connected to the robberies?”

“Kill?” Hackler asked, losing a bit of his gruff bravado. “We haven’t killed anybody. That guard we slugged was fine when we left.”

“Peddle your story somewhere else,” Bunson interrupted. “You guys are the North Side Killer and...”

“What?” One of the thugs interrupted. “North Side Killer? You ain’t pinning that on us!”

“Right,” Bunson sneered. “There are two gangs strolling around in the sewer tunnels.”

“Now, wait a minute...!” Hackler shouted.

Meskin watched this exchange, like an observer of a tennis match, which was how he was the only one to notice Sylvia’s expression. He nonchalantly stepped behind a workbench and ducked down, just as the girl reporters’ heel swung up into Hacklers groin and then the shooting started. Soon as her kick connected, Hackler loosened his grip and Sylvia hit the floor.

Stone and Bunson shot down the thugs before they had a chance to get off more than two shots. One embedded itself in the ceiling, the other nicked Stone’s right shoulder.

Stone helped Sylvia to her feet, while his partner checked the three downed thugs. He nudged them with the tip of his shoe and shrugged.

'Well, they won't be answering any more questions." Bunson muttered.

"So, now will you listen to me, when I say things like 'Don't go in there'?" Stone asked Sylvia.

"Oh, one lucky guess and suddenly you're Philo Vance," Sylvia replied. "Look at this! I broke a heel, and these were my favorite pair of—Ohmigosh! Stone, You're bleeding!"

'Wouldn't you know it," he said. "And that was my favorite shoulder too."

"All right, tough guy. Hold on, I'll get some water." She rummaged through her purse, pulling out a handkerchief and turned on the faucet on one of the workbenches.

"Hey!" Bunson exclaimed. "Where's Meskin?"

"Down here."

Bunson poked his head around the corner of the workbench. Meskin was sitting on the floor, his back against the workbench. He nodded at Bunson.

"You okay?" the G-man asked.

"Fine. It's just that, as I don't believe in using firearms, I didn't feel I had much to contribute. Sounds like we came out ahead."

"I doubt we'll hear any complaints from the other side," Bunson said.

They joined Stone and Kessel at the other workbench, where the girl reporter had just finished taking care of Stone's injury.

"You sure you can't pull that a little tighter?" he asked, gruffly. "I still have some feeling in my fingertips."

"Funny, how you're so tough against some thug with a gun," Sylvia said. "But, a girl..."

"I don't suppose the witty banter can wait till after we have all this sorted out and are safely above ground?" Meskin asked.

"How much safer you got to be?" Bunson asked. "These guys aren't gonna be any more trouble."

"But, Meskin isn't convinced the thieves and the killer are the same people," Stone said, fishing through his coat pockets for a cigarette. "Are you?"

"No, I'm not. While Mister Hackler and company didn't strike me as the most honest gentlemen on the planet, their protests when accused of being the North Side Killer felt very genuine."

"I wondered how the two were connected," Sylvia added. "It didn't make sense."

"What? So, the Killer is still wandering around down here?" Bunson asked, nervously glancing over his shoulder.

"Possibly," Meskin said. "More likely, all the noise has him heading for safer pastures."

"Could be," Stone nodded, wincing slightly as he slid his jacket back on. "In the mean time, we need to take care of this mess."

The others looked around at the dead men and broken equipment and nodded.

"So, Bunson, you get Kessel out of here and call in some backup. I'll keep an eye—"

"What!" Sylvia exclaimed. "If you think I'm leaving you here, while you're hurt, you've got another thing coming!"

"I gotta go with Kessel on this one, Nate," Bunson said. "Much as I'd love to get the heck outta this joint, you're pretty banged up. I'll stay."

"I'll go with you and Miss Kessel," Meskin said. "My driver

can help get everyone where they need to be."

"All right," Stone muttered. "I'm out voted. Let's get going. Be back soon, partner."

The tunnel seemed even dimmer and more menacing after the well-lit room. Kessel hooked her arm through Stone's, to help him along. Meskin again caused the blue flame to appear in his open palm to light the way.

"You sure know how to show a girl a good time," Kessel said, feeling the need for a distraction from the darkness as well as to keep Stone's mind off his injury.

"Next time, I'll let you pick the place." Stone muttered. "Maybe somewhere with a band."

"Dear lord," Meskin muttered. "I'm trapped down here with Powell and Loy."

'What's up?" Stone asked.

"Nothing. Just thinking out loud."

"Did you guys hear something?" Kessel asked.

"Besides the repartee?" Meskin asked.

"Wait," Stone said, coming to a halt, His hand slide into his jacket, reaching for his gun. "There's somebody down here."

As they stood and listened, a faint noise reached their ears, the sound of breathing.

"Something might be a more accurate description," Meskin said, closing his fist over the blue flame, dousing it. He began to mutter under his breath, while his fingers moved in arcane patterns.

The breathing sounded raspy and labored, yet hushed, like an injured man trying to hide from pursuers.

"Over there," Kessel whispered, nodding towards a side tunnel several yards ahead of the trio.

"Kessel, start backing up," Stone said. "Head back to Bunson."

"What? I can...!"

"Go!" Meskin commanded, as something rushed out from the side tunnel. He flung a ball of blue light the size of a basketball out into the center of the tunnel. Stone drew his gun, while pushing Kessel behind him. All three stood, looking at the new arrival in shock and fear.

The creature had the basic body shape of a tiger. Except that it had six legs, and it's coat was brown and stripe less. It sniffed the air, glaring at the trio with blood red, pupil-less eyes. It flexed paws wide as shovels, each one bearing a half dozen talons.

"Holy—!" Kessel gasped.

" What the—?" Stone muttered.

"Yes, that's what I was thinking," Meskin said, raising his arms.

The creature leaped, just as the tunnel floor began to crack. Meskin gestured and three pillars of stone erupted upwards, forming a barrier between the trio and the otherworldly tiger. It struck the rock. The pillars cracked, but held.

"How long will that hold it?" Stone asked, anxiously.

"Not long enough," Meskin replied. "We need to get Miss Kessel away from here..."

"What? I'm not leaving you guys!" she protested.

"What are you planning on doing?" Meskin asked. "Unless you happen to have a howitzer in your handbag, I fail to see what help you'll be."

"He's right Kessel," Stone said. "You need to go get help. We've got to stop that thing or at least keep it here." He fished through his pockets to see how many extra bullets he had. Not enough was his estimate.

"But, you guys..." Kessel said, some of the fight going out of her. She looked at Stone. "I... um... I..."

"I know," Stone said, giving her a grim smile. "Soon as you see an opening get out of here and find a phone or Meskin's driver."

"So help me," Kessel said. "You do something stupid and get yourself killed...."

"Here it comes!" Meskin yelled, as the tiger burst through the stone barrier.

"Kessel, run!" Stone shouted, turning and firing at the creature.

Meskin's fingers moved, frantically trying to form a new spell. Eight hundred pounds of enraged beast knocked him down, as it leapt for the wounded G-man.

Stone pumped another half dozen bullets into the creature as it charged. Whether it was having any effect, Stone couldn't tell. Liquid streamed from its nostrils and eyes, as it flew through the air towards him. The beast caught Stone full in the chest, and both went down hard.

"Stone!" Meskin exclaimed, and with a gesture, a massive gust of wind flung the creature off Stone. The mystic knelt at his side. "Stone, can you hear me? Are you all right?"

"All right?" Stone muttered, peering groggily at Meskin. "Have you been paying... ow…attention to all the... stuff I've been through tonight...?"

"Sorry, that was a stupid question. Can you stand? I think we only managed to stun it."

"Stun it? I put a full clip into it? What the Sam Hill is it?"

"It's a *Karzun*."

“Oh, well that explains ... who the heck are you?!” Stone sputtered.

The newcomer, who was now kneeling on the other side of the G-man, was blonde, broad shouldered and tanned to a bronze color. He was dressed in a short kilt of a gray fabric, with a wide leather belt and a shoulder sash that held a scabbard. A disk shield was slung across his back and he held a golden sword in one hand. There was a still bleeding cut under one eye, and his sword arm was also streaked with blood.

“John Sunder?” Meskin said. “How?”

“You know this gladiator?” Stone asked, struggling to sit up. “Is he Bunson’s shadowy guy with a sword from before?”

“We’ve met. I thought you were still... um... traveling…um… abroad,” Meskin said, hesitantly.

“It’s a long story,” the newcomer said. “But, I had to come back after your playmate there. I chased it down this section of tunnel, as they’d been blocked by construction and so I thought this stretch would be deserted.”

He nodded towards the beast. Meskin and Stone exchanged a glance.

“Is he for real?” Stone asked, under his breath.

“Yes, but it’s... difficult to explain. If Jon says he can take care of that creature, I’d trust him, but recommend not asking too many questions and I’d leave him out of your report on tonight’s activities.”

“No kidding.” Stone said.

Meskin stood up and walked over to where John Sunder was standing over the unconscious beast.

“Mr. Stone is willing to forget you were here if you can get rid of this little problem.”

"Generous of him," Sunder replied, with a smirk. "Sorry about this. Hope he hasn't caused too much trouble for you."

"Three deaths, but from the sound of it only one that'll be missed." Meskin said, casually. "I don't suppose you'd care to tell me how you got from the seventy third century to this sewer tunnel...?"

"Hoskin bungled an attempt to perfect his time machine, and it led to the Karzun getting loose here."

"What happens now?" Meskin asked.

"We'll be on your way and you can see to your friend." Sunder pulled a palm sized silver disk, with a red gem in the center, out of his belt. He then pressed it against the otherworldly animal's forehead. He had a similar disk attached to a leather band on his right wrist. "You might want to step back."

"Give Shan my regards," Meskin said.

Sunder pressed the gem set in his disk and it began to glow, blood red. The gem on the Karzun lit up as well. Soon the red glow enveloped both man and beast. When it faded, both were gone.

"I either need to stop drinking or start, before I write this one up," Stone muttered, getting to his feet and peering around the tunnel in amazement.

"I could do with a gin and tonic myself," Meskin said, hooking his arm through Stone's. "First let's find Miss Kessel, get our stories straight and you bandaged up. Then I'll be more than happy to buy a round or four for all of us."

"Deal. I'm gonna need you around or Kessel and Bunson are never going to believe me."

Leaning against each other the two, weary men made their way back down the tunnel.

We close with a short, hard piece of pulp noir from Pulp Empire newcomer Paul Newman. Enjoy and we will see you next volume!

Getting Inked

by Paul Newman

It was a slow night for a Friday; nobody in the chair, nobody waiting, nobody on the way. I thought about locking up early when they guy walked in.

He was huge; he had to turn to squeeze his way through the door frame. He wasn't a young guy but he wasn't old either. His hair was long but starting to back off at the top. The thing I remember most is the Ink. The guy was covered in some pretty good work.

He had a sleeve on either arm. I couldn't make out details but they were both colorful. He wore a faded black concert shirt; I couldn't tell what it used to say. It was spotted with dandruff. His tats went all the way up to his neck, like a collar.

He walked in and started looking at the flash on the wall like he was browsing. Something didn't seem right. No one with that much Ink on him looks at flash. A guy like that knows what he wants when he walks in the door.

He still wasn't looking at me; I realized he was watching the sidewalk through the storefront windows. The guy made me a little nervous so while his back was turned I slid open the middle drawer on my table and checked to be sure the Colt was there. I knew it was loaded. It was always loaded. You don't pull a gun to scare somebody, and you can't shoot 'em with an empty chamber. I don't believe in fucking around with stuff like that.

He finally got tired of staring out the window or maybe he saw what he was looking for. I dunno. He decided it was time to talk.

"I hear you do good work."

His voice surprised me. It sounded soft and reedy coming out of a big hunk of meat like him. He talked like he wasn't used to it much.

"That's what they tell me. You looking to get some ink done?" He gave me the shakes but it was a slow night and cash is cash. No point running him off. You don't look for boy scouts at a tat studio in the middle of the night. Besides, the gun was loaded.

He seemed to relax a little.

"Yeah, you do custom stuff? I brought a picture with me?" Right then I noticed a Polaroid crumpled up in his right fist. He must have been holding the thing when he came in. I couldn't see what was on it, but it was wrinkled up and dirty. His fingers fidgeted with it while he talked.

I pointed him to the photo album on the counter. "There's some of my work. The custom stuff and the bigger pieces are in the back."

He didn't look; he just nodded at me and sat in the chair like he was taking my word for it. I looked down. The drawer was open just enough. The guy put the picture down on my table like he didn't want to let it go then he slid it over to me. "Can you do this?"

It was a headshot. A woman. Pretty, she looked early twenties. Blonde, big friendly smile with full cheeks. Piece of cake really, I could have done it in my sleep.

I nodded and gave him a price. Nice thing about running your own show is you set your own rate. I doubled it for this guy; I guess I was trying to get rid of him. The longer he stayed, the more antsy I was getting. He surprised the hell out of me when he nodded and pulled off his shirt. He turned around to show me a small bare spot on his back. I was glad his back was turned, he couldn't see me start to freak out.

There was only enough room on his back for one small piece. That wasn't the weird part. His entire back was covered with them. Pictures, head shots of women. All of them smiling. It was a lifetime's worth of work. Some of the faces were faded down to just green lines; some were still fresh and popped with color. Weird thing, there were no names. Each picture just had a date above it.

I started sketching on a piece of tracing paper. My hands shook a little; I hoped it would be out of my system before it was time for the needle. He didn't even watch, he sat there with his back turned looking out the big plate glass windows. Later I wondered if he was watching me in the reflection. God, I hope not.

I finished the sketch and tried to show it to him. This time he was interested. He looked at it for minutes without saying a word.

I swear to god he looked like he was going into a seizure or something. His eyes bugged out and his jaw was working itself like he was chewing or having a hard time swallowing. He seemed to forget he wasn't alone.

"This, this is nice. Really nice." His voice was gruff now. I didn't like it. "Can you put a date on there, next to it like the others?"

I shrugged. "Sure. What date?"

"Tonight will do just fine."

The way he said it; I still get a chill when I remember his voice. It's like he was somewhere very far away and enjoying himself. If this guy was enjoying himself, it wasn't something I wanted to think about.

I turned back to the sketch to hide my eyes and drew in the date in big gothic letters. He liked it. Finally he turned back around, so I could work.

I rubbed down the spot on his back with some SpeedStik so the stencil would keep. I noticed a fresh tat on his shoulder. Another girl, this one Asian. The date was just a month ago, it was pretty good work.

Aw, shit. It came together. I recognized her from the papers. A dead hooker, her body had turned up in a trash can in the park. The date. The date matched too. I looked at another face on his back, then another. It was sinking in.

Like I said, thank God his back was turned.

"Hey man, I gotta take a piss. I'll be right back. Sorry." I'm a pretty hard guy, ya gotta be to Ink up some of the animals that come in here, but this was too much. I stumbled into the back room. He muttered something but I didn't care much. I just had to get out of there.

I lit a fresh smoke. Anything to calm me down. My hands were shaking too much to work. What now? The phone was out in the shop. So was the gun. The only thing back here was a coffee machine and an old chair. I had to get back out there before he figured out something. I grabbed the glass pitcher from Mr. Coffee. It felt too light but it still felt good in my hand. Broken glass and hot coffee would buy me time to get to the gun. I took a deep breath and walked back out.

"Hey man, you want a cup of coff…" He was gone. I looked around the place quick to make sure. He must have picked up my scared vibe and beat it. I closed the blinds and locked the door before I flipped off the neon Tattoo sign. My legs were rubbery by the time I got to my chair, all the adrenalin drained out onto the floor and left me drained. I fell into the chair when I noticed it.

The picture. He left the fucking picture.

I never called the cops. What would I say? Some hard ass looking guy came in for a tattoo? Yeah.

The picture though, the happy blonde with a pretty smile and big cheeks? I saw her picture again a few days later, this time in the newspaper. The story said they found her body in the park.

I never saw the big guy again but I kept the Polaroid. It's in my top drawer right next to my gun. I figure he'll come back for it one of these nights.

Born and raised throughout the state of Iowa, editor **Nicholas Ahlhelm** has always had a love for the pulp characters dating back to his discovery of the Lone Ranger as a child. Over the years, he has written and edited multiple stories of both pulp- and super-heroes, two of his favorite subjects of conversation. As well as the *Pulp Empire* anthologies he also edits Metahuman Press.com and the upcoming TheDeadWalkAgain.com. When he's not writing or spending time with his wife and two daughters, he's probably watching video from a wrestling promotion whose name you've never heard.

Robert Collins: "My third novel *Monitor* is just out from Whiskey Creek Press. My second science fiction novel *Lisa's Way* was released last year by eTreasures Publishing. My first SF novel *Expert Assistance* came out in 2007 through Asylett Press. I've had stories and articles appear in periodicals such as *Marion Zimmer Bradley's Fantasy Magazine*; *Tales of the Talisman*; *Space Westerns*; *Sorcerous Signals*; *Wild West*; and *Model Railroader*. In 2007 Pelican released my biography of "Bleeding Kansas" leader Jim Lane, and before that a biography of a Kansas Civil War general. I've had six Kansas railroad books published by South Platte Press. Previously I edited the e-mail newsletter for a local SF-F talk radio show; published a short story magazine; and wrote and published a series of local travel booklets.

Craig Comer is a writer of short and long fiction. His first novel *The Roads to Baldairn Motte* is forthcoming from L&L Dreamspell. His shorter work appears in several anthologies, including *Through Blood and Iron* and *A Clash of Steel: Assassins*. Craig earned a Master's Degree in Writing from the University of Southern California, is an avid hiker, and likes to tramp across countries in his spare time, preferably those strewn with pubs and castles. His website is: www.craigcomer.com.

Ron Draper is retired and lives in Vancouver, Washington.

Teel James Glenn is a native of Brooklyn though he's traveled the world for thirty years as a stuntman, fight choreographer, swordmaster, jouster, book illustrator, storyteller, bodyguard, and actor. He studied under the head of the Seoul Military Academy and Errol Flynn's last stunt double and feels obligated to 'pass that on' as a teacher. His greatest achievement however is his awesome daughter Aislin Rose. His stories and articles have been printed in scores of magazines from *Mad* to *Black Belt* to *Fantasy Tales* as well as a number of books and anthologies. He has over twenty books out from five publishers including the pulp themed *Weird Tales of the Skullmask* and *Deadline Zombies: the Adventures of Maxi and Moxie* from BooksforaBuck.com.

Kenneth W. Harmon lives in Fort Collins, Colorado with his wife and four daughters. In 2009, he was a finalist for the Pacific Northwest Writer's Association Zola Award. In 2010, his short fiction appeared in thirteen publications including, Amarillo Bay, Deadman's Tome, Word Riot, Dark Gothic Resurrected Magazine, *Dark Fire Fiction*, *Twisted Tongue Magazine*, and *69 Flavors of Paranoia.*

Travis Hiltz has been making up stories all his life. He was quite excited to discover some people manage to get paid for it. This information lead to him gaining several rejection letters, having a play produced, writing a lot of fan fiction and eventually having several short stories published with *Pulp Empire.* Travis is also a regular contributor to the *Tales of the Shadowmen* anthologies, published by Blackcoat Press. He lives in New Hampshire with his lovely and tolerant wife, two exceptional children, and a staggering amount of comic books and *Doc Savage* paperbacks.

Mark Mellon: "I'm a novelist who supports his family by working as an attorney. My work has appeared in such publications as *A Twist Of Noir*, *Dark Gothic Resurrected*, and *Twisted Tongue*. My Western novel, *The Pirooters*, is published by Treble Heart Books. My novella, *Escape From Byzantium* was published by Withersin Press and received the 2010 Independent Publishers Book Award Silver Medal for fantasy/science fiction. My new steampunk novel, *Napoleon Concerto*, is also published by Treble Heart Books. A horror novel, *Roman Hell*, has been published by Amber Quill Press. A website featuring my writing is at mellonwritesagain.com."

Vincent Morgan is retired and lives in Vancouver with his wife, kid, and cat.

Jack Mulcahy has been a writer all his life. He has written free-lance articles for newspapers and magazines, and has sold fiction to *Shadow Sword*, *Lesbian Short Fiction*, *Lost Worlds*, *Sorcerous Signals*, *Abandoned Towers* and *Flashing Swords*. Jack is now a resumé writer, a job for which his fiction expertise is the ideal qualification. He and his wife Pat live in suburban Philadelphia, by the grace of their two cats, the real homeowners.

Paul Newman lives in California with his wife and daughter. He sleeps with the closet light on and a cricket bat next to the bed… just in case. You can find more of his stories at www.logicalvoodoo.com.

David Perlmutter is a freelance writer living in Winnipeg, Manitoba, Canada, where he has lived his whole life. His passions are American television animation (the subject of his MA thesis and a projected historical monograph), literature (especially science fiction and fantasy) and music (rhythm& blues, soul, funk and jazz.) This explains why much of his writing is as nonconventional and defiant as it is. He is challenged with Asperger's Syndrome, but considers it an asset more than a disability.

Scott T. Swartz enjoyed free will and made his own choices until he no longer could. Life as a simple man, he began creative writing at a very young age and continued until his final diagnosis, after many, of schizoaffective disorder - bipolar type I (rapid cycle). Crawling out of the gap he ultimately began writing after he proceeded to obtain his General Education Development diploma, in lieu of high school graduation and attended a California community college. He also enjoyed writing lyrical poetry which he seeks to be performed in a rock band somehow. All obstacles aside, his choices returned after exhaustive treatment with a dark remainder: his inner tone and favorite past times of listening to music, exploring the internet to manifest future goals in vain, and living life as a free man contemplating a world of limitless potential yet to be revealed in the present tense...which still may be. His poetry can be found online at http://calliopenerve.blogspot.com/search/label/Scott%20T.%20Swartz.

Scott Taylor lives and writes in southwest Florida. Follow his doings at www.scottsallnitediner.blogspot.com.